Moon Madness

OTHER BOOKS
BY ALAN TWIGG

Undaunted: The Best of BC Bookworld, ed. (Ronsdale, 2013)

The Essentials: 150 Great BC Books & Authors (Ronsdale, 2010)

Tibetans in Exile: The Dalai Lama & the Woodcocks
(Ronsdale, 2009)

Full-Time: A Soccer Story (McClelland & Stewart, 2008)

Thompson's Highway: British Columbia's Fur Trade, 1800–1850
(Ronsdale, 2006)

Understanding Belize: A Historical Guide (Harbour, 2006)

Aboriginality: The Literary Origins of British Columbia
(Ronsdale, 2005)

First Invaders: The Literary Origins of British Columbia
(Ronsdale, 2004)

101 Top Historical Sites of Cuba (Beach Holme, 2004)

Intensive Care: A Memoir (Anvil Press, 2002)

Cuba: A Concise History for Travellers (Harbour, 2004;
Penguin Books, 2002)

Twigg's Directory of 1001 BC Writers (Crown Publications, 1992)

Strong Voices: Conversations with 50 Canadian Writers
(Harbour, 1998)

Vander Zalm: From Immigrant to Premier: A Political Biography
(Harbour, 1986)

Hubert Evans: The First Ninety-Three Years (Harbour, 1985)

For Openers: Conversations with 24 Canadian Writers
(Harbour, 1981)

Moon Madness

DR. LOUISE AALL, SIXTY YEARS OF HEALING IN AFRICA

ALAN TWIGG

RONSDALE PRESS

MOON MADNESS: DR. LOUISE AALL, SIXTY YEARS OF HEALING IN AFRICA
Copyright © 2019 Alan Twigg

RONSDALE PRESS
3350 West 21st Avenue, Vancouver, B.C., Canada V6S 1G7
www.ronsdalepress.com

Typesetting: Get to the Point, in Minion Pro 11.5 pt on 15
Cover design: Get to the Point
Front cover photo: Louise Aall, solo hiking in Switzerland. Aall family collection.
Paper: Ancient Forest Friendly Enviro 100 edition, 60 lb. Husky (FSC),
    100% post-consumer waste, totally chlorine-free and acid-free.

Ronsdale Press wishes to thank the following for their support of its publishing program: the Canada Council for the Arts, the Government of Canada, the British Columbia Arts Council, and the Province of British Columbia through the British Columbia Book Publishing Tax Credit program.

Library and Archives Canada Cataloguing in Publication

Title: Moon madness : Dr. Louise Aall, sixty years of healing in Africa / Alan Twigg.
Names: Twigg, Alan, 1952- author.

Description: Includes bibliographical references.

Identifiers: Canadiana (print) 20190102632 | Canadiana (ebook) 20190102705 |
    ISBN 9781553805939 (softcover) | ISBN 9781553805946 (HTML) |
    ISBN 9781553805953 (pdf)

Subjects: LCSH: Jilek-Aall, Louise, 1931- | LCSH: Physicians—Africa—Biography. | LCSH: Physicians—Canada—Biography. | LCSH: Epilepsy—Tanzania. | LCSH: Congo (Democratic Republic)—History—Civil War, 1960-1965. | CSH: Norwegian canadians—Biography | LCGFT: Biographies.

Classification: LCC R654.J54 T85 2019 | DDC 610.92—dc23

At Ronsdale Press we are committed to protecting the environment. To this end we are working with Canopy and printers to phase out our use of paper produced from ancient forests. This book is one step towards that goal.

Printed in Canada by Island Blue, Victoria, B.C.

to Dr. Bruce Fleming
& caregivers everywhere,
particularly the staff at
Inglewood Care Centre

ACKNOWLEDGEMENTS

Longtime cohort and designer David Lester was essential.

The care and attention of publisher Ron Hatch was inspiring.

I am grateful for a writer's grant from BC Arts Council.

The unexpected friendship of Father Placid Kindata
was the additional fuel I needed to complete this journey.

Royalties will be donated to aid projects in Tanzania.

"If you have courage you can achieve
what others consider to be impossible."
—THE DALAI LAMA

"For a person who leads a spiritual life,
self-sacrifice brings a bliss that far transcends the
pleasure of a person who lives by the self-indulgent
satisfaction of his animal passions."
—LEO TOLSTOY

CONTENTS

CHAPTER 1

Early Years

LOUISE AALL WAS BORN in Oslo on April 21, 1931, the second child of distinguished professors. Born in a Norwegian village north of the Arctic Circle, her father, Dr. Anathon Aall, co-founded and headed up the Philosophy Department at the University of Oslo. Also a distinguished psychologist, he corresponded with Albert Einstein about international peace. Her Austrian-born mother, Dr. Lily Weiser-Aall, was an internationally-known ethnologist who received the King's Gold Medal from the University of Oslo in 1933 for her book, *Symbol and Psychological Foundation in Religious Experience*. Both of Louise's siblings would have distinguished careers. Her brother Cato, one year older, would become a United Nations-affiliated nutritionist who worked primarily with refugees. Her sister Ingrid, who was born two years after Louise, would become a widely-travelled artist as well as an art historian.

Growing up in Oslo, Louise knew she came from a family who had played an important part in Norway's history. Jacob Aall Street was named after her great-great-grandfather, a leading figure in the National Assembly who had participated in the drafting of the constitution of Norway in 1814. Her great-grandfather, Hans Cato Aall, had been a Member of Parliament and mayor of Hammerfest. From an early age she knew the Aall family crest contained elements of the Norwegian royal family's crest. The surname Aall—pronounced "all," as in the phrase "all or nothing"—was derived from the name of a river in Denmark.

Louise enjoyed a privileged if somewhat cloistered upbringing. From their balcony in the neighbourhood of Inkognitogata, at 24-B-3rd in Oslo, they could gaze from their third-floor apartment and watch the royal family in their private garden. Louise always knew when the royal family was in residence because she could see the Norwegian flag had been raised atop the castle. The Aall family had an orderly existence, timed in part by the palace activities. Precisely at two o'clock each day, a marching band of the royal guards would parade beside the lake in a nearby public park, wearing black uniforms in winter, blue uniforms in summer.

Like her brother and sister, Louise would never attend public schools until her mid-teens. Her relatively free-thinking parents were determined to oversee their children's education. Seldom doctrinaire, they mostly encouraged reading.

"They taught us one thing above all else," recalled Ingrid in 2018, "and that was to be independent." Their father was sometimes more lenient than their mother. He preferred to teach them with stories, including *Aesop's Fables*. A code of behaviour was instilled with these fables: never exaggerate; never cheat.

This style of education meant that the children did little socializing with other children in their early years. A Russian consul occupied a floor of their building but his children were not permitted to speak to strangers. Home life was mostly happy—full of music, laughter and learning—with the exception of occasional beatings from an overly-harsh nanny. Her father had spontaneously hired this nanny, Alfhild, after learning she was also from Finnmark, where he grew up. When her severe punishments came to light, "Affil" was fired by Louise's mother but she remained in touch with the family.

The children looked forward to spending time at their country home called Ospeteig, two hours by train from Oslo. In this forested region they skied in winters and boated on a small lake in summers. Their family rowboat called *Lübeck* was named after the city in which their parents had first met while attending a conference. The children went on walks with their parents on paths through the forest, during which Louise learned a reverence for nature—mostly from her father, who also taught her the Lord's Prayer.

Even though there was a considerable age difference between her parents, Louise was impressed by how well her parents got along in their marriage. Lily was thirty-three years younger than her husband. They had met only a few months after the death of his first wife. Ever since then, the pair had developed the practice of often tossing a ball back and forth as they talked outdoors. Louise hoped she might one day achieve a similar union, born of equality and mutual respect.

Sibling rivalry was almost inevitable given the closeness of the children's ages, and in her early years Louise often felt that she did not come up to the standards set by her brother and sister. She recalls that Cato and Ingrid criticized her, telling her she was boring, her face wasn't pretty, her nose was too long, she cried too much.

Eventually her mother came to her rescue and asked her why she wasn't playing with her brother and sister. With tears in her eyes, Louise told her mother that Cato and Ingrid found her ugly. Lily took Louise by the hand, called Cato and Ingrid to them, and sternly told them that it was cruel to speak that way. "I tell you," Lily said firmly, "that she is the most beautiful of all of you."

The taunting stopped. But Louise felt that she had to continually impress her parents with her mental abilities. On Sundays, when the family went for walks and there could be longer conversations, she tried to show her mother and father that she, too, could be clever, but her attempts to act like an adult only made her parents laugh.

More introverted than her brother and sister, Louise began to take solace from nature. She chided herself for her own petty vanities and she began to dream of one day becoming a doctor.

A crucial early teenage experience occurred when Louise was on a streetcar with her mother and sister. Prior to this incident, Louise and Ingrid had been told very little about sex or men. Lily turned to the girls and pointed to a woman who was dressed in a revealing manner and who was pushing up against her male companion. Lily told her daughters that this was a woman who "was trying to have the man make love to her." She delivered a stern warning: "You have to be careful! Once you let a man kiss you, it's the beginning of going too far into that . . . and before you know it, you are pregnant." The supposedly loose woman or prostitute on the streetcar would loom large in Louise's mind for decades.

Louise decided firmly that she must not become unduly attractive to men and that she must learn to live beyond romance. Although she would never be immune to romantic attraction, Louise vowed not to allow temptation to derail her from what was becoming her single-minded intention to become a doctor.

⌒

IN THE LATE 1930s, the family made a trip together to Baden-Baden in the hopes that the famous baths could have some palliative effect on Anathon's declining health. While travelling to and from Baden-Baden, the children assumed they were on a holiday adventure and little attention was paid to the German warships they saw or the seriousness of their father's condition. Later, Louise commented:

> In Norway, people don't talk about illnesses. They are ashamed when they are sick. I think it has to do with the Protestant Church. It was as if God has sent the illness because they have done something wrong. Even when I was a doctor in Scandinavia, it was often very difficult to get the patient to say what was wrong. Many people feel ashamed to be sick. Here [in North America] people love to talk about illness. I am always irritated when people like to describe all the things that are wrong with them in public. I don't like that at all. It embarrasses me.

The family's quiet life in Oslo was turned upside down when, early on the morning of April 9, 1940, under the code name of Weserübung, Germany invaded Norway and Denmark. The invasion of Denmark lasted six hours—the fastest successful national occupation by Nazi troops. The King of Denmark responded by wearing the Star of David in an effort to protect Danish Jews. Norway resisted for 62 days, longer than any other country invaded by Hitler's forces, except the Soviet Union. The Wehrmacht forces were ostensibly protecting the neutrality of Norway and Denmark by preventing or pre-empting Franco-British governments from taking similar "protective" measures. In reality, Hitler needed to guarantee Germany's supply of iron ore from Sweden and to establish naval and air bases for a possible campaign against Britain.

Louise's father and mother watched with disbelief as a provisional government for civil rule was assumed by the Reichskommissariat Norwegen (Reich Commissariat of Norway) under the Nazi leader Josef Terboven, who ruled Norway during the occupation in conjunction with the Norwegian Vidkun Quisling, who nominally served as prime minister from 1942 to 1945. Over the course of the war, about 80,000 Norwegians managed to flee the country. Crown Princess Märtha crossed the border into Sweden with her three children in April, eventually finding refuge in the United States. King Haakon VII departed Norway, along with Crown Prince Olav and government officials, aboard the British heavy cruiser *Devonshire* on June 7 to establish a government-in-exile in London.

Louise's parents decided that they would be safer if they fled Oslo and took refuge at their country home. Lily was already helping Jews, in particular by arranging for their private libraries to be safely stored in Norway, and by occasionally helping to relocate Jews to England. Her dislike of Hitler might have been known to Louise's uncle, Herman Harris Aall, a prominent Nazi sympathizer. In order to protect their Oslo home from occupation by the fascists, Lily wrote to a friend in Vienna and asked if she would come to Oslo and look after their apartment. "Tante Grete" agreed and she soon found a job in a children's home similar to the orphanage she had managed in Vienna.

She would stay in the Aalls' Oslo apartment all through the war years.

The Aalls' daily life at Ospeteig in their secluded country house was in the beginning largely happy. At the time the children did not know there was another reason for moving to the relative isolation of Ospeteig: their father's health was deteriorating due to Parkinson's disease. Eventually it would have to be explained to the children that their father was susceptible to Parkinson's disease because he had contracted the Spanish flu in 1918. The isolated house had been brought to the site by Anathon who had acquired its ownership after his first marriage to the daughter of a prominent businessman.

The name of the property was possibly derived from five noteworthy trees on the property. (*Ospe* in Norwegian means tree. *Teig* means grove.) One large coniferous tree was designated as the Father Tree. A lovely beech tree was designated the Mother Tree. There were three smaller trees to represent the three children. There were no neighbours. A Finnish mailman brought letters and parcels by car in the summer; in the winter he made his deliveries on skis.

At Ospeteig, Louise occasionally heard gunshots in the forest where members of the Norwegian resistance movement remained active. Once, when a patriot, or possibly someone simply fleeing from the Nazis, took refuge in their barn, Louise left food in the barn for the runaway for several days until he disappeared. She never saw him.

Louise and her brother frequently had to trek down the mountain to buy groceries in the nearest village, Roa, the administrative centre of the Lunner municipality. "I don't think there were many children who walked as much as we did," she has recalled. "Both before the war and after, we often walked long distances, either to buy groceries in Roa, or else to forage for food in the surrounding forests." The family could take the train to Oslo, but it was also possible in winter to make the trip on skis. She and her brother made the latter journey several times in their teens, taking approximately eight hours. In physical activities, Louise was filled with energy and resolution. There was none of the lack of confidence that she had in social situations.

Once her adventuresome spirit proved almost fatal. Louise and a girlfriend were out on cross-country skis and were following a logging road, as instructed, until they realized they had been given the wrong directions. As night fell, they tried to retrace their route, but her companion became exhausted. She begged to rest, to lie down in the snow, but Louise knew that could be fatal. She had to slap the girl to stop her from sleeping. Finally, they managed to reach a hut and found shelter. Her companion thanked Louise for saving her life—the first of many who were to do so.

Even for Norway, the snowfall was heavy in the early years of the war. Initially, when Anathon was still mobile, the family would trudge every day through the snow to listen to the news on their neighbour's radio. On their way back, Louise's parents talked about the war, and she could see that they were worried, but mostly the children were too young to fully understand the conflict. Meanwhile they continued to be schooled at home, far from the nearest school. Their mother was able to acquire school books and materials from the school nearest their home in Oslo. The parents backed each other up if it was ever necessary to stress the importance of education. Louise often struggled with her math. This problem would persist for years, almost preventing her from gaining entry to medical school.

Her mother sometimes grew irritated with her, and Louise remembers crying as a result, but she soon became essential to her mother as a caregiver to her father at Ospeteig. Louise grew to increasingly love and respect her father, especially when he took her on walks to talk about the many plants, trees and flowers. She grew proud that her papa spent so much time with her. As the effects of the Parkinson's disease became more disabling, the task of nursing fell increasingly to Louise. She gladly stayed and read to him. Much of the other time, she and Cato were hired by local farmers to help with their crops and gardens, often receiving fruit, meat or vegetables in lieu of cash payment. Their chores increased with the addition of two goats that were bought for a steady supply of milk.

Their mother also brought home a Greenland sled dog that they named Leo. Louise recalls training Leo to pull a sled loaded with provisions from Roa. That way she and Cato no longer had to carry heavy supplies on their backs. They also taught the dog to ride on the sled with them, like a person, much to the amusement of locals when they saw a very large dog sitting with them like another child.

When the family acquired rabbits, these multiplied quickly, as did the daily work looking after them, cleaning their cages. As the only son, Cato was initially selected to kill one of the rabbits when they needed one for supper, but he was squeamish about using the hammer. Louise disapproved of his method: he did not strike hard enough, decisively enough, thereby prolonging the animal's agony. She became convinced that a swift, hard blow would be far less cruel. As a result, Louise appointed herself chief executioner of the rabbits.

The family did their best with the housework, food preparation, isolation and dealing with Anathon's illness until eventually he became bedridden. Long hours spent in bed eventually caused serious bed sores and Louise's mother had no medication to treat them. The local physician, Dr. Askerud, increasingly made his secretive visits from Roa and Louise saw how the doctor's visits calmed her mother. Admiring Dr. Askerud, she became more convinced that a career in medicine would be the best path for her to follow. In the process, she also realized how important it was to care for people's emotional difficulties as well as their physical problems.

Increasingly, Anathon became confused, even delirious. He was also prone to fits of anger and fear. The children would hear his voice from the upstairs bedroom crying, "Help! Help!" all the while banging his cane on the floor. Until then they had limited understanding about his illness and had never expected him to die. As Anathon drew closer to death, he was prone to hallucinations caused by his Parkinson's dementia.

"We couldn't tell other people that he was mentally sick or take him to a hospital," Louise said. "If the Germans found out, they would have him taken away and euthanized, as they did so many others suffering from mental illness. As a result, our mother took it upon herself to look after him, and Doctor Askerud would come in the dark of night. In winter he came on skis. I remember that feeling when he came: we were so relieved." Ever after, Louise recalled the doctor's selflessness, and later she would keep her promise to return from her medical studies to enable him to take a well-deserved vacation.

One day the children watched as their mother listened to her husband's cries for help and saw how she didn't dare to go upstairs. For some reason their father thought his wife was trying to kill him, and he was becoming violent. Louise crept up the stairs to comfort him. From their walks together, she knew how to calm him. Increasingly, she was sent to sit with her father when he became delusionary. She somehow found inventive ways to explain away his fears to him.

Once, after a tree had fallen and injured Cato, forcing him to stay briefly at the hospital, her father became agitated about Cato's situation. Bizarrely, Louise put her head in the oven and pretended to be on the telephone to the hospital, relaying encouraging words. Strangely enough, these absurd theatrics mollified her father's anxiety.

There was a reprieve whenever their Uncle Cato and Aunt Signe came to Roa and stayed at the fine hotel near the Roa train station. The children were invited to Roa for a sumptuous meal. Lily could not attend because someone had to stay with Anathon. This was the start of a particular bond between Louise and her childless uncle.

One night there was a terrible winter storm. The children could not sleep as they lay in their beds. Louise, Cato and Ingrid grew anxious. Suddenly, the big tree, which the family called the Father Tree, crashed in the wild winds, hitting the roof with a thud. Louise saw that her father was lying quietly with his eyes wide open, staring out in the dark. He was barely able to speak by this time, but Louise heard him whisper, "There died my tree."

The children awoke the next morning to calm, the storm having passed. Their mother solemnly came to ask them to go upstairs to see their father. He was lying in bed with closed eyes and was attempting to say something to them. Their father made a sign with his hand for Louise to come closer. She bent down to be near his mouth. Finally, Louise was able to decipher what he was trying to say: "Be full of love and truthful." Their mother made a sign for them to leave while she stayed behind in the bedroom and watched him die.

After what seemed a long while, their mother came downstairs, tears streaming down her face. The children looked at her, stunned. She never cried. She stood still for a few moments before saying in a low voice, "Children, Papa is dead." Even though she herself did not really believe in God, Louise thought she could feel her father ascending to heaven. Years later, as an adult, whenever Louise encountered difficult times, she would say to herself, "Be full of love and truthful." It usually helped.

Anathon Aall died January 9, 1943. His body was taken to Oslo for burial in the Aall family plot. Although his earlier dream of founding an international journal to promote cooperation among scientists and humanists was never realized, his work in experimental psychology and his co-founding of the Philosophy Department had been progressive and widely recognized.

Lily withdrew into herself, occasionally playing the piano for consolation. Louise enjoyed hearing the music even though sometimes she felt it only increased the sadness in the house. She found herself longing to become an instant grown-up and a physician—and she still wasn't entirely sure why the family needed to be living so far from Oslo, especially after her father had died. The mystery would only deepen when an SS officer appeared and knocked on their door.

⌒

THIS VISIT BY THE German officer Hans Schwalm would turn out to be part of Reichsführer-SS Heinrich Himmler's initiation of the plan in 1935 to found the German research institute Ahnenerbe ("ancestral heritage") to amplify pan-Germanic commonalities. Intent on proving the ancestral superiority of the German race, Himmler sought to accentuate relationships between north and south Germanic peoples throughout Europe.

Ahnenerbe was officially incorporated into the SS in 1939 and it soon encouraged numerous experts to fabricate pseudo-scientific evidence pertaining to Germanic paganism, a subject in which Lily Weiser had been expert while studying in Vienna. For propaganda purposes, it was useful for the Nazis to connect ancient Viking conquests to the legitimacy of Hitler's conquests. With his keen interest in Norwegian history and folklore, Himmler had already visited the ancient rock carvings at Ekeberg, near Oslo, in the winter of 1941. Archaeological ruins and research in Norway were given such a high priority that German troops were instructed to take care not to damage cultural monuments or artifacts when building bunkers and roads.

In 1942, when Himmler needed a competent representative of Ahnenerbe in Norway, he selected Hans Schwalm for the advancement of Norwegian Science. Schwalm, an academic with extensive research credentials, was instructed to manage the Norway contingent of Germanischer Wissenschafteinsatz ("Germanic Science Initiative"), a trans-European department in the Ahnenerbe. Part of this research was to investigate Norwegian folk stories and to show their supposed similarities to German stories.

Not surprisingly, Schwalm tracked down the whereabouts of Dr. Lily Weiser-Aall. As a member of the Norwegian Academy of Sciences since 1937, she was perhaps the country's best-known female academic. Her reputation in the fields of ethnology and anthropology could be helpful in the Nazis' desire to prove the Scandinavians were part of the German "Aryan" race. The inescapable fact that she had been born and raised in Vienna also qualified her as a prime target for recruitment.

Hans Schwalm had the authority to order her to help the Nazis implement the new order (*Die Neue Ordnung*) of National Socialism. Hence his arrival on Lily Weiser-Aall's doorstep at Ospeteig—even though he had significantly chosen to arrive out of uniform—was fraught with peril. Lily was already known as a liberal intellectual who had numerous Jews as friends. If Lily would assist him in his work with folk customs, Schwalm was invested with the power to be lenient or even helpful. If she refused to cooperate, however, well, there was simply no limit to how far he could send her.

Louise's mother must have known about Schwalm's arrival in advance. Louise recalls she and her siblings had been instructed to be especially good and polite when he arrived. There was no telephone at Ospeteig, so contact between Lily and Schwalm had likely occurred by mail, in advance. Louise, Cato and Ingrid were told to remain indoors, keeping visible as much as possible, and to try to make a good impression. To this day, Louise believes that her mother thought that if her children were friendly to Schwalm, he would be sympathetic to her family.

It is highly possible that Schwalm had been instructed to take Lily to Germany to work on Himmler's propaganda projects under the guise of academic research. Her mother later told Louise that she had hid all the letters she had received from her Jewish friends behind her books in the library. When Schwalm found them, he did nothing. And Lily was allowed to remain at Ospeteig with her children.

The local people would not have known about the intricate, scholarly connections between Schwalm and Lily, but they would have recognized that he was a German officer, even if he was not wearing his uniform, and that he was making numerous visits to her remote location. If the pair of scholars proceeded to have in-depth conversations on the subject of Norwegian folk customs, that would hardly become widely known either. It was no secret the high-born Aall family was increasingly short of money for basic necessities. Lily accepted some assignments from Schwalm for paid translation work for scholarly texts, from Norwegian to German, for *Germania* magazine, which was published by Ahnenerbe. This translation work was, of course, not public knowledge.

Hans Schwalm is known to have returned to Germany in 1944, a year before Germany capitulated to the Allies on May 8, 1945. When the war ended, Schwalm's part in the Nazi occupation was brought under scrutiny. To his credit, Schwalm had evidently succeeded in accomplishing very little. An investigation into his conduct led to an interpretation that he had not wanted to work for the Nazis. Schwalm, a reluctant intellectual forced into uniform, was exonerated of any

Lily Aall and Anathon Aall met at an academic conference in Lübeck in the spring of 1926. He was 59; she was 26. They married in 1928.

Louise (left) with brother Cato and sister Ingrid.

Lily and the three children being home-schooled. Louise (right) never attended a formal school until after World War II.

Anathon could be more playful than he looked. Here he poses with newborn Ingrid and her brother Cato.

Louise enjoyed read-
ing, music, nature and
sports. She was a com-
petitive ski jumper and
later played goalie for a
men's soccer team.

Louise stands atop the house at Ospeteig where she nursed her
father until he died of Parkinson's dementia in 1943.

Louise's mischievous brother
was her closest friend. He once
said he'd marry her if they
weren't siblings.

In 1945, while living with only her mother in
Ospeteig, Louise reluctantly agreed to sit for
this sombre portrait by a local female artist,
Raynhild Langmryr, who knew her mother.

Louise learned to tactfully dissuade suitors. Her mother cautioned her that sex was dangerous for any teenager who wished to pursue learning or a career.

Louise's brother Cato drove her to the Universitiy of Tübingen in southwest Germany, renowned as a haven for international students.

Louise's brother was named after her uncle, Cato. She visited London with him after the war. He helped pay for her university studies.

wrongdoing. He returned to his life as a university professor, teaching at the Lower Saxony Academy of Spatial Research at Hanover and then at the Bundesforschungsanstalt für Landeskunde und Raumordnung in Bonn. He then taught Eastern European geography at the University of Tübingen from 1959 to 1968. Born in Bremen, Germany, on August 16, 1900, Hans Schwalm died in Tübingen in 1992.

Louise recalls the difficult time after the war. Norwegian officials decided to interview her mother. It was finally decided that even though Lily had done translation work for Schwalm, she was clearly anti-Nazi. It had also been logical for the family to leave Oslo when the Nazis arrived to get away from possible persecution as liberal academics who were helping the Jews. The translation work, it was apparent, had been for academic texts. Nevertheless, Louise's mother was very upset by the suggestion that she might have been pro-Nazi. She told Louise never to tell anyone about this part of the family history concerning Schwalm's visit. Louise maintains that she has never spoken about this matter until she was questioned for this biography.

Herman Harris Aall, one of Anathon's younger brothers, was investigated by Police Chief Sverre Hartmann, and he was put on trial after the war as a collaborator. The prosecutor called for life imprisonment. The disgraced law professor would eventually be sentenced in 1947 to 15 years in prison for his collusion with the Nazis, although the sentence would later be reduced when he became very ill. Three senior Norwegian political leaders complicit with Nazism were executed for political crimes after the war: Vidkun Quisling, who led the collaborationist government; Ragnar Skancke, Minister of Labour; and Albert Viljam Hagelin, Internal Affairs Minister. There were 34 other executions of Norwegians and Germans who were convicted of murder, torture or systemic informing.

AFTER THEIR FATHER'S DEATH, Ingrid's health deteriorated. The children were prepared to lose their beloved Papa, but possibly Ingrid took it the hardest. It was discovered she had a stomach ulcer that was bleeding. A neighbouring farm woman agreed to let Ingrid live with them where there would be lots to eat, and slowly she regained her health. Louise and Cato repressed any envy they felt at Ingrid's good fortune and they were glad to see her recover.

Then on a Saturday night Louise was stricken with a severe attack of appendicitis. Dr. Askerud advised that Louise should be transported to the nearest hospital. By the time her mother managed to take Louise to the hospital, two hours away, there were no doctors on duty. A nurse or attendant had left a glass of water by the bed, not recognizing that appendicitis patients should not drink liquids. Unaware or else forgetting that she must not drink liquids, Louise woke in the night, saw the glass of water, and drank it. Her appendix burst. By the time the hospital was able to undertake an appendectomy to remove the appendix and clean her abdomen, peritonitis had spread, resulting in septicemia, or bacteria in the blood.

Sedated with morphine, Louise was hospitalized for more than a month. Her doctors wanted to perform a second operation on her but Louise adamantly refused. At one point, the medical staff contacted her mother, warning that Louise was close to death. To be near her daughter, her mother stayed at a nearby hostel. To pass the time, she would read to Louise at her bedside. Something in one story struck Louise as hilarious to such a degree that she suddenly laughed so hard that her body expelled pus. Or, as she has put it, "Horrible things came out of my rectum."

Strangely enough, she recovered soon afterward. The doctors were amazed that she could be saved by her laughter. Years later, when she was a medical student, Louise learned that peritonitis from a perforated appendix could result in female infertility due to subsequent scarring of the fallopian tubes, or salpingitis. When she was unable to conceive, Louise would conclude the bursting of her appendix was the probable cause.

Having worked side-by-side for years at Ospeteig, Louise and Cato grew much closer. They would sometimes repeat the practice of skiing for eight hours to reach Oslo. Their adventuresome spirit would later give rise to a summer bicycle trip in 1948 that would last two months. Having told their mother they would ride as far north as Narvik, where their former nanny lived, upon reaching Narvik they sent a letter saying they intended to go further, all the way to Hammerfest. Ultimately, Louise and Cato went even farther, all the way to Nesseby, where their father had been born, inside the Arctic Circle. After reaching the most northerly point in Norway, the two teens returned by ship, having been away from home at such a young age for more than two months.

The closeness between brother and sister was such that their friends often called them "the twins." Whenever Cato fell in love with a girl, he would ask Louise what she thought of her. If Louise did not like her, Cato stopped going with her. His female admirers consequently gave her a nickname—the crocodile. Their camaraderie included the outgoing Cato helping Louise overcome her awkwardness in social situations. Handsome, athletic and generous, he could be charismatic and impulsive to a fault. Later, when the two were both medical students, Cato would give Louise a book in which he wrote in tiny letters, just for her to read: "If you weren't my sister, I would have married you." She never replied to this compliment, but she was moved. A realist, she would also quip, "A woman would have to be crazy to marry my brother."

AT WAR'S END, people were streaming back to Oslo, but Tante Grete—Lily's friend—could not find housing, and it was agreed that she and her family would continue to live in the Aall's apartment until they could find another home. Lily could have the use of a small room in the apartment whenever she needed to do some business in Oslo. At this point, two of Lily's close friends offered separately to keep Cato and Ingrid, one child each, so they could go to school in Oslo. Lily decided, however, that Louise should remain with her in Ospeteig, ostensibly to help take care of the house. Louise recalls being devastated at first:

I was stunned and envied my two siblings who could stay in Oslo. Mama looked at me with a warm smile and said, "Don't be a fool. We two need to learn to know each other better in a relaxed atmosphere." Then I felt proud and curious about how things would turn out. I had always wanted to be close to her but I had been too shy. We became more relaxed and we grew closer. Together, we worked cleaning the house and packing up things that we wanted to take back home with us to Oslo when it was convenient to return.

That they were able to become closer to one another had a second important aspect, for it was at this time that Louise was able to watch her mother pursuing her research, making contact with circles of the nearby farm women and having them discuss their lives with her. As an ethologist, Lily had worked this way in Austria, and now Louise was watching it firsthand. As the only teenager in the room, she saw how her mother was able to establish camaraderie and trust with groups of women, thereby encouraging them to confide in her. By witnessing her mother's ingenious methods for addressing and solving problems with groups of women, Louise would later be able to replicate some of her mother's methodology for group therapy sessions, both in Africa and in Canada.

Without the pressure of looking after a dying man, Louise and her mother also had leisure time at Ospeteig to read together, and they frequently had long discussions about the books they had both read. When she was approximately age fifteen, Louise read one novel in particular that would greatly affect her life:

I was a teenager when I read Dostoevsky. He was the most influential person of all because of his novel *The Idiot*. He used his own experience of epilepsy to create the character of the "idiot," Prince Myshkin. I am sure it influenced me in understanding people with epilepsy. It was called *The Idiot* because that's what people thought Prince Myshkin was. They had no idea about all the things that went on in his brain. I also read the book that was written by Dostoevsky's wife about him and his epilepsy. He was a very difficult and complicated person. So, when I went to Africa I knew what was going on inside the minds of people suffering from epilepsy. The people in Africa noticed that. They knew I didn't think they were crazy. So, they were able to talk to me.

Louise says that she is sure that it was these books that also made her become better friends with her mother. Lily had often criticized her, and Louise didn't really know why:

> I remember I had read something in *Brothers Karamazov* about Aloysha and I asked her to come in and I talked to her about it. I said, "Let us be good friends again." And it was very nice for both of us after that. I am sure much of my knowledge in psychiatry came from those books.

Many years later Louise would be able to tell her mother how much she appreciated their time spent together and her mother would be much pleased to hear it.

When it finally came time to return to Oslo in December of 1946, and they had to prepare the house and grounds for their departure, Louise decided she must spare Lily the task of slaughtering their goats and rabbits. When they reached Oslo, only half of the Aalls' original apartment could be made available, so Cato and Ingrid had to remain living separately with family friends. But that did not destroy Louise's happiness about finally living in Oslo with her mother.

Having been a member of the Norwegian Academy of Science since 1937—the year she published perhaps her most important book, *Ethnology and Psychology*—Lily Weiser-Aall first found work managing a new system for accumulating sociological data with questionnaires called the Norwegian Ethnological Examination. She was then elevated to work as a Konservator at the Norsk Folkemuseum on the Bygdøy peninsula, on the western side of Oslo, approachable only by ferry. Louise recalls visiting her mother at her office:

I often visited my mother at Bygdøy. I loved to stay with her and I had a sort of job leading tourists around. I talked to them about the farms, the schools and the museums which had been moved there and recreated in their natural environments. There were all kinds of activities. People were doing things in age-old ways with traditional costumes: baking, sewing and carpentry.

For Louise, it seemed possible that now she was finally living in Oslo, she would be able to have some proper schooling. Seeing how badly Louise wanted to go to school, her mother promptly enrolled her in a private school for girls, Berle, only fifteen minutes away from the family apartment. Louise was delighted, but it turned out that killing rabbits was easier. The well-to-do girls laughed at the clumsy new girl with her simple country clothing. They all had fine clothes and silk stockings. Most of her classmates were inattentive and flighty when asked questions by their teachers. Louise earned their disdain because she liked to be well-prepared for her classes and the teachers appreciated her eagerness to learn:

> The other girls had silk. They had very nice things. I wore things that were knitted with wool. So, I was certainly a funny girl. They found me very odd. But jealousy is not something that is in my life. I did not try to be like them. I withdrew from their curiosity. Sometimes I struggled to become light-hearted and chatty but it only stressed me more, causing me to stammer and get confused. The girls soon drew away from me. They laughed at me. I was too naive. They didn't like me. . . . I was miserable in Oslo. I hated being in school. I was intimidated by the other girls. And I was bored! bored! bored!

Once, hurrying to get to their sewing class, she appeared out of breath in the doorway. The teacher asked if anything was the matter. No, she said, she just didn't want to miss any of the lesson. There arose a derogatory outburst from the other girls. "Uhhh, listen to her!"

Often the other girls would respond with the same derision when she answered questions from their teachers correctly. Louise was shocked and confused by the other girls' behaviour. The girls always made a show of complaining that they had not studied enough, as if they were afraid of getting poor results, but they managed perfectly well to achieve passing grades. Louise, on the hand, ever-earnest and eager to please, often had to struggle to get through, especially in mathematics. Her home-schooling had not prepared her as well as her mother had hoped.

Ostracized as a goody-two-shoes, Louise lost her self-confidence once again, and her grades plummeted. It would take her years to recover from the humiliations meted out by those girls from well-to-do families. Eventually her mother agreed she should leave the private school in favour of a co-educational government school with mostly male teachers who tended to be sterner with the girls. By this time, however, Louise had become withdrawn and anxious in the classroom. She felt at odds with her own life. Cato and Ingrid mostly lived elsewhere and her mother was busy establishing herself at work. During this period, Louise often went alone to movie theatres.

Classical music had the power to touch her but it could stimulate such a deeply moving experience that her longing for a friend to talk to was exacerbated. She missed the evening stars and moon that had been so clear in Ospeteig. People in the street seemed to look at her as if she were crazy when she stared up into the night sky, searching. They turned their heads and looked askance at her, questioningly, as they ran busily through the streets.

Louise began to take the train to Roa on weekends, walking up to Ospeteig and visiting their farming neighbours, who were always glad to see her. She preferred walking alone or, in winter, skiing. These trips, however, interfered with her studies and her classroom preparation; her marks in mathematics and physics plummeted. She tried not to care. Increasingly, she preferred reading books to her school lessons. Of all the arts, it was literature that most deeply motivated her to want to find her place in the world.

While Louise absorbed insight from literary classics, she became increasingly bored and inattentive in the classroom. She often had a book from the library hidden under her desktop, as she became acquainted with writers like Tolstoy and Goethe. Frequently, she sat up in the evenings at home reading these library books instead of studying for her classes:

> When I was with my mother for two years alone, after the war, only her and me, she read many books to me. By the time I came back to Oslo, I was naive in reality, but not in my brain. I saw the woman's side. I knew a woman wants to make a man want to feel closer. But that is not the real love. When I spoke to people and I didn't like them, I felt bad that I didn't like them and so on. But I have always liked books very, very much.

> One book that has influenced me very much was Goethe's *The Sorrows of Young Werther*. Of course, *Faust* is fantastic and I have learned many poems by heart from that book. But I think it might have been *Werther* that made me very afraid of romantic love. Reading that book was like a warning—definitely. I never flirted.

Published when Goethe was twenty-four, the epistolary and partly autobiographical novel *The Sorrows of Young Werther* had engendered countless suicides throughout Europe among young men who strongly identified with its protagonist, Werther, who felt so beleaguered and oppressed by romantic love that he took his own life. For Louise, this cautionary tale not only reaffirmed her mother's streetcar warning; it also enhanced her empathy for the opposite sex:

> My mother didn't touch much. And my mother taught me to be careful about sex and that I should be a virgin when I married. She was from Austria and they can be conservative. I took it much more seriously than most girls. I often thought about boys and I saw that the boys who married

early lost something. They were not so fresh anymore. They were not so optimistic. They became ordinary. When they married young, the woman needed the man to say, yes, yes, I love you. The young husband would not see his friends anymore. He would not want his wife to cry and say, you have left me alone, you do not love me. I hated all that. I could see there were a lot of unhappy marriages. In medical school I came to know that quite a lot of men kill their wives. So, I was afraid of men, kind of. I was afraid of making them feel that they wanted to have me.

In contrast, her younger sister Ingrid was lively and attractive. According to Louise, boys swarmed around her. Sometimes Ingrid could be disdainful of Louise's relative lack of charm. "You are so boring," she would tell her sister. But Louise steadfastly refused to participate. Whenever a boy showed any interest in her, she would warn him she was not inclined to intimacy. Some of them thanked her for her frankness.

Louise was not averse to sex. Rather, she believed it was important to wait until she knew what she was doing. Sex was dangerous for both parties. She believed that many men wanted to be friends with women. They did not necessarily want to have sex. She told herself she would not destroy the lives of young men who were full of ideas about what they wanted to do.

Fortunately, Louise finally found one girl at school who became a friend. They travelled to Roa whenever they could, and stayed at Ospeteig where they swam in the lake or skied in the forests, always returning to Oslo refreshed. Cato and his friends also began going to Ospeteig on holidays. But her schoolwork remained the bane of her existence. One day, close to examinations, she was sitting in the classroom with a math quiz on her desk, sucking on her pencil, unable to work up any answers. The teacher who was supervising the quiz stopped at her desk, clearly unimpressed.

"What is your aim for the future?" he asked.

Without hesitation, Louise looked up. It was the one question she knew the answer to. "I want to be a doctor."

He shook his head. "Give that up. You will never reach such a goal."

The teacher continued shaking his head as he walked away. At first, Louise was shocked, then she became furious. *No teacher has the right to say that*, she thought to herself. But this scorn was short-lived; his regretful tone eroded her confidence further. She worried he could be right. She spent several days in a haze, her confidence once again shattered, because he had so easily disparaged her innermost ambition. In 1948, at age seventeen, Louise took refuge in her diary where she upbraided herself:

> Pull yourself together Louise! Do not let this lazy weakness come upon you and take over. Be aware that this time is important. If you do not fight to overcome your own weakness every day, you will never do it.
>
> Read this letter again so that you will have the inspiration to get enough strength to prepare for exams. You must read this letter many times with great attention. Remember, it is you yourself who have written this letter. Then you will be rewarded. Think of your parents and all the other good people you admire who have struggled and worked for years to reach their goals and understand that you must continue to be alert.

CHAPTER 2

Education & First Love

SOON AFTER THE WAR, Uncle Cato's wife, Tante Signe, died of cancer. Feeling lonely, Uncle Cato invited Louise to London. After the privations of the war years—scrounging for food, arranging secretive visits by the local doctor—Louise was astonished by the liveliness of the bustling British capital, even though London was still recovering from the war. They stayed at a hotel at Piccadilly Circus because her uncle could still afford it. Many of the people working at the hotel did not really believe that Louise was Cato's niece. Girls and women came into the hotel, offering themselves to the moneyed guests. At this time, most Londoners were still struggling.

As a widower, Uncle Cato decided he ought to support each of his nieces and nephews who wished to attend university. He still had sufficient money from his former business dealings, and he offered to help them with tuition to study anywhere in the world. Louise was his favourite. After the war, many people wanted to attend university in Norway, and competition for placements was severe. Because her marks were not high enough in mathematics and physics, Louise was heartbroken to discover that she had not gathered enough points to attend the University of Oslo.

She tried repeating the entire grade with the help of a private tutor, but she was so miserable and disheartened that her results were again insufficient. Just the thought of exams made her feel ill. The next year her brother Cato offered to help. He changed schools and shared some of the same classes. Louise felt much better to have her brother at school with her, and his presence helped her confidence tremendously, but mostly on a social level. Cato was so popular that with his support she developed many new friends.

Slowly, she began to feel less awkward. Cato managed to mix parties and schoolwork with relative ease, whereas she did not. She became desperate to gain her Examen Artium, the academic certificate that would qualify a student for entrance to universities in Denmark and Norway. On her third attempt to realize her dream and attend medical school, Louise fell short for qualification by just one point. When Louise discovered that Cato had made it into university and she had not, she fainted.

Seeing her daughter was distraught, Lily wrote and explained the situation to her best friend, Gabriella Wissmann, who was married and living in the university town of Tübingen in southwest Germany. For centuries Tübingen, a two-hour drive from Zurich, had accommodated international students, in keeping with the traditions of Eberhard Karls University, founded in 1477. It was long regarded as one of the top five German universities for medicine and law. One-third of Tübingen's population were students, and almost 20 percent of those were foreigners. Its university graduates included Georg Wilhelm Friedrich Hegel and Johannes Kepler.

Gabriella had been visiting Oslo when Louise was born and she had been chosen to be Louise's godmother. As she had no children of her own, she and her husband agreed in 1951 to have Louise live with them. It was Gabriella's husband, Hermann Wissmann Jr., a painfully shy man who was nonetheless a revered geography professor, who would eventually smooth the way for Louise to be accepted into the medical studies program at the University of Tübingen.

It helped that Anathon Aall had also briefly taught at Tübingen.

Children of professors who had taught at German universities were accorded free tuition if they could maintain high marks from year to year. Louise's proficiency with the German language was not strong, and she would be obliged to teach herself Latin, but she was thrilled with the opportunity to attend classes from 8 a.m. to 8 p.m. daily at a prestigious university:

> Uncle Cato knew how depressed I had been, and ashamed, so he invited me to a very expensive hotel outside Oslo in a beautiful setting. He walked through the forestland with me down to a river where there was a fantastic view. He sat on a bench with me and told me about his struggle with his life. He encouraged me to pursue my dream and study medicine. He gave me a stipend of money so I could buy the books and other materials I would need at the university.

Her brother Cato drove her to Tübingen in an old car that he had bought from a friend. When they arrived and Cato met the Wissmanns, he decided that he, too, would like to enrol. Two years later he would do so, eventually gaining his professional accreditation as a nutritionist. He then completed a medical degree in Spain and thereafter lived in many countries. An idealist who frequently mismanaged his private life, he would spend the rest of his adult life working for the United Nations and the World Health Organization on behalf of refugees.

Meanwhile, Louise's younger sister, Ingrid, went to live as a painter in France. She would develop an international career as a professor of Fine Arts, living in India, China, Israel and other countries, later settling in Long Beach as a professor at the University of California and publishing numerous books. All three siblings kept in touch with their mother by writing letters.

Having her brother Cato join her in the university town raised Louise's spirits, which were already high. This was the first time in her life when Louise felt she was finally coming into her own:

I was so incredibly happy. I was like a flower blossoming because I was able to talk to everybody. At the dances, all the boys wanted to dance with me. It was so different from Norway. I was not at all shy anymore. In Tübingen they didn't know me, they didn't know my background. It was a beautiful town with old buildings and people all knew each other. And all the students very much liked being there. It is very good to come to a place where people don't know you. Then you can experiment a bit. You can learn how to get closer to people. I learned how to be friends, especially with boys, without it becoming dangerous. I had quite a few nice friends, boyfriends, but they never tried anything. They could see I didn't want that. They respected me a lot.

So, there were very, very good things in Tübingen. There were professors and some of my mother's friends. They were highly educated and they just loved me for the way I was. It helped a lot. Maybe I was sixteen or seventeen. I'm not sure. I remember when I got my first medical book. I went up to a tower and I thought, now I am on my way. It was fantastic. I have never been so happy in my life as when I was a medical student in Tübingen.

Each year, when she was at Tübingen, Louise was able to pass the annual tests to maintain free tuition. She nonetheless accepted a job as a house cleaner for a woman doctor, and she also sold soap door-to-door. There was a sociological imperative to this diversion. Like her mother, she wanted to see how different people lived. Selling soap, Louise discovered the rich were the least friendly, whereas the most generous tended to be those with the least money, particularly refugees.

One day, while she was cleaning the outdoor steps of the doctor's home, the head of the student union recognized her and was upset to see her spending time on menial labour. He gallantly proceeded to arrange for the student union to provide her with a stipend—but

Louise liked the manual work and so she kept on doing it.

After a time, Louise felt that she had to leave the Wissmanns', largely because her godmother's mother-in-law, who was also living in the house, resented Louise's presence as a non-German. Attending classes until 8 p.m., Louise was unable to eat at regular hours, and this behaviour angered the widow of Hermann von Wissmann Sr., who would not allow Louise to eat at odd times. In addition, she was jealous of the attention that Louise, as a non-German, was being accorded.

An argument can easily be made that this old woman's hostility was born of the arrogance derived from her husband's celebrated military butchery. While living with the Wissmanns, Louise learned that Wissmann Jr. was decidedly different from his renowned, militaristic father with the same name. A wild game hunter, Wissmann Sr. had treated his son, an academic, as a weakling.

More than twenty German cities had streets named after Wissmann Sr. as a *Volksheld* (hero of the people); a statue had been erected in Berlin. Wissmann Sr. had been essential in helping the Belgian King Leopold to gain his stranglehold on the Congo. As an intrepid African explorer in the 1880s, Wissmann had been hired by Leopold to "pacify" the equatorial tribes. He had orchestrated a reign of terror, the reverberations of which would be felt for generations.

To emulate Belgium and to take its own huge chunk of the African colonial pie, in 1884 the German East Africa Company had taken control of a large territory from Lake Victoria to Zanzibar. Then when the company had difficulty in putting down native revolts, the area was turned into a government "protectorate" named German East Africa. This in turn required a Reichskommissar, and so Hermann Wilhelm Leopold Ludwig von Wissmann was appointed in 1889. By 1890, he was accorded a hero's welcome upon his return to Germany. In 1891, Wissmann was appointed commissioner for the western region of German East Africa. By 1895, he was its governor.

Wissmann Sr. wrote several books including *Afrika: Schilderungen und Ratschläge zur Vorbereitung für den Aufenthalt und den Dienst in den Deutschen Schutzgebieten*. These books were in the home of

Wissmann Jr., where the widow lived. In this way, Louise first learned about an area of the African continent called German East Africa. At the end of World War I, the British had renamed it Tanganyika when they took over administrative control of the country.

From her reading Louise learned that *tanga* in Swahili means sail; *nyika* means wilderness.

Louise's curiosity about East Africa would lead her to books by the British pastor, David Livingstone, who went on foot throughout Africa, from west to east, in the wilderness, to preach to the so-called "wild" Africans.

She also read the work of the Henry Morton Stanley, the journalist who walked through Africa, from east to west, searching for Livingstone until he famously discovered the pastor in the African interior. The romantic ideal of walking alone in Africa appealed to her love of nature and her quest for independence.

As a young Norwegian in medical school, Louise did not always find it easy to remain focused on her studies. She very much wanted to enlarge her social world, and one day she decided to go to a dance:

> I didn't have clothes to wear so I went to a place where they rent out clothes. I had no idea what was fashionable. I saw a red dress that seemed elegant, so I rented it and went to the dance in it. But this time I didn't get people to dance with me. I just sat and I just looked. I became quite sad because I *loved* to dance. It came the time when they announced: "Ladies Choice," which was when the ladies could choose. I thought to myself, okay, I'm going to choose somebody. I began looking around. Finally, I saw a table with several people. I went over to them. It was a table with several teenagers and their father and mother. I said to the father, "Would you dance with me?"

> At first, they kind of laughed at me. "'Ha, look, she you wants you to dance with her." I could see that the father almost said, "Oh, just leave me alone." But he came. And we danced. He was somewhat embarrassed but he knew it would appear

churlish to decline. As we were awkwardly dancing, he began to make small talk. He had learned that I was in medical school, so he asked, "Why do you want to be doctor?" I said to him, "You can't ask me such a big question while we are dancing!" But we started talking anyway. He asked me who I was, where I came from. It became more interesting. He told me he was a Protestant minister, a professor of religion. So, I asked him some questions about that. Of course, my grandfather had been a pastor. We talked and talked and talked. It was very interesting. At the end of the dance, I thanked him and didn't see him anymore that night.

Later I met him again and he had heard that I was having difficulties with where I was living with the Wissmanns. So, he said, "We have a beautiful place, a house, you could have a room there." I was astonished. I said, "Well, that sounds good." And so I lived there with the family.

I loved them all: especially the children. The father and mother were extremely good to me. They always invited me for dinner on Sundays. We had good talks and so on. And he was so interesting to talk to. A thinking person. I lived with them for several years. The children liked me. I spent countless hours playing ping-pong with them. This man, whose name was Steinbach, was like a father to me. Only much, much later he told me: "That was a terrible dress you had on at the dance!"

When her mother visited her in Tübingen, and they travelled together to attend a congress in Passau, Germany, Louise could see that her mother was proud to introduce her as a medical student. As graduation from university approached, however, she learned that the policies of the medical authorities in Norway meant that her Tübingen degree would not permit her to practise in Norway. Louise remained determined as ever, and her resolve was strengthened by a stint, after graduation, working as a medical intern in Oslo. There she was among the throng of 20,000 well-wishers who had serenaded Dr. Albert Schweitzer with a Scandinavian hymn "Wonderful Is the Earth" after he had received his Nobel Peace Prize, first announced in 1952, but presented much later on December 10, 1953.

Along with her professors and fellow students, Louise was also to sit in the big hall of the University of Oslo and hear Dr. Schweitzer deliver an unforgettable Nobel Peace Prize lecture about his work at his hospital complex in the tropical wilderness of what is now Gabon. She proceeded to read Schweitzer's books, and increasingly realized Schweitzer's "reverence for life" philosophy was not dissimilar to her father's Christian beliefs. When the people of Norway matched the $33,000 Nobel Prize money, enabling Schweitzer to build a leprosarium at Lambaréné, Louise did not have any premonition that she might one day be able to see it and work as a doctor there.

⌒

AFTER TÜBINGEN and her brief period as an intern in in 1954–1955, Louise decided to accept an offer to study, with free tuition, at the medical faculty of Saarland University. Founded in November of 1948, the university in Saarbrücken in Germany, near the French border, was created by the French government, under the auspices of the University of Nancy, as a bilingual institution that combined French and German educational traditions in a unique manner. It was the first university to be founded west of the Rhine River in the aftermath of World War II, at which time Saarland was a partly autonomous region linked by an economic and monetary union to France. The French government was enabling foreign students such as Louise to study in French, with French tutors to help foreign students learn the language. Following the defeat of Germany, France was appearing to take an altruistic approach, but there was clearly a political motive: to help the people of Saarland establish a separate political entity that would be reliant on France. The Saarland was rich in resources.

After taking the train to Saarbrücken and getting settled, Louise welcomed the opportunity to acquaint herself with the approaches taken by French medical practitioners. Whereas German physicians had tended to restrict their diagnostic approach to the accumulation of data about the patient, she discovered that French doctors were far more likely to respond to the mental and emotional needs of a patient while they were treating physical problems:

> The French teachers were taking more time to be aware of how patients responded in the mental state. They were making observations about the ways that patients dealt with emotions, with their fears, rather than only recording details of an illness. We were made aware of how to help to relieve anxiety and depression, and to listen to the physicians' assurances that the patients could be helped. I learned the importance of taking a friendly approach.

At Saarland University, unlike what she had found in Tübingen, there were nine small hospital buildings surrounded by trees and flowers, with parks and benches. People with small children were encouraged to use the hospital grounds where there were birds, cats and dogs. Patients with similar illnesses were in similar rooms so they could help one another recover. Louise was mostly assigned to help female patients.

For the sleeping accommodation of the students, all the women students slept in a dormitory with about sixty beds. There were many restrictions and the doors were locked at eight every night. Male students had more freedom. They could stay up as long as they wished, without many rules.

One day, to avoid the constant distraction of conversation in the dormitory, Louise took an hour's walk through the surrounds and was amazed to discover a little village with neat houses and a beautiful church. There, she was soon befriended by an elderly couple who greeted her with kindness and allowed her to stay overnight. A friendship blossomed. The more she helped the old woman with her housework in their little house, the more she became accepted in the picturesque village. A friendly local priest took to calling her *la petite étudiante* and she was soon invited into other people's homes.

Eventually the constant laughing and chatter in the dormitory led Louise to find accommodation on her own in the village, taking care not to create any fuss while doing so. The husband in the house gave her a revolver to defend herself when she walked through the woods between the hospital and the village. There were many rough men who worked in a nearby factory, he said, and they would be keen to approach her. During her walks to and from the hospital, Louise always kept the revolver hidden in her purse.

At the end of her studies in Saarland University, having greatly improved her fluency in French, Louise decided that she wanted to complete a higher medical degree, and she chose the University of Zurich. The reason: this was where the Red Cross was based, and Louise greatly admired the organization and its founder.

On the train to Zurich, Louise thought about all she had learned and what she wanted to achieve. Tübingen had been an education in socializing with her brother Cato and others but often there were too many distractions from her medical studies. She felt she could have studied more for her classes. In Saarbrücken, she had resolved to be more diligent, to study harder and be less involved with other students and friends. She hoped to continue that resolve in Switzerland.

In Zurich, she found a small room in a quiet area on the top floor of an apartment building. She was happy and eager to start her new life. Even though this room was so small she hardly had any room to move about, it afforded her access to a flat roof where she could walk and look out at the entire city and the Alps on the other side of Lake Zurich. It was glorious to be atop the building when all the church bells in town started to ring simultaneously at 6 o'clock. All the bells, big and small, sounded to her a friendly welcome. She often went to the rooftop and had a feast for her ears. At other times she walked on the roof when there was a full moon, with the faint outline of mountains in the background.

In Zurich, Louise expected she would have to write an entrance exam to continue her studies but she was unsure of the procedure.

She saw that there was a list of admission exams and went to the appointed hall. Here she found a room full of students preparing to write exams, and initially it appeared that the supervisor would not permit her to apply because she was female. Then she realized the hall was being used for applicants to the engineering faculty.

When she was finally able to locate the registrar for the medical school, he was personally opposed to helping foreign students, and he tried to dissuade her. Taken aback, she refused to leave. Finally, he asked in an irritated way, "Why do you want to study medicine at our university? Why not study in your own country?"

"I admire and respect Switzerland," she responded, "because it has managed to avoid getting involved in wars." She also told him how much she appreciated the willingness of the Swiss to help suffering people. Henry Dunant was a hero, she said, for creating the Red Cross in Geneva, in 1863, along with Gustave Moynier and others.

The registrar could see the enthusiasm in her shining eyes. "I have often dreamt of being in this country and studying here," she said. "There is no other country I would like so much to study in and learn from the people here." He remained silent for a time, and then he finally gave his permission to stay and study at the university. He looked at her marks at Tübingen and found that they were sufficient for entry. She would not have to write entrance exams. Her heart pounded with happiness. She vowed that nobody would ever be disappointed with her. She was to study in Zurich from late 1955 to 1958.

Her Swiss education began with a course in autopsies, examining cadavers. It was not a task she enjoyed but she found she was good at it. Moreover, she discovered that she could follow all the classes taught in German relatively well. After that, every day, for three years, she looked forward to her classes and the new teachers. She was careful not to involve herself with too many friends, not to go to the theatre, films or other distractions, as she had done in Tübingen.

She also learned how to make patients have confidence in her, because she herself was confident. She loved her small room where she could study undisturbed for hours, reading and learning about medicines and illnesses. To her delight, she was able to concentrate so well that she did not forget what she had read. Her knowledge about illnesses and treatments grew quickly.

During her stay in Zurich, Louise once set off on a prolonged hike into the Alps, unescorted. Her naive, intrepid experiences in Norway with her brother had taught her to improvise, to trust in her own inventiveness. She carried few belongings. To her surprise and alarm, she discovered the Swiss were not at all friendly towards itinerant strangers. In this post-war period, a solo wayfarer with a backpack was viewed with suspicion. At one point, unable to find a place to sleep, she was reduced to asking a farmer if she could sleep in his stable. Later that night, he attempted unsuccessfully to rape her. While physically resisting, she outwitted her attacker by shaming him.

AT ZURICH, THERE WAS a big auditorium, the *Aula*, where students gathered for important lectures. One day Louise noticed a slender boy enter and look for a place to sit. He walked as if he were trying to hide, as if he wished he could be invisible. And yet when he smiled, Louise saw that his face was beautiful. Each time he came into the auditorium, Louise noticed him and became curious to know his story. There was something deeply serious about him. He looked as if he were carrying a big problem. But she told herself she must not approach him, to let him know she was fascinated by him. It could be dangerous to become friendly with somebody who was really lonely; he might cling to her—except this boy did not appear to ask much for himself. He was humble and this appealed to her. In the cafeteria, if there were two things on a table to eat, he was the sort of person who wouldn't take the biggest one.

The more she watched him, the more she found to like about him. Finally, one day Louise talked to a friend of his and learned his name was Eric. The friend told Louise they were planning a trip to the Alps. Eric didn't have any skis so she volunteered to lend him hers:

I thought that would be all right. It would be a safe thing to do. They could come and see if the skis would work for him. So, the two boys came to my place. Eric sat himself in the corner of the sofa and retreated into himself. But the other one was a Norwegian boy. He drank some alcohol—I don't know what it was—and he became very lively. He tried to kiss me.

Louise became furious. She stood up and flung the Norwegian boy onto the sofa. Eric looked astonished. He had never seen a girl do that. She appeared like some Viking fury. After they left, she worried she would never see Eric again, but the two boys did return, visiting for a cup of coffee and *Kuchen* (cake). Eric said that he would like to reciprocate her hospitality.

When the threesome met at Eric's apartment, she was pleased to see everything was clean and that he was a good cook. Better yet, when he put on music, it was Mozart. So, Eric loved Mozart, too! The friend was there talking and talking, saying silly things, while Louise ignored him and listened to the music. It had been so long since she had heard her beloved Mozart. She lifted her eyes and met Eric's. And she could see in his eyes that he had the same feelings about the music: "When his eyes met mine, it was like something went through my whole body. And I thought, ah, that is *love*. I was *very*, very taken with that. We were like the same souls."

These feelings of uplifting mutuality only increased. They went out together, conversing in German. They listened to music. They became very good friends. It was a deep feeling they both had for one another. They were surprised to learn they could be so consistently happy. It went on like this for a long time.

They discovered that they read and liked the same books, *The Brothers Karamazov* and others. They were happy on a spiritual plane until, after several months, she realized it was always Eric asking her what they ought to do. She started to wonder why he couldn't sometimes make a plan for them? Annoyed, she brought this matter to the fore. Why couldn't he instigate anything? There was something missing in him. Louise still did not know the secret of his background, and would not learn about it for some time.

Soon after this, Eric would come to her room in the mornings so they could walk to school. Zurich was not a place for loose morals. Someone reported their behaviour to the local police, presuming Eric was sleeping with her. Fortunately, there was someone who knew Eric well and told the police he was innocent. It was recognized they were a very "nice" couple, simply friends.

It was Louise's idea to take a trip together. They went to a town in northern Italy, by the ocean, to go swimming. It all went well for a time, but then Eric became ill with flu—very ill! She contracted the flu too, but she wasn't nearly so sick. They came back as soon as possible to Zurich but Eric couldn't recover. She started to get worried. He said, "No, no, no, I'm fine." But his health didn't improve. He refused to take anything. When she pressured him further, he reacted with some hostility. Finally, she demanded that he see a doctor, and Eric said he would go. But he didn't go. Instead he went to the pharmacy and bought some over-the-counter medication.

Eric was weakening. Against his wishes, Louise went to a colleague at the hospital. This doctor came to see Eric and was taken aback. Why hadn't Eric seen a doctor before! The doctor forced Eric to be admitted to the hospital where they learned that when Eric had contracted the flu in Italy, it had affected his entire constitution and, as a result, his kidneys had begun to fail. As Louise thought about the situation, she realized that only a short time before, she had been treating another young man in the hospital who had much the same problem, and he had died of kidney failure. That made it worse. She told herself she should have known.

Not allowed to visit him when he was in acute care, Louise told the nurses to let her know if Eric became overly anxious. A few times she stayed with him during the night, unbeknownst to the doctors. She kept telling him he would be all right. Finally, one day he said, "No, I am going to die." He felt bad about it all, as if he were letting her down. No, she said it was he who had given her so much.

Louise's father had died upstairs in his bedroom at Ospeteig, out of sight, so she had never seen anyone die until Eric died in her arms. After Eric's death, she would never again be afraid of sitting by people who were dying. But when it was over, Louise was exhausted and fell into a deep sleep for hours. It became clear that she, too, was very ill. Her mother came to Zurich to take care of her and when she saw Louise's condition, she didn't dare leave her daughter alone. Louise recalls the terrible ordeal:

> It was awful, awful, awful. It took me a long time to get over this loss. This relationship was so beautiful. With him I had been terribly, terribly happy. I learned much from his character. I learned humility from him. Because I had been a very, very proud person.

Distraught and in mourning, Louise wrote to some people Eric had known in Paris to tell them what had happened, and they wrote her a lovely letter saying, "We have never known a person as beautiful as that boy."

Eric had never told anyone about his past, including Louise. Only by accident, looking through some medical records in Zurich years later, did she come across the medical files for Eric's father. Only then did she learn that Eric's father had tried to poison all his children, including Eric. When Eric's father killed himself in a mental hospital, Eric had illogically felt he was somehow responsible for his father's death. Louise recognized then that the poisoning attempt by Eric's father could have accounted for Eric's inability to make decisions. The poison could also have contributed to the weakness of his kidneys.

For the rest of her life she would have dreams about Eric. In one particular dream he was sitting on a stone, hunched over, downcast. "Oh, Eric, it's you!" she would say. "Why do you look so sad?" And he would reply, "It's over. I can't come back. Because I know you don't really want it." It was a strange dream, as dreams often are, because Louise knew in her waking moments that she had truly loved Eric and really had wanted him to come back and stay with her.

One of the two people who soon after examined her in her oral medical exams was a doctor who was a specialist in kidney failure. When she was unable to answer any of his questions, another student had to whisper to him about what had happened with Eric.

Eventually Louise went to the bench where she and Eric had looked out over Zurich together. She vowed to herself, loudly, because there were no people there, "I will get over this. I am going to become a doctor!"

Sixty years later, asked directly if her relationship with Eric and his death had any correlation with her decision to go to Africa, she did not hesitate to respond. "Oh, yes, sure. This had to have some bearing on my decision to go to Africa. I had to get away and do something completely different. Otherwise I might have killed myself."

In Zurich, as she proceeded to treat patients, some of whom were close to death, Louise found it helped to stay with the patient to listen to what the patient wanted to say. Sometimes, just the friendly touch of a physician's hand could work wonders. By listening intently to what the patient said, she could decide how much each patient could tolerate when learning how serious their illness was. It was especially important not to frighten the already fearful patient.

After their exams were finished, medical students continued working as interns in various hospitals where the older physicians helped newcomers. She was surprised to discover that one hospital had very little food for the interns. After working her shift one day, she was ravenous. One of the nurses took pity on her and found her four eggs. She ate all four quickly, including the shells. The nurse was shocked. But Louise just smiled, saying, "In Norway we eat all of the egg, including the shells."

Female interns had to learn some lessons on their own. Once a severely mentally ill patient grabbed her and tried to kill her; another time when she leant over to examine a twenty-year-old man, he grabbed her forcefully and tried to kiss her. It was important to know how to fend them off.

INSPIRED BY HER MEMORIES of Albert Schweitzer at the Nobel Prize ceremony when he had talked about his hospital in Africa, Louise eventually decided to leave Zurich and go to Basel, Switzerland, to obtain a certificate in tropical medicine at the Swiss Tropical Institute. Basel was scenic with a beautiful river through the town, lined with old houses and crossed by several picturesque bridges. She vowed well in advance to proceed with even more assertiveness than she had displayed in Tübingen, Saarland and Zurich, not to allow herself to be distracted by beauty or friendships, even if it resulted in loneliness.

At the Swiss Tropical Institute, established by Rudolf Geigy in 1943, she would not only learn about tropical diseases in Africa and its treatments for people, she would also be able to study diseases related to other animals such as cats, dogs, sheep, cows and pigs. She had discovered how much she loved animals while working with her brother at Ospeteig. Another advantage of studying in Basel was that the diploma program for Tropical Medicine could be completed within a year.

Switzerland in general, and Basel in particular, had long been home to pharmaceutical companies, including J.R. Geigy AG. This international firm had employed the chemist Paul Müller, who established the insecticidal properties of DDT, a compound that had been first synthesized by a German chemistry student, Othmar Zeidler, in 1874. The effectiveness of DDT to counteract tropical, insect-borne diseases had resulted in Müller receiving the Nobel Prize for Medicine in 1948. It was not until many years after that the disastrous effects of DDT on the bird and animal populations came to be widely understood.

Most of the courses at the Institute were taught in German and French. Classes often lasted for three hours without a break. Then there would be a brief mealtime, followed by more classes, often into the evenings. Louise learned about insects and worms, pathology, bacteriology and histopathology. She often studied late in the library that was filled with African history books, increasing her curiosity.

There was little time for friendships but Louise did come to know Rudolf Geigy's wife, a beautiful and highly educated Russian who, as a refugee, had married Geigy, possibly in part to gain Swiss citizenship. It was Geigy's wife who arranged for Louise to meet her husband at their estate. When Geigy asked Louise what she wanted to do, she expressed her wish to work somewhere in Africa. Geigy then described to her the small hospital he had built in Ifakara, Tanganyika, 600 miles south of the equator, for research purposes after his visit to Tanganyika in 1949.

The centre at Ifakara undertook a wide range of projects. For instance, when mosquito nets were first introduced in Africa, many mothers would make a hole in the nets in order to talk to their children, not understanding that the tiny mosquitoes were the source of malaria. The Ifakara research hospital had helped to develop an anti-mosquito spray that could be used on mosquito nets if a net had holes. "Papa" Geigy suggested that Louise could be paid a small stipend if she would agree to go to Ifakara and conduct some research on behalf of a firm called Hoffmann-La Roche. So, at age twenty-eight, Louise agreed to conduct tests in Africa for a new and unproven medicine to counter amoebiasis, or as it is more commonly called, amoebic dysentery.

Before she sailed on a freighter from Genoa, Italy, following the advice of the pharmaceutical firm, Louise wrote to the Archbishop of Tanganyika for permission to provide medical services as an alternative to the medicine men. Although she was not a Roman Catholic, the Swiss-born Archbishop Edgar Aristide Maranta wrote back to agree that she could help the nurses at the Ifakara Mission Hospital and conduct her research on amoebic dysentery.

Soon there would literally be no end to the number of people who wanted her medical attention.

CHAPTER 3

Becoming Mama Mganga

AFTER SAILING VIA THE Suez Canal and the Red Sea, Louise disembarked in Dar es Salaam in 1959. It was still a coastal town, not yet the teeming metropolis of five million it would become when she would be attacked on the street almost fifty years later. As she walked down the gangplank of the *Kenya Castle*, Louise saw amongst the small crowd gathered to greet the ship, a Catholic priest waving at her, waiting to help with her luggage. He had been sent by the Archbishop to drive her to the mission compound to stay the night.

The following morning, Louise eagerly left the coast to drive inland in a truck driven by a Capuchin friar who kept a figure of Saint Christopher dangling above the dashboard. The proliferation of wildlife on both sides of the road—and often crossing it—was astonishing. The continuously bumpy and bone-jarring, fourteen-hour drive entailed a near-collision with an elephant. Lions, buffaloes, waterbucks, zebras and antelopes were abundant. Decades later she would recall the journey:

> I got a thrill out of watching the white birds walking up and down the backs of the brown buffaloes, peacefully picking flies and other insects off their skin. The huge buffaloes

would lift their heads and watch the truck as we passed, their broad horns showing clearly against the sky. The waters were crowded with crocodiles.

Upon reaching Ifakara, she was less pleased to discover her smelly, rudimentary room would be shared with bats. Droppings strewn on the tiny bed were problematic, but as she was soon to discover they were nothing compared to the fact that the female doctor who had previously been at Ifakara had been widely disliked. Louise would have to find ways to show them that she was different. One way, she decided, was to add Swahili to the other languages she spoke. To this end, Louise found a bilingual version of *Aesop's Fables* and sat down to study it. After Louise had been working on the language for some hours each day, Sister Arnolda, the oldest nurse, who had been watching Louise poring over the text, said to her: "Forget about the language for a while and just follow me on my rounds." Louise agreed this was a good plan. After all, she had to know the hospital routine and how to fit into it, and this way she could learn the language by listening to others.

Much preferring humans to her bats, Louise stayed at the hospital in the evenings, fraternizing with the African staff. During the day she bolstered her confidence with medical tasks, doing her research on amoebic dysentery, but also finding that she was mostly needed in the delivering of babies. After dusk, she felt how the rational world of European medicine could give way to the mystical world of the African bush. She could feel the emotional stress of the families who had gathered for their loved ones, particularly after medicine men had visited and advised a family that a patient would recover only at home.

Often, patients disappeared out of the hospital into the night. Having learned much of her mother's techniques as an ethnologist, she was curious to learn where their homes might be, what they ate, where they slept. After a day's journey in a Land Rover, when Louise arrived at Merera, her first village in the bush, the priest whisked her away from the people who had hurriedly assembled to see her. She was disappointed by his protectiveness and assured him she did not mind their curiosity. She did not wish to viewed as being aloof.

As night fell, and she walked to her sleeping quarters, she discovered a crowd of women and girls had gathered at her hut. One young woman put her foot in the door as Louise was about to enter, making it impossible to shut the door. Not wanting to hurt the woman by slamming the door on her foot, Louise found she was soon surrounded by excited women who were talking in a flurry of words and laughing for reasons she did not understand.

The women reached out to touch her hair and stroke her arms. At first she accepted their attention. After all, they were curious about her in much the same way she was curious about them. But before she could stop them, they had lifted up her skirt. When they saw she was white all over, the throng uttered cries of "oh" and "ah." Some of them were so curious about her white body that they even poked their fingers into her mouth, her eyes and her ears. More people pushed forward and stretched out their hands to touch her. She tried not to appear as frightened as she really was. When a scuffle ensued, she dashed inside and was able to lock the door. There were cries of disappointment and knocks at the door, but she did not dare open the door.

The small window openings were soon filled with dark faces peering in. When she saw the reflection of her lamp in their staring eyes, it gave her an eerie feeling, the like of which she had never experienced before. She was like a circus attraction, hardly a person at all. With so many people watching, she felt too uncomfortable to undress. Instead, she crept under the mosquito net, fully clothed, blew out the light and lay motionless, like a prisoner, hoping the onlookers would eventually go away.

When she woke in the morning there was still one pair of eyes watching her from the window. As news spread that she was awake, more laughing faces returned to watch her. She washed and dressed as best she could. But when she began to comb her hair, the women outside went into hysterics. They pulled at the door and shouted in unison for Louise to open it. They had apparently never seen long hair like hers before. She opened the door while she continued to comb it. All the women gazed in astonishment. Some swooned in a trance-like state, glassy-eyed, and mimicking her every movement. For reasons she would never be able to comprehend, others literally turned themselves upside down, standing on their heads.

After all this, Louise hurried across the yard to the priest's house. As soon as he understood the frenzy of the women who were following her, the Father came out and reprimanded them. He told them that it was bad *heshima*, that it was disrespectful, to behave so unmannerly towards a stranger. They finally began to disperse, laughing as they went and discussing what they had seen. Louise could not help feeling violated.

Once she returned to Ifakara, she discovered that the hospital laboratory accommodated her research tasks, but the actual town of Ifakara was stifling. Louise much preferred the cheerful atmosphere of Igota, where there was a smaller dispensary about an hour's drive from Ifakara. Two African-trained nurses—called "dressers"—were unusually competent at Igota, and the priests were friendly and appreciative. After a few weeks of travelling back and forth, she accepted their offer of a room in Igota, closer to the mountains and the town of Mahenge.

Children from the nearby school loved to knock on her door, just to have a glimpse of her. Whenever she opened the door, they would shriek with delight and run away laughing. From her window she had a lovely view of the wide plain and trees. Sometimes lions roared and she often heard the grunting of hippopotamuses and the howling of hyenas. This was the Africa she had dreamed of as a girl. It began to feel like her new home. People called out to her, "*Jambo, Mama Mganga?*" (How are you, Mama Doctor?), and she had learned to reply, "*Mzuri, asante sana*" (Very well, thank you).

One day not long after, when she went for breakfast, she found the staff was unusually excited. Apparently Archbishop Maranta would soon be arriving in his splendid car for a visit. People from all over the countryside were coming to the mission in anticipation. When the beloved Archbishop arrived, the dispensary staff filed out to greet him. First, the priests came forward, followed by teachers, maids and others. They all kneeled, one at a time, and kissed the Archbishop's ring on his outstretched hand. After being blessed, they made the sign of the cross and stood up. Not being Catholic, Louise stood respectfully aside. Because her European shoes were too hot, Louise often went barefoot or in sandals. At the moment when she finally went forward to pay her respects to the Archbishop, she felt an excruciating pain in her toe. Looking down, she immediately saw what was wrong. She had been bitten by a scorpion.

Tears of pain filled her eyes. The Archbishop was puzzled. What on earth was wrong with this poor woman? Embarrassed to let him know what had just happened, Louise grimaced as she feigned a smile, determined not to unduly draw attention to herself. The sympathetic and astonished Archbishop assumed this newly arrived doctor must be feeling very lonely in a foreign land. The Archbishop took her hands and leaned forward, with kindness and respect. "Pray, Fräulein, pray," he said.

Mortified by both the piercing pain of her scorpion bite and her tears, Louise retreated to her room as soon as possible. As she ministered to her scorpion sting, she worried she might be a dreadful failure in Africa. A letter from the Archbishop arrived soon afterwards, inviting her to Dar es Salaam so that she might accompany him on a safari. He politely suggested that she might wish to see more of the country. If only to be polite in return, Louise felt she had to agree to go along.

One of the Fathers happened to be driving to Dar es Salaam the next day, so it would be easy to get a ride to the coast with him. The resultant safari in southern Tanganyika proved unforgettable both for what she saw and her companion. The Archbishop was famous for having a big car that he drove himself. Everywhere they went, men, women and children ran to the roadsides and knelt down.

He took care to drive slowly. That way people could see who was in the remarkable car and they could spread the news of his visit. The Archbishop constantly made the sign of the cross, blessing everyone, while talking to Louise beside him. It struck her that he would make an excellent Pope.

Initially, Louise had felt uncomfortable, because it might look as if she was pretending to be royalty, but Archbishop Maranta was so distinguished and loved, and he made so many people happy, that she grew to admire him and relax. By the time they had parted in Dar es Salaam, she felt buoyed by their friendly, unsentimental talks. It turned out he had been gauging her character. The Father who was driving her back to Igota confided that Archbishop Maranta had told him, "From now on, I allow the Padres from the missions to take her along wherever Dr. Aall is needed. She is honest and sincere."

DURING LOUISE'S TRAVELS in the months that followed as she visited the many outlying communities, she sometimes slept in a tent, sometimes in a sacristy. Occasionally, she made her house calls in a canoe or a riverboat. Once she slept in a boat. There were countless occasions when, as an itinerant doctor, the conventional rules of medical practice simply did not apply. Once, at the end of the day, a chief with several wives insisted on seeing her, but when Louise saw him she could not diagnose his problem. He looked thin and worn out. Could it be worms? His diet?

Using the local priest as a translator, Louise was able to determine finally that the chief was distraught about his inability to perform for his wives. One of her orderlies had previously mentioned to her that impotence, aggravated by anemia, was a common problem taken very seriously by the men who were affected. With no iron pills ready at hand, Louise put a Redoxon effervescent tablet in a glass of water and told him to drink it. With wide eyes, the chief watched the tablet dissolve into a myriad of bubbles. With trepidation, he agreed to swallow the brew in one gulp. After managing to keep all the bubbles inside, the chief opened his eyes and smiled, exclaiming: "*Dawa ya nguvu!*" Yes, Louise told the chief: powerful medicine.

With the help of the priest, Louise told him to drink a glass of this powerful medicine every night before bed, and she gave him a blue tube containing the Redoxon tablets. The chief was thrilled. His problems were now solved. As he was leaving the room, another man who had been listening outside the door announced that he, too, had come to her about the same problem. Louise told him there was no more *dawa ya nguvu*. To prove her point she showed him the empty cabinets in the dispensary. That's when the chief slowly unwrapped his tube of Redoxon tablets and carefully gave the other man exactly half of the tablets. Each tablet promised one night of potency. Everyone was happy.

In her research on amoebic dysentery cases, which she had been asked to do for the institute in Basel, she found that the best results seemed to come from several groups of drugs which she found killed the amoebas in the blood and in the wall of the intestine. She sent the results of this work back to Rudolf Geigy in Basel.

When working with the local people, the only group who made her ill at ease were the towering Maasai tribesmen who struck her as the personification of Africa: enigmatic and beautiful, and potentially dangerous. Because they were a pastoral people with their large herds of cattle, they often suffered from bovine tuberculosis and tape worms. They would walk hundreds of miles to Ifakara to get the best treatment available. To Louise, they had a strange way of walking, as if constantly wading through high grass. They moved along slowly and graciously, raising their heads haughtily and holding their long spears with a firm grip.

The Maasai were difficult as patients because the men always demanded to be treated before everyone else. If a Maasai felt insulted or provoked, he would swell like a turkeycock and suddenly tear apart his clothes to expose his male attributes—the Maasai gesture of aggression, especially towards women. Their women were never allowed to go anywhere without male company. Louise later recalled:

When Maasai passed under my window in the morning on their trek to the hospital, I could hear the copper bangles of their women clanking with every step, as if they were prisoners walking in chains.

Gradually, Louise learned how to deal with the Maasai. The males had to be treated first, but she also made sure that their wives were treated fairly in the clinic, and she found she could chuckle about the confidential stories their wives told her.

Misconceptions occurred almost daily. The local women in Igota began to feel sorry for *Mama Mganga* because they assumed she would want to have a man in her life. They were also distressed when she attended the church services because, evidently, she was not permitted to take communion. They did not understand that she was not religious and she simply went to services because she liked to hear the wonderful music and singing. When Louise asked them to explain their pity, they were too embarrassed to explain. Finally, one of them told her, "Well, you must have done something very bad so that you were excommunicated." This misconception was not disadvantageous. The more dangerous and fearsome a medicine man was, the better his treatment was presumed to be. Louise was thus imagined to be very dangerous and thus all the better as a doctor.

Soon she was travelling on her own to attend to difficult cases, or else priests came in their own vehicles to fetch her. She was not always successful. Once a woman was brought to her on a homemade stretcher from a long distance, and Louise could not at first ascertain the problem. The poor woman was acutely agitated by the slightest touch. The local priest was consulted. It turned out the patient had tried to hang herself from a tree. People had cut her down, but by this time her neck had been broken. Louise was unable to help her. The possibility of someone in the wilderness wanting to commit suicide had never crossed Louise's mind.

Although she could detect malaria and other parasitic diseases without knowing much of what her patients said, misunderstandings about treatments were inevitable: such as the time a young man with a small abscess on his stomach rushed out of the room, knocking people aside, when he saw her approach with a scalpel for a minor procedure. The female patients awaiting treatment gleefully exploded with laughter. Other situations deeply upset her:

> I was faced with the most horribly infected wounds and broken limbs, situations where I had to use all my courage to clean and disinfect the wounds and for the painful manipulations necessary to set the broken bones. I could not stop marvelling at the patients' endurance of pain.

Remote parishes and dispensaries were connected by shortwave radios, so her reputation spread quickly. While travelling among the villages of the Wapogoro people as a reluctant celebrity, Louise soon developed meaningful friendships with Father Prosper and Father Celsius at Igota; Father Oskar and Father Willibald at Iragua; Father Esaias at Merera; Father Richard and Father Diego at Mchombe; Father Sigisbert in Mwaya and Ruaha; Father Zeno and Brother Kumbert in Taweta; Father Emeran at Tabora; Father Wolfram at Luhombero; Father Theopher at Gauranga and malaria-ridden Father Oswin at Itete. The well-educated priests naturally looked forward to their conversations with the unmarried and unaccompanied *Mama Mganga*: "People have always come to me and told me things they would never say to anyone else. I have learned never to tell anybody any of the things that people have told me in private," Louise explained. Whatever these priests were telling her, Louise remains determined not to divulge their secrets.

There was always the danger that her medical cures would be mistaken for witchcraft. During one of her numerous visits to faraway Luhombero, where the local tribe still used poison darts, some of the local people accused her of being a witch because she had been seen out walking past the graveyard in the moonlight. Father Wolfram had to explain that she had only been out for a stroll beneath the stars and she had not even known about the graveyard.

Father Wolfram at Luhombero reminded her of St. Francis. He eked out a spartan existence with one helper, a Brother, but he never complained. It was obvious the Africans loved him. Whenever he took Louise on his motorbike to visit patients who were unable to come to the dispensary, he was always friendly with everyone as a matter of course. When she and Father Wolfram visited in a village hut, she would notice how all the women would be happy that he was there with them.

Once in a very hot village, when she had to treat far too many patients, Father Wolfram came to offer her a cool drink. "You must be very thirsty and tired," he said. None of the other Fathers would ever risk such a display of kindness to her in public because they felt compelled to show how they rejected any degree of intimacy with women. With requisite modesty, she expressed her gratitude.

Because Father Wolfram was Swiss they spoke German to each other. Once he mistakenly used the informal, personal pronoun *Du*, rather than the required, impersonal *Sie*. Much embarrassed by his inadvertent impropriety, he blushed. Louise continued talking as if she hadn't noticed. During their many years of religious training, the celibate priests had been forced to read books that forewarned them that all women were keen to seduce them. Knowing this, Louise always took care to wear modest clothes and use appropriate language. She did not need to be told that as an unescorted white woman in East Africa, she would have to exercise caution. To advance in the male-dominated field of medicine had required similar restraint.

For the next three years, other than letters to her mother in Norway, the expression of her private thoughts and feelings would be severely restricted—and sexual behaviour would be self-prohibited. Archbishop Maranta would cross paths with Louise several times thereafter, even visiting her in her room in Igota. She would later describe him as an "exceptionally relaxed and correct person." She hoped others who had seen him enter her room would describe her the same way.

For rest and refuge, Louise frequently visited the Kwiro mission

In Tanganyika, when Louise opted to leave the Ifakara Hospital for the bush and mountains of the Ulanga District, she quickly learned to improvise for both accommodations and medical treatments in 1959.

The frequently flooded Ulanga River was a transportation hazard for anyone travelling from Dar es Salaam to Mahenge—until the Kilombero Bridge was finally completed with expertise and funds from China in 2017.

Crossing the Ulanga River, 2016, during Alan Twigg's first visit to Tanzania.

Another method of crossing the Ulanga River, without any fee.

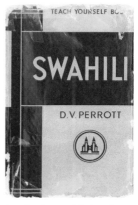

Louise kept this book with her when she was teaching herself Swahili, one of ten languages she has spoken: Norwegian, Danish, Swedish, English, French, German, Italian, Spanish, Swahili, Lingala.

Louise has always enjoyed playing the piano and drawing. These two sketches show the *maskini* boy (left) who inspired her curiosity about epilepsy and served as her translator; and a local teacher named Susanna.

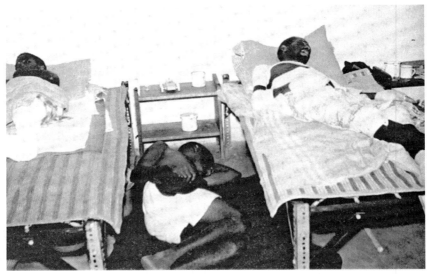

Louise first encountered patients with epilepsy at the crowded hospital
at Ifakara, 600 miles south of the equator, where she went to
conduct research for Rudolf Geigy.

After treating the *maskini* boy, who became her interpreter, Louise treated
these women with epilepsy at the Kwiro mission in 1959.

Louise pioneered her treatment programs with phenobarbital in 1959 with these men who had been treated as outcasts. At first, she feared them.

From her mother, Louise had learned the importance of bringing women together. She convened group sessions with female patients so they could share their stories of suffering from epilepsy.

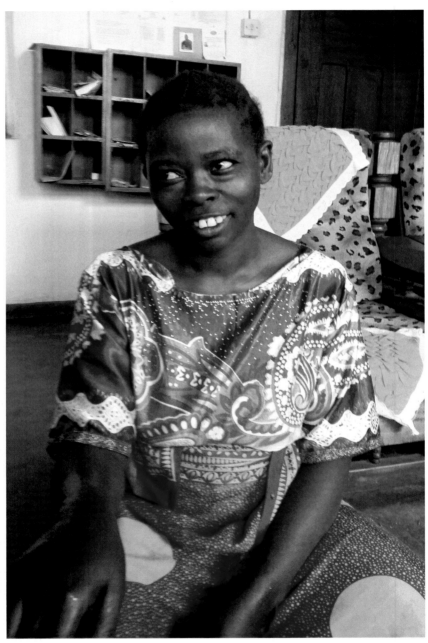

Fatiha Maokola has been through the epilepsy rehabilitation
program and is seen here working at the Kasita seminary.

in the Mahenge Mountains where, because the air was much cooler and fresher at night, it was easier to sleep. Two unusually competent nurses at Kwiro called upon her only for the more difficult cases, so she was free to go for numerous walks amid the beautiful scenery, wandering past banana groves, fields of manioc, beautiful flowers, lush vegetation, astonishing birds and the long-forgotten coffee plantations abandoned by Germans decades before. Little children invariably giggled and whispered behind her back, following her at a distance as she greeted old women carrying heavy loads of firewood on their heads, or younger women returning from the fields with babies on their backs.

One day, when she was at Kwiro, she lost her way amid the trees. Sunset was nearing. As she continued walking along a narrow path, she remembered having been warned that leopards were prone to attack their prey at dusk. At one moment she wondered if she had glimpsed a leopard in the bushes. Her apprehension about the leopard turned to dread when she saw a large black snake gliding towards her on the path. As if paralyzed, she waited as this creature stopped a short distance in front of her and appeared to look at her knowingly. The snake was fearlessly majestic. She was shocked to be thrilled by it. Sometimes it felt as if every living thing in Africa had a spirit. The snake decided to turn off the path and disappear into the bushes, as if they had somehow just had a conversation.

Before she could attempt to gain her bearings, a third creature disturbed her. This time she was certain something or someone was watching her from the bushes. Then the bushes moved and the creature emerged in rags. It was a young boy with the face of an old man, very much undernourished. His skin was horribly wrinkled, dry, and cracked, especially on his legs. He appeared to be filthy with lumps of dirt on his skin. It was as if flies were stuck to his body. The doctor in her realized he had thick keloid scars from poorly healed wounds. She approached the boy slowly, wondering if the meeting with the snake had been an omen. She saw a makeshift hut behind him. This must be where he lived. He was evidently surviving alone in the bush.

She felt spontaneous sympathy. What sort of wild creature was he?

Louise was taken aback when he spoke to her in English: "Good afternoon, Memsahib." She responded with the information that she had lost her way. The boy nodded. He understood and wordlessly set about walking along the path in front of her, guiding her, but keeping his distance so that further conversation was not possible. Sometimes he would turn and look over his shoulder to make sure she was still following. At one point her guide turned and gestured to her that he would carry her bag. Already feeling indebted to him, Louise at first instinctually declined his offer. But when this humble and bedraggled waif looked so disappointed by her refusal, she relented and let him carry it for her.

With her bag balanced on his head, the boy walked awkwardly along the trail until they eventually reached the edge of a village. He put down his load and whispered, ever so politely, "Goodbye, *Mama Mganga*." He disappeared quickly. Louise noted there was a young woman in a nearby yard who had seen both of them approach. "Who was that boy?" Louise asked. The woman, who had been pounding maize, shrugged with indifference. Only when Louise persisted would she deign to answer. With some contempt in her voice, she said, "Just a *maskini*."

Louise knew this word referred to someone who has been reduced to the status of an outcast or a beggar, someone who has been wretchedly ostracized due to some misfortune or illness. A *maskini* must remain unobtrusive, and never approach a fire unless invited. Sometimes families would look after their own *maskini*, while others were expected to survive without any responsibilities or rights, abused and reliant on crumbs.

Maskini were often required to survive in hidden places, far removed from any help. Louise was curious about this boy because he seemed to be mentally alert, certainly polite and hampered only by his appearance. No doubt banishment and severe loneliness had prematurely aged his face. But why? During another stroll, in a different area, she met the boy a second time. Then a third time. Soon enough, she saw him every time she went for a walk, no matter in which direction she went from Kwiro. Except for a greeting, he preferred to keep his distance. Even though he seemed to be stalking her, Louise was not alarmed because his behaviour was so gentle and humble. She never felt any sense of aggression.

Although he disappeared in the bush as soon as anyone else approached, he always returned and began guiding her to beautiful places. Attempts to improve personal contact seemed to upset him, but when she offered him food he would obviously be pleased, reaching for it with trembling hands. As an alternate approach to contact, she brought along her charcoal pencil and paper. He was not averse to sitting still for a portrait. When he saw the result, he smiled for the first and only time.

Weeks and months could pass but this relationship did not dissolve. She still had no idea what his thoughts were. One morning while Louise was attending Mass at the mission in order to hear the singing, a terrible cry interrupted the proceedings, horrifying everyone. The pews emptied. Children were screaming. Fear was infectious. The general panic made her wonder if somebody could be dying. She reminded herself that she was a doctor. She waited until everyone was outside and the stampede ended. The church had fallen silent but she heard strange noises from a dark corner. She advanced to investigate and found the *maskini* boy having convulsions. And she suddenly understood his problem.

Epilepsy. Moon madness. Louise knew from her medical training that, according to the World Health Organization, approximately 80 percent of all epilepsy sufferers in developing countries were not receiving medical treatment. In Africa, that percentage was likely higher. Non-scientific or indigenous attempts to counteract epilepsy could sometimes be more harmful than the affliction. As reported from West Africa, these included burning the soles of the unconscious convulsing patients, dropping acid in their eyes to "wake them up" or forcing cow urine down their throats.

Globally, it had been believed for centuries that epilepsy occurred as a punishment for wrongdoing, which could mean either a sin against God, or transgressions against ancestors or supernatural spirits. Misconceptions about the causes and contagiousness of epilepsy had yet to fade in Africa, where most people still believed epilepsy resulted from the bodily invasion of a malignant spirit that caused the seizures. For Muslims it could be the *jinn* spirit; in the Judeo-Christian realm, it was the devil.

Fear of contagion from the saliva or urine of the afflicted person had been ubiquitous since the Middle Ages. Therefore sufferers were usually liable to severe punishment if they dared to act against restrictive rules for isolation. Naturally, everyone had immediately fled from the church for fear of contagion from the writhing *maskini*. It had been that way for centuries.

Louise tried to soothe him as best she could. As his attack was abating, she succeeded in getting him carried to the dispensary where she was able to give him an anticonvulsive injection. When the boy awoke about half an hour later, and he realized she had witnessed his seizure, he shamefully mustered his strength and rose to his feet.

His eyes widened with fear. Now she knew, too. He staggered out of the dispensary as soon as he could, disappearing back to the furtive ignominy of the bush. The nurses at Kwiro explained to Louise that the boy felt ashamed by his convulsions. At the same time, many persons suffering from epilepsy believed they mustn't be touched.

The nurses told her that medicine men in the Wapogoro region traditionally used the bark of a particular tree to have an emetic or purgative effect on the epileptic sufferer. Patients who failed to respond to the medicine man's treatments were those who failed to have diarrhea or to vomit, but they knew little more than that. The bark treatment was always undertaken at the change of the moon.

The Wapogoro people were particularly fearful of seizures. They believed that an adversary should not be struck too hard on the head during a fight or scuffle. Children should not spin around too vigorously in games. Birds that circle in the air prior to plunging to kill their prey should not be killed. A potentially epileptic person should not cut a chicken's neck because headless chickens have what appear to be convulsions. If someone with epilepsy killed a chicken, its meat would have to boiled with a certain root which had preventative properties.

Louise knew that phenobarbital tablets can be effective as an anticonvulsive treatment, so she took a small bottle of them back to the place where she had first met the boy. It took some time before she was certain she had found the place where she had encountered the snake and the boy. Finally, she found his little hut amid the trees. She called out to him but he refused to answer. The squalid hut was empty. She found him crouching in his small garden. She spoke to him gently but he behaved as if he did not hear, as if silence could render him invisible. "Listen, my friend," she said. "I know the illness you have, and I am not afraid of it."

Tears were running from his lowered eyes. She wanted to reach out and hold him but she could not take the risk of having him run away. She kept speaking in a soothing voice. Eventually she held out the bottle of tablets and told him to take one every night before going to sleep.

"Will you take the medicine?"

Finally he nodded. She left some food, promising to return in two weeks. It marked the beginning of her treatment of epilepsy in the Mahenge Mountains for another sixty years. For the boy, the treatment went well. Two weeks later, he reported he had not had a single seizure. He eagerly accepted another batch of tablets. He soon fixed the roof of his hut and began keeping himself clean and tidy.

His family history turned out to be all too typical. The boy had been a promising student, accepted into the mission school. He had learned some English quickly. His parents were proud of him but his mother had made the mistake of bragging. A neighbour whose son had been rejected by the mission school became jealous and resentful. This woman took revenge by entering the boy's home while the boy was studying and pressing her hands onto his head, predicting he would soon become sick and have fits. The boy and his family became fearful. A few days later he had his first bout of convulsions.

55

After the boy had a second attack in the classroom, the descent into shame was immediate. His teacher and classmates fled. Everyone knew. The next day the teacher refused to teach him. None of his closest friends would speak in favour of him. He was banished because everyone believed that evil spirits could leap from an epileptic person to a bystander during convulsions, or that these evil spirits could be transmitted by saliva or urine.

The boy's father took him to a medicine man, to no avail. It was too late. The boy had already suffered burns on his body after falling into a fire during an attack. The father tried to lodge a formal complaint against the neighbour at the village court, a *baraza,* accusing her of witchcraft, but the elders could not rule against her because there were no witnesses. The neighbour simply denied any wrongdoing.

At first, the family had tried to feed him, but his brothers and sisters had wanted nothing to do with him. It was a nuisance to feed him with a separate set of dishes. He was instructed to fetch his own water from a distant well. Eventually even his mother avoided him. His parents took him to the abandoned hut in the woods and left him there to fend for himself. For a year or so after that, his family would help by delivering some food. Fearful of making a fire in case he fell into it again, he grew embittered and depressed. To relieve his wretched existence, he sometimes hid in the corner of the church to hear Sunday Mass. Even after Louise had intervened with the phenobarbital tablets, he remained forlorn, isolated and hopeless.

Having seen the community's response to the boy, Louise came to realize that the condition had to be treated as much as a social disease as a physical disease. Tablets were not enough; it was clear to her that social rehabilitation had to be part of the treatment. To relieve the *maskini* boy's apprehensions, in order to make him feel as if he could be re-admitted to society as a valuable contributor, she told him she wished to start a treatment centre for epileptic patients—and she needed him as a helper, someone who could speak English well, someone who knew the local people and customs. He pondered this offer for a long time before responding.

"Then I would not be a *maskini* anymore," he said. "I would be able to go home." There was hesitancy in his voice, not elation or triumph. Louise realized it was not enough to be rid of seizures; epileptic persons had to be accepted by their families. The boy would also have to feel that he could contribute to his parents. So she offered him a salary as well as permanent residency at her proposed clinic.

"All right, *Mama Mganga*," he said. "I accept. You help me by letting me help you."

⌒

AFTER TREATING THE *maskini* boy for some time, Louise realized that she would have to make her work on epilepsy a priority and she would have to develop a strategy to deal with it. Unfortunately, the text books did not offer much help on the subject. It was all new ground as she set out to establish the first East African clinic for the treatment of epileptics at Kwiro. She decided that she should start out by working with a test group. She had noticed that there was a group of epileptics who performed menial tasks around the mission grounds at Kwiro in return for food and shelter. She often saw them in the fields or stables. From a distance, these cloistered *maskini* struck her as strange and pitiful creatures. Some were lame, others appeared to be half-blind. They were covered in sores, and they all suffered from seizures.

There were about fourteen of them living in a stable. She was forewarned that some of the men could be seized by anger and suddenly lash out at anyone near. Her first visit to the stable was unforgettable. Timid and trembling, the men gathered around her. As she expected, their bodies were covered with burn scars and full of sores. They had crippled hands or feet, but she was not prepared for their bewildered, swollen and distorted faces. Years later, she wrote:

> One young man practically lived in a flour sack. He crept into it, tightened it firmly around his neck and rolled on the ground, gnashing the red earth between his teeth without uttering a word. Many of these men were plagued by con-

vulsive attacks day and night. One young man used to spin round and round before falling down. Another danced around wildly going off in different directions, not aware of the direction in which he was running. Upon regaining consciousness, he would find himself with bleeding feet far away, somewhere in the bush.

The extent of their injuries was so severe that she felt fearful and wasn't sure what to say to the assembled men. It took a while before she found words to explain what she intended to do, that she would find a way to cure their conditions.

An old man with spindly legs stepped forward, with a staggering gait. He folded his hands, as if praying, and spoke with a thin voice. "Let us thank *Mungú* (God) that he has sent *Mama Mganga* to us." At this, the others also folded their hands as best they could and spoke words in an attempt at unison. Their simple and earnest prayer moved her to tears.

A young boy with a withered arm rolled a log towards her, inviting her to sit. Mama Doctor took out a notebook to record their names. That way she could keep track of their treatment trajectories. It was easily agreed that the old man should be their leader. Mama Doctor explained the phenobarbital treatment to them, and asked them to tell the leader all about their attacks and other symptoms. The leader would keep a supply of medicine and be responsible for its daily distribution. For her trial treatments she had only phenobarbital, one of the oldest and most economical anti-epileptic drugs. She would have to order in a large supply of the pills. Other antiepileptic medications were not available and at any rate would have been too expensive for the people of the mountains.

Louise soon decided she must also try to provide phenobarbital to the women with seizures who worked in the garden. About a dozen of these *maskini* lived in a small house close to the vegetable garden where a kind-hearted old nun looked after them in the same way that one mission brother, who attended to the cattle at Kwiro, kindly guided the fourteen forlorn and lonely men with their daily chores.

For weeks she was tense, worrying about the results, or if there would be any with both the men and the women. She was taking a risk, trusting her instinct. Perhaps it was preferable to stay on the sidelines, doing nothing, watching people suffer. She knew that these patients had all sorts of concomitant diseases. She worried about possible repercussions if they forgot to take their medications. A series of violent convulsive attacks could ensue, sometimes ending in death. Their ability to tolerate phenobarbital could be decreased due to unknown factors. Or perhaps other aspects of their illnesses could become more prominent if their attacks were suppressed.

Meanwhile, Louise remained astonished to see how many people came to her for treatment of severe burns. She knew that people in rural Africa cooked their food on small open fires in front of their huts and were used to handling fire from early childhood, and yet dozens of people were coming to see her with limbs deformed from burn scars:

> Many people came with horrible, fresh wounds from burns often reaching to the bone, or covering large segments of the body. It took some courage to clean and treat these severe burn wounds, often festering and buzzing with flies.

Patients with serious burns were generally malnourished, dishevelled and depressed. Other people retreated from these "wretched ones," including family members, who generally showed little sympathy. They often addressed the burn victim with harsh words. These patients barely spoke. They kept their heads lowered and their eyes fixed on the floor. Why these burns? And why such an attitude? Louise realized that people seemed bothered by her questions and withdrew, until one day a woman, looking around as if afraid, whispered in her ear, "It is *kifafa!*"

The Swahili term for epilepsy was derived from *kifa*, the verb for "to die." The addition of a syllable made that word into a diminutive term, for "little dying." The woman hesitated, looked around again, and then said in a low voice, "Even talking about it can make the *kifafa* spirit angry. It may jump onto the one mentioning its name." Louise found that when there weren't any epilepsy patients around, then people would answer more of her questions.

She learned that *kifafa* referred only to grand mal seizures; other forms of epilepsy were not recognized and did not provoke similar dread as a person who was convulsing with frothing saliva. The burns, Louise soon realized, were caused by individuals having a seizure and then falling into the cooking fire. Only a few close family members sometimes dared to rescue a convulsing person when they fell into the fire. People were also convinced that *kifafa* was strictly an African condition, and therefore not treatable by Western medicine. Families often sought help from a traditional healer for *kifafa*. They would bring *kifafa* sufferers to the clinic only for treatment of burns or other physical ailments even though the burns had been the result of a seizure causing the individual to fall into the fire.

⌒

AS WEEKS PASSED, Louise was delighted to see that her patients in both groups—the men in the stable and the women who worked in the fields—became bright and lively, filled with hope. Everyone was astonished when a few of the workers, free from convulsive attacks, went home and were accepted by their families. The news spread that the little white tablets could indeed defeat the evil *kifafa* spirit when strict treatment rules were followed.

Contrary to predictions, families began to bring their epileptic patients for treatment, but not always during the day when the clinic was open to everyone. Due to the social stigma attached to the disease, they were sometimes dropped outside her quarters at night. There she would find them in the morning, too frightened to say a word, hovering in fear, but also hopeful. Often they would be lying on the ground in their wet and dirty rags, shivering with cold and fear. Overwhelmed with embarrassment and timidity, they hardly dared to move. She literally had to lift them up and drag them indoors.

Because of other people's fear, she could not easily take the *kifafa* patients to the dispensary, and saw no other solution than to examine them in her own room. The smell of poverty and illness would hang in her room long after the patients had left.

The social isolation of her patients was the next hurdle to overcome. She found it heartbreaking to observe how roughly these usually gentle people treated their relatives with *kifafa*. Such conduct arose as much from social pressures as it did from fears of contagion. Brothers of a *kifafa* sufferer would be denied brides from healthy families; sisters would be unable to secure a high bridal price. She had to convince the families and all the people in the villages that unless someone was willing to take responsibility for the patients, to accompany and care for them, she could not provide treatment. She had to steel herself for a few days, leaving abandoned epileptic patients outside her door. As more people knew for certain that Mama Doctor's pills clearly worked, reducing attacks, or eliminating them altogether, families became willing to show their faces and take shared responsibility for treatment outcomes.

As word spread about the effectiveness of Mama Doctor's treatments, the work load increased to the point where Fridays at the Kwiro dispensary were exclusively for epilepsy cases. This enabled the mission nurse and her helpers to keep records of the epileptic patients. Initially, each patient was given only a week's supply of pills, but gradually seizure-free patients were given supplies for a month or more. In a few months, it was a marvel to see how the people with epilepsy gained a sense of community, sometimes singing together and dancing with drums, perspiration glistening on their bodies. Louise remembers how their cheerfulness and happy smiles, their never-ending thankfulness and warm attachment to the clinic staff made these Fridays unforgettable.

After the dispensary had been operating for a considerable time and Louise's reputation had spread widely, a most unusual event happened. Louise was out walking some distance from the clinic when she met a tall, well dressed individual with a dignified bearing. As they passed one another on the path, Louise recalls being startled:

> Our eyes met and something like an electric current went through me. I nearly stumbled and turned around to greet him. But he continued on his way unperturbed, and I was convinced he had not even recognized me. I could not explain what had happened, but I now understood why people were afraid of his look.

Louise learned that although the man did not have any of the symptoms of her other epilepsy sufferers, he was in fact suffering several seizures a month. He asked to come to see her. After three months of treatment with Louise with the phenobarbital tablets, the man waited until everybody else had left the dispensary before requesting a private consultation for early the next morning.

Before sunrise he knocked on her door and she hurriedly dressed. He wore a colourful blanket with a chain around his neck, a strange headdress and he had painted his face. In one hand he carried a bundle; in the other he had a chieftain's cane. He went straight to the window and closed it. Then he closed the curtains and placed his cane against the door.

Addressing her as *Mama Mganga*, he solemnly told her he was a *mganga*, a healer who had treated many people suffering from *kifafa*. He wanted to share some of his knowledge with her. She respectfully remained silent as he untied his bundle. No other medicine man had ever divulged his identity to her.

The *mganga* explained that his father was a famous medicine man and he had inherited a great deal of knowledge from him. "When my father grew old," he said, "he would take my oldest brother along and shortly before his death my brother inherited all his secrets. I left home when I was a young boy and was working on the coast when my father died. Shortly afterwards I had my first epileptic attack. One night when I felt very lonely and upset, my father appeared to me in a dream. He took me by the hand and led me through a thick forest until we came to an open space. There he pointed to a tall tree and told me that its bark contained a very strong medicine against *kifafa*.

"He showed me how to prepare the remedy from the bark. In this dream my father told me he wanted me to help people who suffer from *kifafa*. When I woke up I could hardly wait for daylight before I started out to find the tree."

He described to Louise how he had wandered around in the forest until he came upon a clearing which resembled the place his father had shown him, and where there was the tall tree he had seen in the dream. He explained what he did then: "I took some of its bark and hurried home to my village. When my brother saw that I had the bark and heard about my dream he realized that our father wanted me to be a medicine man. He taught me everything he knew about the treatment of *kifafa* and sent me to other medicine men to learn more. When I returned home after a year, people began to come to me for treatment of *kifafa*. Some I have been able to cure. Some I cannot. And I include myself among those I cannot."

He picked up a piece of bark and continued: "This is the bark of the tree my father showed me in the dream. I always use this medicine first. When boiled in water it produces a foam like the froth of saliva on the mouth of a convulsing person. The patient must drink large amounts of this brew. If he gets diarrhea and vomits, he will be cured. He has to vomit until he expels a lump of slime and blood. That is the toad of *kifafa*.

"We think there is a supernatural toad in the stomach of the patient. It has to come out or the patient will not be cured. The treatment, which lasts a few days, has to be repeated after a month, and again after six months. But several conditions must be met if the treatment is to be effective. The patient must start the treatment as soon as he contracts *kifafa*. If he waits until he has burns from falling into the fire, the prospect of a cure will definitely be very poor. Moreover, the treatment must be undertaken by the entire family. It begins when a bunch of roots, bulbs and leaves are cooked together with a chicken. The whole family must eat of the stew. During the year of treatment, the patient must refrain from hard physical work.

Drinking home-brewed beer and other alcoholic beverages is forbidden and the patient should stay quietly at home avoiding anything that might be upsetting."

Many of this man's medicines were for the patient's relatives, to strengthen them against the *kifafa* spirit. Certain dreams, especially those of being chased by wild animals, were considered ominous forebodings that somebody in the family might come down with *kifafa*. A medicine man had to be consulted immediately. The right kind of medicine had to be taken by the whole family. There was one dream in particular, called the dream of *kifafa*.

"If you ask the *kifafa* patients," he said, "you will find that most of them have had this dream. The dreamer is about to wash himself. He pours water from a vessel over his shoulders with a feeling of pleasure. Suddenly he sees that the water turns red, like blood. He wakes up in a panic and he might fall into convulsions right then. In any case, he should hurry to get medicine against the dream." The medicine man picked up a root with a repulsive smell. "This root is called *nefuzi*," he explained. "It is hung by the bedside. Its bad smell will chase away the evil spirit of *kifafa* and prevent bad dreams from harming the sleeper."

The medicine man explained to Louise that his medicines were most effective at the time of the new moon. This statement impressed her because she knew that Hippocrates, centuries before, had taught that the frequency of seizures varied with the moon phase. Since the Middle Ages, it was generally believed in Europe that epilepsy and mental disease were aggravated during the time of the full moon, hence the word "lunatic," but this medicine man believed *kifafa* became more problematic and prevalent during the *new* moon.

The medicine man told her nobody would consider treatments to be successful before at least three full phases of the moon had elapsed without attacks during a new moon. Phrases she had heard, such as "Let us wait until the moon is starting to grow" or "I am all right because the moon is full," now became more meaningful to her. She decided that she would more closely monitor the moon and would later come to the conclusion that her *kifafa* sufferers had more attacks during the phase of the new moon.

By this time, it was almost dawn. The medicine man stood up and said he would have to leave. Before he bundled up his remedies, he gave Louise the piece of bark from the tree his father had shown him in the dream. He suggested she should take it with her back to Europe. Maybe it could be made into tablets like the ones she had given him. Louise put the bark in a box and promised she would deliver the bark to the pharmacology department at the University of Zurich. She always kept her promises, whether made to herself or others.

EVEN THOUGH LOUISE had never received any training as an artist, she loved to make sketches and portraits. One day Father Berthold at Malinyi invited her to go with him on a hunting safari. Louise had no interest in shooting a rifle or killing wild animals but she readily accepted his offer because she rarely missed an opportunity to marvel at nature and make new sketches.

After the safari, Louise was seated in a wicker chair on his verandah, putting some finishing touches on one of her charcoal drawings, when she was distracted by shouting. A lean young man was running towards them on the dirt road. The messenger's forehead was covered in perspiration when he arrived and thrust a crumpled envelope towards Father Berthold. Although her Swahili was still rudimentary, she thought she heard him say that he had travelled all the way from Dar es Salaam. But no, he was saying the *message* had come all the way from there.

Father Berthold looked at the envelope and handed it to her. By now, she was accustomed to emergencies. But as soon as she broke the seal of the envelope and realized the message was written in Norwegian, it was impossible for her to appear calm. Father Berthold noted her distress. He had to restrain himself from touching her bare forearm out of sympathy. Was her mother ill?

There was an awkward silence. The messenger also began to fear something was seriously amiss. He backed away, understanding he could be the bearer of dreadful news. Father Berthold leaned over and recognized one word only, KONGO. "It's from Oslo," she said. "From the Norwegian Red Cross."

In western Tanganyika, many people had heard about the atrocities in the nearby Belgian Congo. All Belgian nationals, including the doctors and many nurses, were fleeing for their lives. The Congolese wanted independence. Belgium had strengthened the armed forces; then all the soldiers had mutinied because they weren't being paid properly. The BBC called it a bloodbath.

The entire message was KAN DE TSENESTEGSOERE VAART LEGE-TEAM KONGO SNAREST 3 MAANEDER STOP BREV FUELGER. NO, R KROSS.

"I'm being asked if I can go to the Belgian Congo," she said. She sounded strangely wistful, as if remembering a dream. Of course, it was a frightening prospect, and of course her mind quickly considered how she might draft a letter to decline, but there was a third voice inside her head that was completely at odds with her survivalist instincts:

> *This is a message you have always wanted. It is from the Red Cross. This telegram is really coming from Henry Dunant, of your greatest heroes. Everything is meant to be. If you deny this request, you will be denying who you are.*

Having grown up in Norway, the home of the Nobel Peace Prize, Louise had been taught at an early age that Swiss businessman Henry Dunant was one of the first two recipients of the Peace Prize. After seeing the aftermath of the 1859 Battle of Solferino in Italy, he had written the book *A Memory of Solferino* that gave rise to the International Committee of the Red Cross in 1863, and the Geneva Convention one year later. She could not refuse to respond to a letter that, in her mind, was coming from Henry Dunant.

Everyone around advised her not to go. All her new friends at Mahenge, Ifakara and Igota tried to persuade her not to leave behind her clinic and the progress she had made. It was foolhardy, reckless, because the Congo was an extremely dangerous country in its present condition. But she wrote a reply in English, accepting the assignment, which was taken by the messenger back to Dar es Salaam.

Instructions in English arrived for her from Norway about one week later, a cryptic summons to risk her life:

PROCEED LEOPOLDVILLE SOONEST, CONTACT MR. KAI NOR-REDAM, INTERNATIONAL RED CROSS. LEAVE FRIDAY, ARRIVE LEOPOLDVILLE SATURDAY.— NORCROSS.

On the morning of her leave-taking, Louise opened her door at dawn and found a huge, grey toad sitting motionless on her doorstep. This, she thought, was the spirit-toad of *kifafa,* prophesying doom. It looked hideous. But she told herself to rise above superstitions. She stepped over the slimy toad and into the waiting Land Rover.

During the long drive to the coast, she was able to take some satisfaction in what she had learned and what she had achieved. In Tanganyika, some of her most remarkable work had been scientific, as much as it was medical.

⌒

WHILE OPERATING HER Kwiro clinic, she had deduced that people living in close proximity to fast-running mountain streams had a higher number of *kifafa* cases than those who lived in Mahenge or other places where there was no running water. Having studied tropical medicine, she knew that the flies which infest people with the filaria parasite breed mostly in fast flowing rivers—and thus people living close to such waters were more frequently bitten than others. Therefore, her own rudimentary research was able to reveal that an unusually high percentage of *kifafa* sufferers were infested with the filaria worm—*Onchocerca volvulus.*

In parts of Africa, eradication of this filaria worm was already being undertaken by the World Health Organization to prevent *Onchocerciasis* or "river blindness." Therefore, if she could gather scientific evidence that the high incidence of epilepsy was indeed linked to the filaria worm, it was conceivable that the WHO could radically reduce the number of epilepsy sufferers by undertaking an eradication program in Mahenge. Unfortunately, it would take six decades before this causative connection between *Onchocerciasis* and *kifafa* was corroborated by further medical science.

Equally prescient had been her discovery of the "Nodding Syndrome," a seemingly unique form of epilepsy. During her fieldwork at Kwiro and Mahenge, mothers had often brought small children to her with symptoms that local people described as *amesinzia kichwa*. In Swahili this meant "he/she is nodding the head." Mothers told her that *amesinzia kichwa* was a well-known sign that their child would eventually suffer from epileptic seizures. Louise observed that children before the age of seven who exhibited this peculiar nodding condition did indeed succumb to epileptic seizures that were mostly therapy resistant.

Although she would proceed to publish descriptions of this "head nodding" syndrome in medical journals in the 1960s (Aall-Jilek 1964, 1965), the existence of this syndrome would long be ignored by supposed epilepsy experts. Her own field research in 2005 would eventually confirm the presence of this epileptic disorder in Mahenge. Nevertheless, although the World Health Organization would recognize this affliction in East Africa and Sudan, adopting "Nodding Syndrome" as a technical term, her role in its discovery would seldom be acknowledged in 21st-century medical literature.

At Kwiro, Louise had similarly deduced the extent to which epilepsy in Africa was also a social disease. Children were denied any further schooling after having their first seizure, and young people who had an epileptic parent or sibling were not able to find a mate from a healthy family. With such crumbling self-esteem, chronic epileptic sufferers nearly always came to despise themselves as much as the others despised them. Like the *maskini* boy, these people were chased away by their family to live in desolate places, or as street beggars or with other outcasts in graveyards—all of which resulted in a lifespan much shorter than half of that of the average African.

The need for some rehabilitation initiatives struck Louise as obvious. The so-called wretched ones required not only medical interventions to reduce their seizures but also paid employment to raise their social stature and self-esteem, and to release them from being a burden on their families. But before she could gain any support to introduce social programs to encourage reintegration into society, she would first have to verify the unusual extent of the malady and prove effective treatment was feasible. To do so, Louise had kept detailed notes and graphs for her patients and she had trained her assistants to do the same.

To maintain a prescribed therapeutic regime, reminders had to be given on a monthly basis to both the patient and to the person or persons who accompanied them to the clinic at the outset of treatment. To further ensure collective involvement, Louise had tried to think of small tasks for family members to do in order to keep them involved in the epilepsy treatment. Such tasks could include guarding the medicine bottle from children or anyone who might want to take the powerful little tablets. Louise also asked relatives to note seizure frequency and report it to the clinic nurse on their next visit, enlisting the family to report any change in the patient's behaviour. A clinical staff member was delegated to visit the home of any patients who missed their appointments, thereby honouring the importance of those individuals in the process.

Louise had also experimented with group therapy sessions, divided between men and women. Unaccustomed to revealing their thoughts in public, the reserved mountain people of the Wapogoro tribe were initially mortified because they had never dared even to mention their affliction in the presence of somebody outside the immediate family, but they soon benefited from these "out of the closet" discussions. It was particularly groundbreaking for women to gather and share stories in a public forum. Generally, after *kifafa* sufferers were accustomed to listen to what others had to say, they mustered enough courage to speak about themselves.

Her overall collective approach to care had proved effective. During the clinic's first two years of operation, about 200 epilepsy sufferers were identified and treated by the clinic's staff; of these, 164 would stay in regular treatment, scheduled for Fridays at the clinic. The majority of patients did not forget to take their daily medicine. All the so-called experts who had predicted this could never happen were proven wrong.

CHAPTER 4

The Belgian Congo:
La Petite Doctoresse

BY THE TIME SHE WAS in a window seat for a connecting flight to Nairobi and on her way to the Congo, Louise was filled with a sense of purpose. She would be living up to the standards of Henry Dunant. It was as if one of her heroes had reached out to her personally and asked *her* to dance in the ballroom of destiny. It felt as if her entire life had been a prelude to this moment. As she rose through the clouds, she had the inner satisfaction of knowing she was living up to her wildest dreams. She was *meant* to go.

But as the moon rose as she was landing in Kenya, she was receiving interior messages that cautioned her not to be reckless. She wrote a postcard to her mother. "Shall I always be on the go, full of tension, always struggling with new problems? Always trying so hard to do my best? Shall I never find peace and a happy family life?" The next day Louise proceeded on a southerly flight over Lake Victoria, over steppe land and large tracts of jungle, peering down at valleys and rivers—David Livingstone territory—until she saw the surging Congo River below.

A serious man who introduced himself as Mr. Kai Norredam was waiting for her at the Leopoldville airport. He introduced her to another serious man, a Norwegian surgeon, Dr. Niels Stensrud, with whom she would be stationed. Dr. Stensrud had come directly from the cool climate of Oslo and he had no experience in Africa. She could see he was unprepared for the heat. Whereas Norredam was formal and respectful, Stensrud was aloof. Louise also sensed that he had little experience working alongside female physicians.

Mr. Norredam explained that their hospital was located at the country's main seaport, Matadi, a town of approximately 600,000 people. There could be as many as 300 to 400 patients in the hospital at peak periods. Dr. Stensrud would exclusively perform surgeries, while Louise would handle everything else, including administration. They would be the only foreign doctors for a hospital complex formerly overseen by eight Danish doctors. Louise was curious about the town they were going to be living in and asked how Matadi could be a seaport when it was not on the ocean. Mr. Norredam explained that Matadi's position was important because it was the last town before the Congo River became impassible because of the river's rapids. In fact it was located some 150 kilometres upstream from where the Congo flowed into the ocean.

Mr. Norredam was direct and honest: he described Matadi as one of the hottest places in the Congo and a place "where European women did not live." That statement was less intimidating to her than the fact that she had no experience in administration. If she didn't speak the local language, Lingala, it was going to be difficult to organize an African staff. And would they, she wondered, be prepared to take orders from a young woman?

While Mr. Norredam checked them into one of Leopoldville's few hotels, Louise kept such questions to herself. She sensed that any expression of doubt or insecurity would be used against her by her older colleague. There was a sullenness to him that bordered on overt antagonism. Such men needed to feel superior all the time. They lived to be in control, for fear of showing any weakness. When they were comfortably settled at dinner, to put him at ease, she asked both men why the Congo had deteriorated into such vicious chaos.

Mr. Norredam, sensing her strategy, remained quiet as Dr. Stensrud provided a cursory history lesson. Leopoldville was named after King Leopold II of Belgium. European countries had been duped into according control of the entire Congo River region to a private company that was controlled by King Leopold II. So it wasn't really a country but a personal fiefdom of the King. At first, the King was concerned solely with cornering the world trade in ivory. He hired mercenaries who operated as despots throughout the huge tracts of land that were connected only by the Congo River, the country's only highway. Later the King did the same with rubber. The butchery and slavery that ensued for decades was condoned, incited and often conducted by a private military regime, ironically called the Force Publique, which still remained in force.

In Tanganyika, Louise had enjoyed not knowing what was going to happen on a daily basis; in the Belgian Congo she would always be apprehensive. Especially in Leopoldville, there was nowhere safe to walk unescorted, and they were instructed not to leave the hotel at night for any reason whatsoever. As her room was uncomfortably hot, she was not pleased to hear that there would also be a layover of several days until transportation to Matadi could be arranged and they could begin their work.

The following morning, when she went to the breakfast room, another guest, who appeared to be an African businessman, came and sat at a nearby table. He was self-confident, imposing. They were the only two guests in the breakfast room. Contact was unavoidable. First, he tried to engage her in French. She pretended not to understand. He tried German. Then he tried Swahili. She foolishly wanted to impress him and replied.

First, he wanted to know her name. It took him only two minutes to ask her if he might visit her in her room that evening. Louise was shocked to be so directly propositioned by an African in public. She tried to be calm. In Tanganyika, first managed by the Germans, then by the British, this sort of thing simply would not happen. As coolly as possible, she said she had work to do. She hurried away. She sensed he could be the sort of man who gained excitement by a refusal. She locked her hotel room door. She would use her time to learn some phrases of Lingala.

That evening, her phone rang. Once again, she declined his invitation, this time with more firmness. That might have been another mistake, inciting his determination, but she had to give some vent to her feelings. She was feeling trapped. She imagined her mother's voice: "You see, Louise. This is what can happen to someone who is naive, someone who insists upon having good intentions." But how silly that was! Putting the blame on her own shoulders. Without consulting Mr. Norredam, she went to the hotel manager and asked to have a guard to keep her admirer at bay. Within an hour, a guard was designated to protect her, and the African businessman finally took the well-armed hint.

The following day the Red Cross representative, Mr. Pepe, decided it was time for Louise to see something of the city, and he hired a car for a brief tour with Louise and Mr. Norredam. Dr. Stensrud seemed uninterested and remained behind. Mr. Pepe began by explaining that the larger section of the Congo west of the river was controlled by Belgium; the French controlled a smaller but still huge section on the east side. Leopoldville and Brazzaville, the respective capitals, were across from each other on the Congo River. Now there were no Belgians, or at least none that she could see, walking the streets. Mostly she noticed the blue berets and the blue helmets of the United Nations forces, essential for some semblance of order but mostly deployed within the vicinity of the international airport.

Louise was also taken to see the great Congo River and the impressive new university complex. It was completely empty. The education system was one of the first institutional casualties of the civil war. Through the car window, Louise saw only a few white faces, manoeuvring through the crowded streets, as if nothing had changed. Meanwhile the dishevelled Congolese around them, hungry and without money, looked prepared to rob and kill. Once the language of diplomacy, French was no longer a sign of superiority. Anything foreign could be designated as evil. Louise was shown the home of Mobutu, head of the Force Publique, and also the home of Patrice Lumumba, who at this time was being kept under house arrest.

Louise, of course, still had little knowledge of Congo politics. That night she asked Mr. Norredam to explain the present political situation in more detail. He told her that Patrice Lumumba had served as the first prime minister of the Independent Democratic Republic of the Congo until just recently. He had played a significant role in the transformation of the Congo from a colony of Belgium into an independent republic. However, Mobutu Sese Seko, serving as chief of staff of the army, and supported by Belgium and the United States, had deposed the democratically elected government of Lumumba, and had turned the country into a killing field. What no one knew at the time was that Mobutu would have Lumumba assassinated soon after their tour of duty was finished.

On the next day, Louise was finally given the news that it was time to get ready for the trip to Matadi in order for them to begin their medical work. Travel by river, however, was judged too dangerous, and on November 4, preparations were finally in place for Louise and Dr. Stensrud to fly to Matadi.

At the airport in Leopoldville, they met their Red Cross team consisting of two Swedish pilots, Finn Kristoffersen and Richard Stromberg, their main mechanic, Sven Johnson, and the older officer in charge of their mission, Stig Garbrand, who was also a pilot. The two younger pilots were keen to tell an attractive and unattached Norwegian doctor about their adventures helping the Red Cross transport food to hungry people in the war-torn province of Katanga, taking refugees to safety, taking the wounded to Leopoldville for treatment. They told her their small planes were frequently over-filled, and that it was dangerous work, partly because there was never enough time for proper maintenance of the aircraft—a detail she would have preferred not to know.

Once they had taken off, the plane bobbed up and down, not unlike a bottle in the waves. The air inside the plane was sweat-filled. Finally, though, they burst through the clouds and she could see why ocean-going freighters could not manage to navigate the fearsome rapids upstream from Matadi.

Adjacent to the European part of Matadi she could see an African village of small earth huts sprawling along the riverbank. Sven, the mechanic, leaned over and told her that when the Belgians opted to flee, they had done so in a hurry, abandoning their beautiful bungalows in the hills, leaving behind their cars and their belongings. Approximately 80,000 Belgians had evacuated.

Some of the remaining Europeans had taken refuge in the one big European hotel close to the harbour where she would be staying. They had barricaded themselves inside, and when hostilities had ensued, United Nations soldiers had arrived to rescue them. When these Europeans were successfully evacuated, the soldiers had remained in place to protect the UN and Red Cross personnel.

The hospital complex she would oversee was situated on a hill outside of town. She would require a United Nations escort in jeeps to go to and from work. She would also be obliged to visit, via helicopter, four remote dispensaries in the tropical forest. These were several hours' flight away. She would not be able to stay in the hospital after dusk and she would not be safe beyond the hotel.

In Matadi, commerce had dwindled as few ships were arriving. This situation further impoverished the Africans since many had been employed at the docks. Because food was scarce, hostilities easily flared when local representatives boarded the freighters to inspect the cargo. To the hungry Africans, those who were white were *les Belges* and therefore to blame for their misery.

United Nations peacekeepers were stationed between the harbour and the hotel. The 20,000 UN troops in the Congo were from thirty countries, constituting one of the UN's largest peacekeeping missions ever undertaken. Use of deadly force would eventually be sanctioned for self-defence, a rarity in the history of UN peacekeeping.

Louise disliked the hotel. It was a huge, ugly structure with lofty hallways and stairs facing an inner courtyard. She was told it was the best place to say in Matadi but it felt like a prison. As the courtyard was open to the scorching sun, it warmed up the plaster like an oven during the day. This prevented the air from cooling in the night. The rooms had iron beds and unattractive furniture. Nevertheless, the staff were friendly. Not only did they have guests in their half-empty hotel, guaranteeing their continued employment, but now they had two doctors to help them should there be an emergency.

Louise knew that most of her patients, and many of the hospital aides, would speak only their native tongue, so she mustered her energy to continue studying the Lingala language. She knew from teaching herself Swahili how advantageous this would be socially, not just for medical purposes. Someone would invariably start laughing at her efforts to speak the language and tensions would vanish.

The following day, when a military cavalcade escorted them to visit the hospital for the first time, the Red Cross representative, Mr. Pepe, casually mentioned to her that she would also be expected to provide medical services to the contingent of United Nations soldiers who were her designated protectors. For reasons that were unfathomable to her, the soldiers assigned to protect her were all Moroccans, but it did not strike her as problematic.

She hoped her arrival at the Matadi hospital might be greeted with open arms, but there was no one at all to greet them. Eventually a hospital orderly, seemingly embarrassed to be addressing them, suggested they might like to wait for the chief physician who was conducting a surgery. As they waited for a long time in the office of the chief surgeon, they had to listen to blood-curdling screams from the operating theatre. Eventually a friendly African introduced himself as an assistant and explained that a woman was suffering from a botched abortion. "The bleeding would not stop," he said, "so they took out the uterus."

The "chief" finally appeared, well-dressed and with dark glasses. He politely asked who they were and what they wanted. Mr. Pepe explained he was from the Red Cross and that the two Norwegian doctors would appreciate an introduction to the hospital before they started to work. There was a pause, then in a cool voice the hospital boss said he preferred to wait until he received a written explanation from the Red Cross in Leopoldville.

"We are very busy," he said, looking at his watch. He frowned at them with irritation. "What use could you be to us anyhow?" he asked, addressing no one in particular. "You'll be staying here only three months, just until you will have learned our procedures, then you'll be gone." Louise had to admit his point was well-taken but she remained silent. Quite possibly there had been a previous Red Cross physician whose brief tenure had gone badly. Mr. Pepe was furious but he tried to speak quietly and politely. This was not the time to question the credentials of the surgeon whose work had just elicited hideous screams for half an hour.

"If these doctors come and work with you and your staff, coming from a different nationality," Mr. Pepe said, "that way your hospital will learn new methods of working." Surprisingly, the chief agreed and became a bit friendlier. During this truce, they were told the working hours of the hospital for foreigners would be strictly enforced, from nine o'clock in the morning until five in the afternoon. It was agreed that their delegation should return at a mutually convenient time. Mr. Pepe firmly stated the physicians would arrive at nine o'clock the next morning and they expected to be introduced to staff and procedures. There was a handshake and they left.

Before she fell asleep that night, Louise kept thinking about the poor woman who had had her uterus removed, seemingly without proper anaesthetic. Whether the operation had been necessary or not, she would likely suffer more from emotional damage than extreme physical duress. So much of effective practise depended on empathy and the skills of psychology, not just one's knowledge of the body. In Tanganyika she had increasingly found herself resorting to psychological strategies to resolve problems that were not strictly medical. Never once had she regretted doing so. She was convinced a human connection had to be made before any medical treatment; it was mutual respect and trust that opened the door to healing.

The next morning UN soldiers once again escorted Louise and Dr. Stensrud to the hospital grounds where she saw the rows of patients in the enormous hospital wards. Many had not seen a physician for weeks. The suspicious and sullen looks of the Congolese attendants were even more deflating. It was like being asked to play poker or bridge, and someone had just given you one of the worst hands possible. The chief again warned them to be ready to leave punctually at five because tensions after dark were extreme.

There was an administration building, an emergency ward, a surgery building and separate hospital wards for men, women and children. Louise was in charge of three buildings and three nurses. The male ward was clean and had a high ceiling. It was not overcrowded or too hot. There were only about forty patients. Many had war wounds, others were lame, some had tuberculosis, and some had tetanus, which often resulted from small foot wounds. Mostly these patients were thankful and greeted her with curiosity. The male nurse, Vidal, was a thin, bony and friendly young man who seemed to be well-informed.

Her spirits fell, however, when she visited the female ward. She saw that there were some ninety patients and that their ward was dreadfully overcrowded. It had a low roof, too many beds and poor ventilation. These women felt neglected as second-class patients and appeared anxious or close to tears. They were more suspicious of her than the men. Wasn't she far too young to be a real doctor? The male nurse, Thomas, appeared friendly enough, but he was unsure of himself. She saw almost immediately that he did not listen carefully to the women's complaints. When some of the women tried to go outside to get some fresh air, they would be rudely ordered back inside.

The biggest ward was for the children. Resounding with cries and coughs, babbling and laughter, it was overwhelmingly overcrowded, with countless babies, and yet the atmosphere was much friendlier than in the woman's ward. Here the nurses were mainly Belgian nuns from a nearby convent who had stayed put, refusing to leave the little ones. They were excellent. Louise bonded with them in a matter of seconds. It was a huge relief to meet these brave, sweet, friendly Catholic nuns who knew how to nurse children better than most mothers. They would require little direction.

At the hospital, most of the surgery patients were in the male ward, attended by Dr. Stensrud and the "chief," of course. She already knew Dr. Stensrud could be cranky, and he drank, so a friendship would not evolve. As she had suspected, Dr. Stensrud was not fond of women and his people skills were lacking. He was not much concerned with getting to know people. Louise, on the other hand, soon learned to distinguish between those female patients who mostly required "talking therapy" and those who required immediate treatment. She showed the nurses how to make the requisite small talk, asking how patients had slept, so as to move more quickly to the patients who needed more extensive examination.

The first few days were the hardest. She could not visit even half of the cases in one day. Each day she wanted to stay longer, but her guards simply would not allow her to remain on the premises after five o'clock. Louise spoke French fairly well, but the nurses in the male and female wards often said only, "*Oui, docteur.*" She couldn't be sure if they followed her directions or not. Possibly they just continued their treatments as before—and possibly they were often right in doing so.

Her confidence was shaken. She was feeling nervous and inadequate. But the nurses and the patients soon understood her willingness to help was genuine. Frequently she did not take her lunch break in order to see as many of the women and children as she could. As she had done with the orderlies in Tanganyika in the outpatient clinics, she accorded her staff friendly respect, first asking them easy questions about the patients to make them feel at ease. She would then encourage them to reiterate the patients' complaints to her. It was almost impossible for her to read what the previous doctors had written about the patients. The scribbles of the nursing staff were also indecipherable. She encouraged them to make their own observations and treated them as equal colleagues during each bedside visit.

Gradually she began to feel more comfortable. Her reputation grew. She always had a staff member, usually a nurse, accompany her on her rounds, asking their advice and listening carefully, with thanks, when they voiced their opinions. She was particularly diligent about ordering medicines as quickly as possible, everything from painkillers, sleep medications and the more serious drugs, so patients knew they were getting help quickly. She asked the pharmacist for new drugs and had them ordered from Mr. Pepe at the Red Cross.

She was under the impression she was gaining control of a complicated situation until one day she opened a door in the men's treatment area, a door she had not noticed before, and there she found a seriously ill young man in a single bed in a small room. This was a Congolese officer of some sort, judging by the uniform strung over the chair. He spoke French. "So, you finally found the time to see me!" he sneered. She did not know anything about him; she had been kept in the dark.

Possibly her African helpers were so afraid of this person they had wanted him to die? Possibly this man was known to have done terrible things? She turned to the orderly who had followed her into the room. She expected him to appear sheepish. Instead he looked as hostile and defiant as the patient. Was this patient in some sort of quarantine, she asked? The orderly shook his head. When asked why this man had been kept in hiding, the orderly just shrugged.

No matter how much she devoted herself to the work, it appeared some people at the hospital wanted the worst things to happen if she was to be involved in any way. Too much had happened between blacks and whites in this country that she could never grasp. The surly patient and the unapologetic orderly were steeped in hostility, so much so that she did not dare approach the bed of this marooned patient, not until she knew more. She'd have to examine him with one of the UN guards in the room.

There were still some days when she felt she was taking two steps forward, one step back. The turning point was the death of a young boy that everyone liked. He had been admitted too late with tuberculosis. The nuns felt very sad because this particular child wanted so much to live. Louise did not hide her grief either, or her tears. A male African orderly at her side instinctively reached forward to comfort her, stroking her arm. It was just for a moment. When she turned to look at him, she saw fear in his eyes. It alarmed her.

"What is it?" she asked. "What is the matter?"

The orderly looked down. He said in a low voice, "If you would have been a Belgian doctor, you would have given me a slap on the face because I touched a white woman's skin."

Louise shook her head. "No, it was just nice of you."

Watching this, patients and staff scrutinized her, then they smiled. From then on, communication with the staff and patients was less complicated; trust came more easily. She was greeted with friendliness and hope by all the staff. Her confidence was restored. Even the difficulties of transport back and forth between the hotel and hospital became easier to bear. Nothing was ever simple but life became more bearable. Even so, she sometimes dreaded visiting the children's ward because so many children were in such dire need.

Often, she did not feel she had enough time to stay long enough and make proper diagnoses. Nurse Vidal told her that there was a Danish physician who worked in a private hospital in Boma, a small harbour town down the Congo River. Perhaps he could help? And so it was arranged to have a Red Cross helicopter bring Dr. Kai for consultations for some difficult cases.

Dr. Kai turned out to be a Danish professor from the Copenhagen University Hospital. On the morning he arrived, everyone felt happy with renewed courage. He took his time, meticulously studying each patient, and looking at X-rays and fever curves. He frequently went into the laboratory to look through the microscope and make rigorous assessments. He was used to seeing only about 20 to 30 patients a day at the Copenhagen University Hospital, noted for its highly specialized research.

Soon Louise began to feel nervous about the amount of time he was taking. She tried politely to remind the new doctor to move on to the next patient but it did not help. The nurses began to excuse themselves because they knew they should look after the patients who were waiting in vain for the doctor. Given Dr. Kai's exhibition of thoroughness, Louise initially felt ashamed about how quickly she often made a diagnosis, but then what else could one do in Africa under such conditions? Guilty feelings had to be put aside as one simply had to use all one's knowledge and skill to make a diagnosis in accordance with time pressures.

Often they had to compromise and use the best medication which was available in the hospital; and sometimes, when she asked the Red Cross to deliver special medicines, they came too late. Fortunately, many of the hospital staff had worked there for many years and had been well-trained by the Belgian physicians. Knowing the limitations, everybody could stand by one another when a patient died after much long suffering.

The worst was facing the small children. Most of the older children were transferred to the women's ward as soon as they started to improve to a certain degree. Nevertheless, the children's ward was still over-crowded. The calm and friendly nurses worked steadily in the constant din of crying babies and infants. Mothers sat by their children's bedside, caring for them for hours until they were gently persuaded by the nuns to leave the hospital for the evening, telling the anxious mothers to get rest at their family homes, and that there were enough nurses to keep watch on the suffering babies.

The mothers clearly trusted the nurses and went home, returning early the next morning. The nuns, as well as the nurses, had steadfastly refused to abandon the helpless children and stated it was their duty to stay and take care of them and their mothers. The most painful situation was when a child could not recover in spite of all their help. Then the nurses and nuns would be there to help the child to die in peace. They would comfort the grieving mother and give her courage to turn to her other children.

Louise grew to trust one nurse in particular: Sister Solana. She cleaned wounds, gave infusions, ordered antibiotics and other medications and taught body care and diets for babies to the caregivers. She routinely comforted the crying children and encouraged the anxious mothers. She was always on the ward when Louise came in the morning and was still working when Louise left in the late afternoon. Whenever Louise felt overwhelmed, there was Sister Solana to give her strength. She went with Louise from one bed to the other. In advance, Sister Solana usually made up her mind about who Louise ought to see, which cases most required her advice. As Louise would discuss alternatives for each patient with her, Sister Solana warded off the anxious relatives flocking around the bed, trying to pull and push Louise along to see their child instead.

When Sister Solana realized that a child was too far gone, she would put a firm hand on Louise's arm, urging her to pass on, murmuring under her breath: "Not this one." Even the mothers often sensed a hopeless situation and understood. "Necessity makes one hard," she kept thinking. They had to concentrate on treating those who had a good chance to survive.

On the second day of the visit made by the Danish consultant Dr. Kai, Sister Solana sent for Louise, urging her to finish the other wards quickly and help them on the children's ward. Louise found her flustered and indignant, running exasperated to and fro, while Dr. Kai desperately tried to insert an infusion needle into a collapsed vein of an obviously very sick child, who looked as though it was close to death. It was unlike Sister Solana to appear so distressed. The young doctor with European standards was set on saving the baby's life. When Louise suggested giving up the fight, he became upset with her. Sister Solana anxiously brought him what he needed for surgery to open the vein. He worked on it for hours and succeeded finally in getting the fusion to work. He was very happy and proud. He did not seem to notice the staff's rising tension about his disregarding all the other waiting mothers with their children. Wearily, Sister Solana and Louise looked at each other while Dr. Kai was examining another child, marvelling at the many ailments it had, ordering unrealistic laboratory tests which would take far too much time. The tension between them became palpable.

Finally, when the little baby, who Dr. Kai had worked on for hours, died after all, the mother, in her grief, reacted with rage towards the doctor. Louise was worried that their young colleague, unaccustomed to such anger, was going to have a mental breakdown himself. The mother's reaction was not strange to Louise and Sister Solana; they had learned to cope with such feelings. But Dr. Kai looked baffled when the mother cried out, accusingly, "Why did you have to torture my child so much!" The mother continued her tirade: "We all knew that my child was going to die!"

The grieving mother pressed the lifeless child against her breast, tears of grief and anger running down her cheeks. She looked as if she were going to hit the young doctor. In turn, he grew pale, his mouth opened as if to say something but then he shut his mouth firmly and walked slowly away. Sister Solana spoke gently to the mother and put her arm around her. The mother leaned on her and sobbed. Sister Solana turned to Louise and said, "Please continue to visit the children. I will take care of him."

Eventually Sister Solana walked over to Dr. Kai. She talked to him for a long time, like a mother to her son, until he finally regained his composure. He resumed his rounds. But it was evident that he was not ever going to adapt. He was too accustomed to being in a hospital where children are always properly fed and they only have one illness at a time.

⌒

LOUISE WAS VERY impressed with the Moroccan soldiers detailed to protect them. These soldiers stayed in barracks on one side of the main road, near to the hotel. On the other side of the road they provided protection for the harbour and the workers. Sometimes gunshots could be heard from the harbour, and Louise worried about being caught in a crossfire.

At other times, crowds of Congolese soldiers lined the roadway and the tension between the local soldiers and the UN troops was palpable. Whereas the Congolese were anxious and suspicious, unpredictable, sometimes stopping the transport car with threatening gestures, the UN guards were disciplined, firm and predictable. With their clearly visible blue berets, they repeatedly had to explain that the two Europeans were doctors on their way to the hospital, pointing to the UN flag and the Red Cross insignia, before they were grudgingly permitted to drive on.

She increasingly felt admiration for these young men who were committed to guarding her wherever she went. Whenever there was even a hint of trouble or violence, they would unfailingly risk their lives to stand beside her. Some of them were handsome young men, but she knew she did not want to start any romance. Although she felt drawn to some of them, she always felt embarrassed when they looked up and down at her figure and her face, as if craving something. Who were they and where did they come from? How did they explain to their families what they were doing playing policemen during some godforsaken civil war in sub-Saharan Africa?

It was true that they tended to walk through the wards with their heavy boots, treating the hospital staff with contempt, and all the Africans were afraid of them and disliked their noisy behaviour, but the conditions they endured in the intense heat, languishing in their steamy barracks day after day, homesick and unhealthy, bordered on being intolerable. They had indigestion from poor food; they were susceptible to diarrhea and malaria.

The Moroccan guards were also on duty at the hotel day and night. This was a mixed blessing. As the days turned into weeks, it soon became apparent that the Moroccan soldiers, who did not have any other medical staff, were asking to see Dr. Louise far more frequently than had been expected. Many were accustomed to a cooler climate, and they suffered from the unhealthy hot air in their crude barracks. But others were simply bored. Many became listless. They had little appetite and could not sleep at night. There were also some serious illnesses, such as typhoid and jaundice, but she surmised that many of these young men, many of whom had never been far from home before, had quite simply become depressed.

Paying a visit to the lovely, white doctor became a form of entertainment. They all referred to her as *la petite doctoresse*. Of course, some of them naturally hoped to woo her, charm her, seduce her. This was beyond a nuisance; increasingly they were wasting her valuable time. In her position, she could ill afford to chastise or alienate them, so eventually she contacted their commanding officer—not accusing them so much as expressing sympathy for their plight—whereupon their commander asked for a medical report on their collective symptoms. She wrote out the following short report: "The symptoms of these young men are characteristic for persons not used to a moist, hot climate. The listlessness and poor sleep that follows make them bored and depressed. Add to this some fever from malaria and loss of appetite and these men begin to feel weak most of the time. I recommend you give them a pint of good beer to drink in the morning together with better food."

The officer was taken aback. "Alcohol! Don't you know these men are Muslims?"

She responded firmly. "Well, in this case, beer is medicine."

She explained that beer had lots of good vitamins and it would help with their appetite. It would cheer them up. And when they started to feel stronger, he should give them more to do, to create some sports for them. She predicted their sleep would improve and their strength would return. And so it was done. "It's the best medicine we ever had," the soldiers would tell her, cheerfully. Soon the officer thanked her for this advice.

But this re-invigoration of the Moroccan soldiers brought with it a new problem. Whereas the other members of her team tended to socialize in the bar of the hotel, she avoided that area, often preferring solitude. If she was the only woman, alcohol could easily become problematic. Late one night there was suddenly a loud knocking on her door. Who would be disturbing her at that hour? Was there an emergency? Her instinct told her not to answer immediately.

There was another knock. She silently approached the door and looked through the keyhole. She was able to distinguish two Moroccan uniforms. Two men were smoking cigarettes and whispering to each other in the hall. She decided if she opened the door at such a late hour it could be misinterpreted as an invitation. There was another loud knock while she hovered in silence. It was a new terror to be frightened of the soldiers who were protecting her. Tension in the hotel that evening had been high. There had been some sort of a scuffle in the bar. Threats had been uttered. She hadn't been there but she had learned of it second-hand. Their fragile semblance of order was disappearing.

The door did not seem to be very solid. In survival mode, she suddenly wondered if it would hold. The decision to cry out or remain silent seemed fundamental. Had she brought herself all the way through medical school for *this*? Was she somehow to blame for being naive? She could smell their cigarette smoke. They were talking in hushed tones. Then they seemed to laugh a bit. Was that a good sign? Or was it no sign at all?

She opted to follow her first instinct. Stay silent. Wait. Wait. Wait. Louise had no idea how long this situation lasted. It seemed an eternity. No matter where she went on this planet, no matter how well-intentioned some human beings could be, there would always be this tension between men and women.

They must have got tired of waiting. Perhaps they concluded she wasn't there? Perhaps they knew of some other place they could go for diversion? Perhaps their intentions were not violent? Perhaps they were simply drunk and lonely? She'd never know.

The next morning, their team leader, Stig Garbrand, came to fetch her for breakfast. Outside, in the hallway, was a heap of cigarette butts. "What is this?" he asked.

"I think it was the devil," she replied. Nothing more was said.

Eventually one of the Moroccan officers overtly pursued her, hoping to go to bed with her. After an attempt at brief kissing, he, too, was dissuaded. She told him not to bother. She had no interest in risking her independence. He accepted and withdrew.

If there was to be a love interest, it would have to be Stig Garbrand, a sober, clean, well-educated man who didn't talk much about himself. He didn't seek closeness but he was reserved in a positive way. Everyone immediately respected him. One night, when the Force Publique soldiers entered the bar at midnight, pointing their weapons at the Red Cross men, nobody dared protest, but then Stig had arrived and reprimanded the soldiers. The intruders had left at once, and he had escorted Louise to her room, a complete gentleman.

Then one morning, at breakfast, she noticed he was pale and he ate very little. He barely spoke and did not get up when everybody else left. Stig was a very private person, who had a difficult time admitting he had been sick throughout the night. Eventually he told her he had a severe headache. Suspecting that he might have caught malaria, Louise suggested he should lie down until she could find out what was the matter.

She phoned the hospital and asked that somebody be requested to bring the necessary instruments. She proceeded to take a drop of blood from every team member's finger to check for malaria. It turned out that Stig indeed had malaria, but fortunately nobody else did. She gave him Nivaquine tablets and ordered him to stay in bed. When she went to see him the next day, he was sweating and shivering with a severe headache. He looked anxious and felt weak. She instructed him to stay in bed until the attacks were gone and gave him some Aspirin for his pain.

Bored and restless, he constantly begged to be allowed to get up. She eventually allowed him to see how he felt—as a passenger only— in the helicopter. She hoped an outing would lift his spirits. The plan was to see her daily and continue with the medication. Unfortunately, he was too eager to fly again and soon took over piloting. She was anxious about it, but Stig was a strong and independent person who did not make foolish decisions.

A little while later, while coming down for a landing, his helicopter suddenly canted, and one of the propellers crashed onto the ground with a terrible noise. There was an explosion and the helicopter was engulfed in flames. One of the other pilots saw Stig hop out and rush around the side, opening the door and pulling out the two passengers to safety. Both were stunned by the crash, but Stig had worked so quickly that they were not badly hurt. Stig, however, was not so fortunate. Both his hands were severely burned.

Stig was quickly taken to the hospital in Boma and treated there by Dr. Kai. After many days, he showed up at their table in the hotel with bandages on his hands and arms. They could see that he was still in pain but he was happy to be back on duty. It was looked upon as an accident and, as the helicopter was completely destroyed, the Red Cross gave him a new helicopter. Louise wondered if she had made a mistake allowing him to go up in the helicopter when he was still ill. They never spoke about it.

One day their work was interrupted by the arrival of a helicopter in the yard of the hospital. The pilot hurriedly found Dr. Louise in the wards and hastily explained a strange emergency: a Congolese officer was about to arrest the captain of a Norwegian ship. The crew and captain did not speak English or French. They needed an interpreter immediately.

In a matter of minutes, the helicopter deposited her alongside an old freighter in the docks. Surly soldiers were milling about, cradling their weapons, seemingly as ignorant of the circumstances as she was. She followed the helicopter pilot up the gangplank and entered the small captain's cabin where she was the only woman among a crowd of angry and tense men.

Having played goalkeeper for a men's soccer league during her school days in Oslo, Louise was not unduly intimidated by the prospect of squeezing her way through two opposing groups of men. She knew it would take only one aggressive nudge, one slur or sneer, in order for either side to incite a conflagration. She had seen some of the most gentlemanly, civilized men off the pitch transformed into irrational warriors when the tensions were high in soccer just before a corner kick was taken. It was always the goalkeeper's challenge in that situation to literally rise above the fray, leaping above the heads of both sides, either securely catching the ball with both hands or elegantly punching it away with one fist.

Everyone seemed to be speaking at once. And there was no referee. She could easily converse with the captain and the crew but she refrained from doing so. Instinctively, she understood it would not be advantageous to be seen to take sides against the Congolese. If she was going to serve as an intermediary, her first challenge was to establish communication with the militia.

The captain of the military police knew some English so she resorted to a trick she sometimes used when there was a tense situation in Tanganyika which could trigger violence. "Please speak louder so I can hear what you say," she blurted out loudly over the din. There was an astonished silence.

Then there was laughter among the Africans as the joke was explained to them. They liked this kind of teasing, harmless humour. The tension was immediately diminished. She formally introduced herself, using a combination of French and English. She was a Red Cross doctor. She could speak Norwegian.

Using his fractured English, the soldier in charge explained that the ship had entered Matadi harbour without first providing notice of what they were doing there, and who they were. They were naturally suspicious. Therefore, they had boarded the ship to "arrest" the captain. This meant they wished to take the Norwegian captain into custody for questioning to learn the nature of his business.

Louise said she understood. Then she turned to the ship's captain and asked him in Norwegian to explain his presence in the harbour. The much-relieved captain said that for many years he had been bringing dried fish from Norway to many harbours, mainly in Spain, but also as far south as Matadi. He had always been able to unload his cargo of dried fish at the Matadi harbour without any difficulties. He had anchored at the same place as usual.

It turned out that neither the captain nor any of his crew members had listened to the radio or read any newspapers since their departure from Spain. They knew nothing about how the Belgians had fled across the river to the neighbouring Brazzaville. His crew had simply followed their usual course. Now that he understood, he simply wished to offload the fish. He diplomatically asked to be pardoned for the commotion and confusion.

On his side, however, the inexperienced Congolese officer needed to behave in such a manner that would impress his soldiers. Louise understood he must not be viewed as a man who had fallen under the sway of a woman. Whenever Maasai men had appeared at her remote clinics, demanding to be treated immediately, she had learned the efficacy of letting them have their way. Placating male machismo was sometimes the most prudent survival technique.

And yet, subservience was not *always* the only remedy. Having consulted with so-called medicine men, adopting a strategy of mutual respect rather than confrontation, she knew the degree to which the mysterious powers of a healer were revered and feared in Africa. With a pounding heart, she resorted to a second trick. In front of all the men, she stamped her foot, stared into the eyes of the Congolese officer, and made her eyes appear to be half-closed, as if in a trance.

Appearing to receive her words from another realm, Louise recited, in an altered voice: "The men on this ship do not mean you any harm. They are harmless, honest sailors. For years they have brought fish to Matadi for your people to eat. They did not know about the war. Therefore, if you do not immediately leave the ship without doing these men any harm, and you do not allow the captain to unload his fish, I will pursue you for the rest of your days!"

The Congolese officer stepped backwards, obviously frightened. "All right," he said, "let the crew unload the merchandise as usual. But tell this captain the next time he sails into an African harbour he must study the country first. He must take necessary precautions!"

The Norwegian captain did not need to be instructed by Louise to appear suitably chastised and rebuked. He bowed respectfully. Afterwards, the captain and his much-relieved Norwegian crew members invited Louise and the helicopter pilot to stay for lunch which, by the standards of Matadi, was sumptuous.

News of this drama spread quickly. After that, the entire Red Cross team was frequently invited for a good meal aboard the foreign ships that were still landing in Matadi harbour. The captains and crews always had a good laugh when they asked her to re-tell the story, retold, of course, as self-effacingly as she could manage.

Possibly her humility was ingrained due to birth order. To be different from her charismatic brother and her vivacious sister, Louise had long since devised a personality that disguised her considerable ego with a feigned modesty. She seldom brought attention to herself. To do so approximated bad manners. By rejecting competitiveness, she was equally well-liked by men and women. It also kept her at a safe distance from those who imagined they knew all about her.

WHEN THE RED CROSS required the resumption of medical service to remote clinics, two helicopters were assigned. Finn Kristoffersen would be the pilot to carry the Moroccan soldiers for her protection; her pilot would be Richard Stromberg. Dr. Stensrud, who had come with her in the beginning, was kept at Matadi doing surgeries. On the morning of the first flight, Richard took care to fasten her seat belt and also to adjust the microphone atop her helmet so they could converse during the flight over the noise of the engine and propeller. After making a sign to Finn that he was ready, with a firm grip Richard revved up their engine, and the propellers began to whirl so quickly they became invisible.

Initially, the heat inside the glass cockpit as they lifted off was stifling. The hospital was clearly visible below but then they turned diagonally, and the foaming water of the river was beneath her feet. They ascended quickly. That way, if there were problems with Congolese soldiers firing at them, they would be able to glide to the other riverbank.

Richard had instructed her to wear a life jacket "just in case." With the windows opened, the air cooled and she could relax. A wonderful aroma drifted up from the primeval forest. The lush landscape was intoxicating. For the first time she looked at the young pilot and realized he was handsome.

At Seke-Banza, their first destination, Finn landed first so the Moroccans could ensure it was safe. Richard's whirlybird hovered and gently touched down next. Louise ducked under the still-whirling blades and instinctively ran towards the small crowd that had gathered. Outside the small dispensary, the orderlies and a nurse looked tense and unfriendly. She took it personally, not stopping to think that a contingent of armed, foreign soldiers dropping from the sky would be unsettling even in the best of circumstances.

They were told that help from Europeans was not needed. It was an embarrassing situation for both sides. Louise could not know for certain whether these people had been told to refuse help, or if their reluctance to engage was genuine. She waited to see if she would be asked to look inside the dispensary or not. To remove any obvious threat of aggression, the UN soldiers lifted off in their helicopter, leaving her temporarily unprotected, but this made little difference.

Louise made some polite and friendly inquiries about the patients, and asked if any particular medicines were needed, but it remained clear that these people—for whatever reason—were hoping the second helicopter would also disappear as soon as possible.

Recognizing that they were not wanted, Richard and Louise both climbed in, and Richard started off. After about ten seconds, however, with the helicopter tilting slightly to one side, she heard a whistling sound just behind her head. This high-pitched noise disappeared out the other side of the helicopter through the pilot's open window. Immediately, Richard ascended as quickly as possible. Neither of them commented. Could it have been a bird? More likely it was a bullet. If so, that might have been the reason the people had not wanted them there. Were rebel soldiers hiding in the surrounds?

En route to their second and final destination, Inga, they flew into dark clouds and were pelted with rain. Visibility was nil. She noticed the rain ran upwards on the front glass, creating strange patterns. Her stomach tightened when the helicopter suddenly plummeted to take them out of the cloud. "Look down," said Richard, smiling. On her side there was an antelope running. It was scared, not knowing which way to go to escape the menacing sound of the helicopter. Less than a minute later she saw Africans running, too, in much the same manner, dashing into their huts.

It was possible these people had never seen a helicopter before. That alone might have accounted for the distrustful reception at the previous dispensary. She could imagine them mistaking the helicopter for some enormous, mythical, man-eating mosquito of their ancestors. How could one explain the concept of the United Nations to people who had little concept of nationhood to begin with? Louise and Richard agreed they ought to discuss with Finn, the other pilot, a different strategy for approaching Inga.

The decision was that the two pilots would first land in a large field a considerable distance away from the village. Here they could check their fuels and allow the Moroccans to stretch their legs and relieve themselves. They agreed that Richard and Louise should then go back up and land first just outside the village. Richard could remain in contact with Finn in case of trouble.

Needless to say, the head of the UN entourage was not consulted on this change in protocol. Louise's helicopter proceeded to land not far from the dispensary at Inga, where a crowd of people, including a nurse, some orderlies and even some patients, all cheered when she appeared. The lone obstacle was a Congolese soldier. At first he looked quite fearsome. Here, this far out in the countryside, it was not likely he was fluent in French or English. Possibly he was a lone constable in charge of a large swath of territory. She had absolutely no way of knowing what she ought to do or say as she approached.

He must have seen her apprehension because he came forward with a smile, took her arm with a friendly gesture, and motioned her to come with him for a photograph outside the dispensary. There was considerable laughter as everyone shuffled together.

It was easy after that. The patients had all gone to their beds in anticipation of being introduced to a real doctor. She used her methodology from the Matadi hospital: engage the nurse and orderlies at the bedside; question them as the patient was examined; and encourage them to ask questions if her directions were not fully understood. As usual, she apportioned her time in accordance with the gravity of each ailment. The head nurse was assured that if a patient became gravely ill in spite of their efforts, the pilot would not only come and take the patient to the hospital in Matadi, but also return the patient when he or she improved.

After several hours, the orderlies and the nurse thanked her warmly and invited her to lunch in their little cafeteria. Here, as she listened to a litany of stories of anarchy, turmoil and violence all around, it felt to everyone present that they had collectively won a victory for sanity and civility. Louise and the pilots were invited to return.

On the way back, feeling relieved and happy, they took a longer route so she could snap some photos of the swirling, whitish, wild water around the sharp, black stones in the Congo River. Some stretches of the great river were peaceful and calm; people in small boats were fishing. Then came violent stretches where the waters surged through gorges with incredible force.

Richard explained that there were plans for a hydroelectric dam. The outside world, the European/American/United Nations world, believed there could be a future for the Congo, as if it were a place like the other colonies that were shedding their French, English and German overseers. Politics was not her forte and she nodded politely to the idea of a dam, but from what she had seen and heard, the Congo was far different from Tanganyika or any other such colony.

She caught herself glancing at the bare forearms of the capable pilot. Once again she told herself not to start a romance. There were so few distractions and pleasures for these men who were far from home. Fresh trouble could be kindled in just one second, as fast as squeezing a trigger. She had taught herself to literally look away. But after their successful adventure, her eyes lingered. Some of the young

Moroccan men were courageous and attractive, too, but she had already decided they were out of the question. A Swede, however. Was that different? The following day she allowed Richard to fly her to a beach in neighbouring Angola for the day for a lunch on the beach and a swim. But it was nothing more than a friendly picnic.

Another time, when the roadway to the hospital was deemed too dangerous to drive, Stig decided their entire Red Cross team should be rewarded with a visit to a restaurant with a swimming pool. After a refreshing swim, most of the men sat at the table to eat, with bare chests. She felt uneasy in her short swimsuit so she went and changed into her usual clothes. She returned and naturally sat beside their senior officer, Stig. She flushed with a realization: maybe *this* was the man for her.

She hardly dared to look at him. From an early age she had been prone to lecturing herself, so the intrusion of her objective voice was almost commonplace. It was her voice but it was also the voice of her faraway mother: "You do not want a life full of passion in Africa. You have saved yourself for something else. You need your full strength to do your job well with the Red Cross, as you did in East Africa. You will eventually find the right time to find the right man. But not now. You must wait."

When they all went swimming again, later that afternoon, she felt relaxed and freed from confusion. She loved the cool, fresh water. With renewed confidence, she swam underwater and laughed when she surfaced. She gazed into the beautiful brown eyes of the men and felt they liked her. She had not felt such youth and vibrancy for a long time. As they were leaving the restaurant compound, she felt something soft and wriggling under her right sandal. She jumped aside. It was a thin, green snake, one of the poisonous jungle snakes.

"A snake," she announced, just loud enough to warn everyone.

As the others drew closer to investigate, she called the African server who had brought the food to their table. Most Africans knew what do with snakes. Nobody else dared to move or talk. The waiter found a stick in the grass and split one end of it, making a fork. He proceeded to pin the head of the green snake as it wriggled violently. Instead of asking one of the other men to find a rock and pound it to death, he deftly whirled the stick and the snake into the bushes.

"Most women would have shrieked," said Stig.

Nobody needed to make the point any clearer. She was *not* like most women. But would she ever be?

To further aggravate tension, the Force Publique troops had made their headquarters close to the hotel, opposite the UN troops' barracks. This meant Louise and the surgeon, Dr. Stensrud, as well as their Swedish pilots and mechanics were increasingly sequestered in the hotel.

The hotel was also a refuge for relatively well-to-do Congolese who had gravitated to Matadi, hoping for maritime passage out of the country. It only stood to reason that Congolese families staying in the hotel were carrying their savings. They were easy pickings if they left the hotel, so messengers were constantly going to and from the lobby. Sometimes the Force Publique raided the hotel late at night. Louise would wake up in her room to shouts and cries, and the breaking of doors. At times, shots were fired. Twice she heard heart-breaking wailing from women and children.

The UN personnel tried to protest the late-night raids of the Force Publique. But when they tried to intercede one night, the Congolese officer shouted at them, "The hotel is full of communists and foreigners. Just wait!" Conditions worsened to the point where Stig decided nobody from the Red Cross should frequent the bar. It was common for men in the hotel to drink too much out of boredom and frustration. Some played billiards in the evenings. Louise occasionally went to the games room where it became apparent that she was an accomplished ping-pong player. She enjoyed games of skill, but had less interest in card games.

Her swift volleys humiliated the men time and again, until it was grudgingly acknowledged that she was unbeatable. There was invariably an audience. Eventually they collectively opted to take it as a matter of pride that she was *their* champion, a shared possession, like some prize race horse. The reputation for her prowess at ping-pong soon spread through the hotel.

One evening, as they sat down for another of their over-cooked dinners, Louise noticed an extremely large black man at another table with a number of his friends. "If you want to see a real bear," whispered Louise, jokingly at the table, "turn your head and look over there!" The man was huge. A behemoth. His skin was of the deeply dark colour characteristic of the people from the interior of the Congo. He had a pock-marked face, friendly brown eyes and greyish, curly hair. When he talked, he gesticulated freely with his hands, roaring with laughter. He was a comical titan, seemingly harmless. This gargantuan man appeared wholly impregnable to an attack from another man. She felt for him immediately. He seemed to have an elephant kindness, elephant wisdom.

Over dessert a little later, the heavy steps of soldiers sounded through the halls. The Force Publique noisily stomped into the dining room, bristling with their weapons. When she looked at their eyes, she thought some of them might be on drugs. Or was it the drug of machismo? Either way, she felt her life was in danger. Louise and her companions were armed only with forks and knives. On strict orders, they were not to carry any arms in the hotel. This proved beneficial when the rag-tag contingent of Force Publique commandos proceeded to approach them with their metal detectors, looking for guns.

A commotion arose at the neighbouring table. A metal detector was beeping. The soldiers ran towards the elephant man. A Congolese officer shouted something. Many weapons were pointed at the dark-faced man and his companions. They were told to stand with their hands lifted above their heads. Individually, the soldiers would have been afraid of the elephant man, but as a pack of jackals, they held the upper hand. A sickening dread spread through the room as the jackals circled their prey.

"Keep quiet! Stay where you are!" said Stig, sensing his people were ready to run away. "Don't move!"

A soldier slipped behind the big man and swung his rifle like a club against his head. He tumbled with a crash. The soldiers threw themselves at him, beating on him blindly. One of them got hold of the weapon the large man had concealed.

Triumphant, the invaders hoisted the battered man to his feet. His face was covered in blood but he did not utter a word. He did not make any motion to protect himself. The soft brown eyes of the poor giant seemed to stare at something far away. At this point, when their captive was most subservient, the commanding officer proceeded to bash him again with the butt of his rifle.

The big man bowed his head. His tormentors appeared emboldened by the sight of blood. The raw brutality that followed was unforgettable. They pummelled him in a frenzy until he dropped to his knees. He was kicked and pushed and dragged towards the door.

Everyone at the table was still standing, uncertain if they should do something or not. "Keep quiet. Stay where you are," Stig repeated. "Don't move unless I tell you to!"

It was impossible to know whether the behemoth was dead yet or not. They heard his giant body being rolled heavily down the stairs. The other men who were with him were hustled away to their uncertain fates. They all knew better than to resist. Through the windows of the dining room Louise and the others watched as the soldiers loaded the men into the back of a truck.

More cries and shouts echoed through the lofty halls of the hotel. Then the smartly-dressed Force Publique officer who had been in charge re-entered the dining room. He was grinning, with a revolver in his hand, as he picked up one of the ping-pong paddles in his other hand. He motioned for Louise to do the same. The officer laughed at her bewilderment. He made a show of displaying his revolver, his rifle, his heavy ammunition belt, another handgun and a huge bush-knife. The weapons clattered as he dropped them on a small table, their weight causing it to wobble. Again, he made signs for Louise to begin to play. His challenge struck her as ridiculous. She trembled with fear and indignation. Her instinct was to stubbornly refuse, but she knew the officer would not allow that.

Stig gave her an encouraging nod. *I have to play with the howling wolves*, she thought.

Tears were blurring her eyesight. The officer easily won the first few points. She could barely make contact with the ball. But very soon the disparaging laughter of her opponent made her furious. A cold calmness came over her. She began to observe and analyze how he played. It took her back to all those games she had played in Tübingen, and against her brother. *I will show you*, she vowed to herself.

Her opponent was adept at taking direct shots near to his body but he was weaker with sideways volleys that were low over the net and only barely touched the edge of the table. These were her favourite shots. Her opponent had to respond with agility rather than power. The ball sped back and forth with increasing speed. She did not pause in her efforts between points. Each time she won another point she was emboldened. *This is what you get for killing the elephant man!* she said to herself. *Smack. Spin. Twist. I'll play you under the table!*

The officer jumped up and down between points like a boxer in the ring. He was breathing heavily and uttered small cries as he played. The audience for this curious spectacle dared not express its loyalties for fear of being on the losing side. The momentum was shifting as the ball ricocheted harder and faster. He was faltering, exposing signs of frustration. Louise moved ahead in the score. When she took a moment to glance at her supporters, she was anticipating seeing signs of support. Instead she saw her senior officer frowning, shaking his head slowly.

She was mortified. Of course! What was she thinking! Suddenly she came to her senses. It only took a moment for her to see that the Congolese soldiers were dismayed. What could happen if their commanding officer was to lose to a *woman*?

Louise understood she must lose. She changed her tactics accordingly, but not obviously. Her victory would have to be a moral one of voluntary self-restraint. She started to make herself miss shots. Because she had given him such a good fight, his victory would be all the sweeter. After he won the final point, she quietly put down her paddle. "You have won the game," she told him, in Lingala. The winner beamed with pride and his men cheered.

With nonchalant confidence, her opponent rearranged his uniform. He meticulously picked up his blood-stained weapons, put on his ammunition belt, tucked his knife in place and slung his rifle over his shoulder. He placed his two revolvers back in their holsters. Victorious, his rejoicing men marched out of the room with the victor, proud as a peacock.

⌒

SOON AFTER THE GAME of ping-pong, Louise noticed that distrust of foreigners was turning into sanctioned hatred. Whether in the hospital, on the roads or in the hotel, the Red Cross team was increasingly beset by tensions. It didn't help matters when the Luba tribe in Katanga was threatening to outdo the fierceness of the Force Publique.

During more raids on the hotel in the wee hours, Louise heard doors being broken down amid more shouting. It became an ugly routine: suspicious strangers, always men, were dragged out and beaten, as women wailed and children cowered. The Force Publique claimed soldiers from Katanga were taking refuge inside. They charged that firearms were being stowed in the rooms. "This hotel is full of people from the Peace Corps!" screamed one of them, in French. "Just wait! We will clean you all out!"

By February, Louise was fighting anxiety and depression. She didn't have sufficient time for all her patients; every week there were difficult cases that challenged her level of knowledge and experience. A feeling of despair gradually weakened her resolve. Her best was simply not good enough.

She was secretly glad to be told by Mr. Norredam that she should make her preparations to go when she reached the end of her predetermined tenure. Nurse Thomas, during her farewell visit to the hospital, told her, "We all will miss you very much. You understood us Africans. You saved many children and so many other patients for us." Certainly, she had done her best, but it had never been enough.

Louise hastily learned Lingala to communicate with her Congolese staff
and patients when she became the sole attending physician at the
Red Cross hospital in Matadi, Belgian Congo, in 1960.

The Matadi Hospital was left without doctors after nearly
all the Belgians fled the Belgian Congo.

Along with assistance from nuns who chose to stay in Matadi, Louise relied on her "dressers" such as Thomas to perform the nursing duties.

Skills as a diplomat sometimes took precedence: here Louise feigns friendliness with a member of the Force Publique. King Leopold had originally created this militia to maintain his murderous fiefdom.

Relaxing beside a co-worker, Louise felt duty-bound to live up to the ideals of one of her childhood heroes, Henry Dunant, who co-founded the Red Cross.

Along with a contingent of United Nations soldiers from Morocco, Louise was protected by her Swedish helicopter pilots and mechanics.

This is one of two United Nations helicopters used to transport Louise to four clinics far beyond Matadi.

Matadi, main port for the Belgian Congo, as seen from a Red Cross helicopter.

Matadi is located just below the rapids that make the Congo River impassable.

The daily influx of tourists who took unwarranted photos at Lambaréné greatly
disturbed Dr. Albert Schweitzer and his staff. Consequently this blurry image
is the only photograph of Louise at Dr. Schweitzer's hospital in 1961.

A separate hospital compound at Lambaréné provided treatment
and segregation of patients with leprosy, such as this man.

Dr. Albert Schweitzer (left) and Silvio Mittner who felt compelled to climb trees, as seen in 1960. He presented Louise with one of her most bizarre cases.

Louise was awarded the Henry Dunant Medal along with this Citation from the League of Red Cross Societies, Geneva (showing map of the Belgian Congo).

Eventually the various members of the Red Cross team said good-bye to one another, promising to write. It felt like a defeat. Her pilots persuaded her it would be dangerous to leave the country via Leop-oldville where killings were rampant. Stig agreed. Moreover, fewer ships were taking the risk of docking at Matadi.

There would, however, be some freighters arriving at the Congolese port of Pointe-Noire, to the north, or perhaps at Boma, formerly the capital of the Congo Free State. Boma had been founded as a slaving station, on the north bank of the river, upstream from Muanda on the Atlantic. Either way, Louise imagined languorous days aboard a freighter to recuperate.

As soon as they learned a Dutch freighter had docked at the Congolese port of Pointe-Noire, Richard offered to fly her there, and without anyone's permission, gallantly landed his Red Cross helicopter right in front of the hotel to pick her up. Farewells were said hastily. Before anyone could object, they were in the air. Richard assured her it would be easy once they were over Pointe-Noire to spot the Dutch flag of the freighter from the air. The only trouble was, there was no way they could get word to the captain of the ship in advance. She had grown accustomed to trusting Richard in such circumstances.

When Pointe-Noire came into view, the dockside was crammed with people and goods, but the Dutch ship was clearly visible. Richard pointed to an open area on the top deck of the ship, a recreation area for shuffleboard or gatherings of the crew. As they descended, the Dutch sailors fled like a flock of birds in all directions. At first, it was comical. As they drew closer, Louise could see that many of the sailors had retrieved rifles. Didn't they see the Red Cross symbol? She tried to wave. As they hovered, none of the crew members moved out of hiding.

Once on deck, the blades of the helicopter took several minutes before they stopped spinning. The engine finally sputtered, coughed, and died. Less likely to be shot at, Louise descended first. Unable to speak Dutch, she called out hello in Norwegian, then shifted to German. The captain, it turned out, knew who she was. Evidently the episode in Matadi harbour, when she had served as a translator, had been written up in some European papers, casting her in a very favourable light. The captain emerged and said it would be wonderful to have their own Norwegian doctor aboard.

Trouble arose only when a small troop of local soldiers boarded the ship. Their captain angrily asked how she had landed without permission from the harbour master. It took time to explain she was a representative of the Red Cross. The captain of the ship invited the officer to inspect a ready-made cabin, explaining that everything had been arranged well in advance. This did the trick.

The Dutch captain was amused. "I have never had a passenger arrive with such pomp," he said with a good laugh. All her problems appeared to be solved. Given the circumstances, it seemed prudent for Richard to make a hasty lift-off. There was no time for sentimentality. To her relief, he embraced her quickly, kissing her once on the cheek, and left. There was only one problem. The freighter was still awaiting its cargo and she would not be able to start her voyage around the Cape of Good Hope for another week.

The following day, around noon when most people were taking their lunch indoors, Louise found herself walking, unescorted, in Pointe-Noire. If she had talked to the Dutch captain, she could have easily had any one of the sailors on board serve as an escort, but for too long she had been treated as some precious object. Pointe-Noire was much smaller than Matadi; there was no fear of getting lost. For the first time in more than three months Louise found herself walking freely. No appointments. No obligations. No emergencies. She had no one to look after except herself.

Just strolling along the street with no particular destination, putting one foot in front of another, felt like a healing reprieve. It made her nostalgic for Europe, Zurich in particular. She did not need to see a psychiatrist to know her equilibrium had been shattered by the strain of repressing her fears. The descent of the Belgian Congo into barbarism had caused nightmares. She needed rest, rehabilitation.

As she was strolling along the road that followed the coastline, looking out to sea, a man on a motorbike slowed down as he passed. Louise did not like the way he looked at her. A few minutes later, the same motorbike returned. Oh no, she thought to herself. Not again. As there was a steep drop-off to the beach from the roadside, she skidded down, away from the road, in order to make herself no longer visible. Possibly the man on the motorbike would assume she was meeting someone.

She had brought an orange. She sat down on a rock and began to eat it. She assumed the man would have kept riding. He would not have wanted to leave his motorbike unattended on the roadway. But she heard rustling in the bushes by the roadside. She saw the man, a big, dark-skinned man, come sliding down the hillside, as she had done. He was out of control and crashed down nearly beside her. It was somewhat comical so she laughed.

He was shaking a bit. Spontaneously, she offered him a piece of orange. Astonished, he took it. They sat and ate together. She had no idea what language he spoke. She didn't want to know. There was nobody else on the stretch of rough beach but they were viewable from the road. Then the man spoke with his threatening eyes. He motioned her to follow him to where there was more space. That way he might have his way with her.

She was frightened but rose as if to obey. It was like a bad dream unravelling beyond her control. If they began to fight, he would easily overpower her. Following him, like some obedient dog, she saw stairs leading back up to the road. She bolted and ran. She was halfway up the stairs when he caught up with her. He assumed he could manhandle her with ease. He was not anticipating she would turn so quickly and kick out at him. Caught off-balance, he went tumbling back down the stairs. While he was recovering, she raced up to the roadway, hoping there would be a motorist passing. She ran into the middle of the road and waved frantically. In a movie, this scene would not be believable because a car appeared almost instantaneously, as if preordained.

The driver stopped. "Are you crazy!" he said, through the open window, in French. She opened the passenger door as quickly as possible and leapt into the front seat.

Louise gave no thought as to who this man might be, or what he might think of her. All that mattered was to be rescued. He sped away, towards town. Only a fool would refuse a ride to a white, European damsel in distress. But she was accustomed to her Moroccan protectors. As they were driving, the man reached over, as if to comfort her, and his hand rested on her thigh. It proceeded upward.

As soon as they reached the city, she jumped out of the car at one of the town's few stoplights, leaving the amorous motorist to reflect on his ways. What she needed was some place to calm her nerves. She did not want to return to the freighter and blurt out her story, making herself look foolish. Finding herself in a part of Pointe-Noire that had some shops that catered to Europeans, she paused to look through a window. On the table inside she saw a large map of Africa. It was a travel bureau of some sort, she realized, so she went inside, curious to look at the various ports of call she might be visiting on her way.

As soon as she examined the map closely, she saw that Pointe-Noire was about 100 kilometres northwest of Matadi. Not much further to the north, just 75 kilometres south of the equator, she saw the village of Lambaréné. Since her teens, Louise had known that Lambaréné was where Dr. Albert Schweitzer had his jungle hospital on the Ogowe River.

Yes, the shop manager confirmed, there was a direct flight between Pointe-Noire to Lambaréné in Gabon, a new country independent from France for less than a year. Knowing she had a full week before sailing, Louise could choose between remaining in the tiny port of Pointe-Noire, as the only woman on a freighter, or making an unexpected pilgrimage to meet the most famous doctor on earth.

CHAPTER 5

Gabon:
Wonderful Is the Earth
& Dr. Albert Schweitzer

IN 1947, *Time* magazine had described Dr. Albert Schweitzer as "The greatest man in the World." Winston Churchill had called him "a genius of humanity."

Louise bought a ticket.

The following morning, the Dutch captain invited her for a good Dutch breakfast and arranged for a taxi to take her to Pointe-Noire's little airport. Once inside the plane, Louise saw that her fellow passengers included a few African women with children, accompanying their serious husbands in business suits, along with some khaki-clad Frenchmen. The tourists were the ones with cameras and sporty clothes. Evidently, the great doctor had become something of a major tourist attraction.

As her plane rose and headed towards Gabon, Louise recalled the thrill of hearing him speak in Norway. Oddly, she had never fully considered the extent to which his vow to "work in a place where a doctor would be desperately needed" might have influenced her life. In her mind, she had always wanted to be a doctor, long before she knew he existed, and his appearance had little to do with her choice of vocation.

Only after she'd heard Schweitzer speak did she learn his story: with his wife, Helene, an anaesthetist, working alongside him daily as his only nurse, surgical assistant and secretary, he had toiled in relative obscurity, at their own expense, in one of the most humid climates of tropical Africa from 1913 to 1917, establishing their improvised headquarters on the Little Ogowe River. It was not long after the area had become known as French Equatorial Africa in 1910, nowadays as Gabon. They had chosen the site due to the proximity of the Andende French Protestant Mission Post, established by the Paris Missionary Society.

Because he had been born in German-held Alsace, Schweitzer and Helene during WWI had been put under French supervision, and when both of them fell ill at Lambaréné in 1917, they were taken to Bordeaux and interned first in Garaison, and then from March 1918 in Saint-Rémy-de-Provence for the remaining months of the war. At this time Schweitzer went into a deep depression from which he needed several years to recover. Helene was infected with tuberculosis and never fully recovered.

In the post-war years, Schweitzer, who was fluent in both French and German, undertook fundraising trips throughout Europe. Audiences were as attracted by his concerts as much as by his lectures. Schweitzer was renowned as an organ builder and musician, especially as an interpreter of J.S. Bach. Louise assumed she was likely the only person on the little plane who knew that long before Schweitzer had published his first book about Lambaréné, *On the Edge of the Primeval Forest*, in 1922, he had written a well-known book about organ building.

Before their little plane descended through the clouds in the late afternoon, Louise made up her mind not to appear at Dr. Schweitzer's hospital until later the following morning—in keeping with her belief that it was usually best to approach important places on foot. Therefore, as the tourists sped across the muddy Ogowe River in an elegant motorboat, she joined the African passengers who boarded a slow ferry that would take them to the picturesque village of Lambaréné. Her French host at a tiny hotel reassured her that Dr. Schweitzer was renowned for treating each and every visitor with the utmost respect.

It was the beginning of the rainy season. The following morning the Little Ogowe River was swollen with water and the air was heavy with humidity. She soon regretted her decision to walk for several hours in order to make her entrance. By the time she arrived, she would be drenched in perspiration. Finally, however, she came to a lush meadow where there was a Catholic priest in a white cassock, watching a gaggle of laughing school boys swimming in the river. Sunlight glistened on their brown bodies.

Greeting the surprised priest in French, she asked him to guide her to the hospital. He pointed across the river. She saw a few low buildings, like crude barracks. Everything blended into the big trees. It was very rudimentary. It did not seem at all possible that there were seventy buildings accommodating about one thousand people.

There was an old African nearby in a canoe. With only a few words, the priest asked him to take Louise across. The old man agreed and, once Louise was in the canoe, he set off paddling in silence. Louise sat in the front. At first, she thought the rough conglomeration of low, wooden structures—more like over-sized chicken coops than houses—were too close to the water. What if it flooded? But then she realized their proximity to the river made it easier for seriously ill patients to be off-loaded.

At the bow of the canoe, she had a peculiar sense of not only looking forward to meeting a celebrated humanitarian but also contemplating the mystery that was the rest of her life. She was still not thirty years old. Prior to age thirty, Schweitzer had gained degrees in philosophy and theology. From 1905 to 1908, when he took up the study of medicine, he had found mastering a new field in his thirties to be difficult. What unknown challenges and adventures lay before her?

She clearly recalled that moment when Albert Schweitzer and his wife had stepped onto the balcony at the City Hall in Oslo. Even from a distance, she could see that he had been clearly moved and taken aback by the throng in the square below. When a group close to the balcony began to sing, their enthusiasm had rippled through the crowd like an infectious wave, and soon everyone was joining them, an ocean of voices.

Upon being named winner of the Nobel Peace Prize the year before, Dr. Schweitzer had announced he would allocate all his prize money to building a leprosarium next to his hospital. In November of 1954, he delivered one of the most inspiring speeches in the history of the prize. The people of Norway were so moved that their donations collectively matched the amount of the Nobel Peace Prize award to enable him to build his leprosarium.

"Recognize the will to live in yourself and in others!" he had said. "Not the thoughtless, egocentric and hedonistic wish to enjoy life for yourself, but the deep urge to be part of Life itself, in all its manifestations. When you discover in your heart compassion for other living things because they also want to live, and when you feel the wish to help those who suffer, then you will experience a mystic reverence for Life. Each of us can serve Life individually, on a larger or smaller scale. We can deepen it through our thinking, beautify it through our actions, relieve it from pain and further it through progress in science and technology."

The rough-hewn canoe nudged into a sandy shoreline. There was no greeting committee, nobody there at all. She was an unexpected pilgrim, making an unanticipated pilgrimage. The old man helped her ashore with her few possessions. She wanted to pay him for his troubles. He waved aside her offer.

"How long are you going to stay," he asked, in French. These were the first words he had spoken to her.

"About three days."

The old man shook his head, muttering more to himself than to her. "Three days . . . I don't believe you."

With his face wrinkled with laughter, the ferryman pointed to a narrow path up the hill, a trail that had been followed by many people before her. She soon realized why the compound had been criticized for its lack of sanitary precautions by former visitors. The living quarters for the staff were wooden barracks with chicken-wire windows. Rusty sheets of tin were used for roofing. The complex looked more like an African village than a hospital. Everywhere there were chickens, ducks, goats, dogs and cats. Two chimpanzees in a tree shrieked as if to announce her arrival.

Women smiled and nodded as she passed; children rushed forward smiling. It all felt satisfyingly familiar, like camps and villages in Tanganyika. Here were people who lived in harmony with both wild and domestic animals and nature. It was untidy, over-crowded, seemingly dirty, but nobody was on alert. Everything seemed peaceful. Albert Schweitzer had been overseeing everyone's well-being here for fifty years without any serious problems.

A thin, ghost-like, pale woman emerged and introduced herself as Mademoiselle Mathilde Kottmann, Schweitzer's secretary and long-time companion who unofficially managed protocol at the camp. Louise resisted the urge to mention her own middle name was Mathilde. As the work routine was over for the day, everyone was assembling in the courtyard for dinner. She was surprised by the number of foreign hospital workers and recognized some of the tourists. Mademoiselle Kottmann introduced her to everyone.

As they all awaited the arrival of Dr. Schweitzer, a large pelican swooped down from the forest and landed on the porch. This was Parsifal, she was told. He, too, seemed to be waiting for the great man with his well-known black bow tie, his white shirt and his pith helmet. A door eventually opened and out stepped the eighty-six-year-old doctor in a baggy, khaki shirt and trousers that no longer fitted his dwindling frame. He smiled to see Parsifal and he gave the pelican some food from a bag that he carried for that purpose.

When the stooped patriarch noticed her, his frowning, thick eyebrows twitched ever so slightly but he didn't say anything to her. He was, however, quite curious about her, as if she might be a creature almost as worthy of his attention as Parsifal. Like the pelican, she had arrived unbidden from the sky, like an attractive bird.

"*Guten Tag, Doktor* Schweitzer," she said, extending her hand.

"Who are you, young lady?" he replied in German, shaking her hand graciously. Louise introduced herself as Louise Aall, but wishing to be modest, she did not mention she was a doctor. Accustomed to hurrying such conversations along, Mademoiselle Kottmann intervened, indicating their visitor was not simply a tourist but was herself a medical doctor. Then he looked more intently at her, obviously appraising her now.

"And what do you want to learn from me?" Dr. Schweitzer asked.

She was taken aback. She had planned to bring up the hymn in Oslo. That would be safe and congenial. But so many times, alone, in the bush, she had struggled with patients who needed dental surgery. Without any forethought, she blurted out, "I would very much like to learn how to extract teeth."

A light sparkled in his eyes and he started to laugh. He laughed so loudly that Parsifal flew away and the dogs began to bark. "That's a girl," he said, delighted. "A true bush doctor!" The other doctors and nurses were surprised, too. Apparently, the old man had not been seen to laugh like that for a long time. "You've come to the right place," he chortled. "We have an excellent dentist. You can pull teeth with him all day long!"

Evidently pleased by the encounter, Dr. Schweitzer turned and walked across the yard to the dining hall, lit by kerosene lamps, with a long table for about fifty people. The seating arrangements were carefully managed by his secretary: Dr. Schweitzer always sat at the centre and, facing him, on the other side of the table, were the guests and visitors. The most important or favourite guest was usually invited to sit directly across from him in order to converse. Most guests who were given this privilege remained there for one day, two at most, seldom three. Louise would be repeatedly accorded the favoured position and would never be removed more than one chair away from him during the duration of her stay and that was when especially important guests arrived from abroad.

He said a brief prayer in German. There were rules and customs. Even the big, old dogs knew not to beg openly, but sat patiently beside the diners, hoping for charitable scraps, playing up to the new, innocent guests. When she politely caressed one and provided a tidbit, the amused staff of medical personnel waited for Dr. Schweitzer's predictable reaction.

"In the tropics," he said, "you must never handle dogs while eating. If you want to touch the head of a dog during mealtime, use only the back of your hand. Never touch its mouth." She felt embarrassed but it was not a rebuke. A kindness shimmered in his eyes. She watched as he overcame what she understood to be an innate shyness. She noticed that he tried to make some comforting or complimentary remark to nearly every new guest during the course of the evening.

When the plates were cleared away, he opened a huge old Bible and read aloud a pre-selected passage. This was not spontaneous. Nearly every day he devised a different philosophical talk based on some Biblical theme. On this evening he discussed the apostles' reaction to Jesus' death as a martyr. He suggested that the notion that Jesus ascended to heaven in body and spirit was false, a later reinterpretation of visions generated by his grief-stricken closest followers.

Louise was likely the only person in the dining hall, with the possible exception of Mlle. Mathilde and Nurse Ali Silver, both of whom had worked with him for decades, who knew that Schweitzer's topic for his doctoral thesis in medicine was "A Psychiatric Study of Jesus." In this paper he refuted the supposition that Jesus could have been suffering from a psychiatric disorder. Louise recalled her father had also written scholarly papers on Jesus.

For Dr. Schweitzer, Jesus Christ was a remarkable, very real human being. An inspiring example for all. Hence his lecture led to a necessary statement about the difference between Catholics and Protestants. Whereas the Catholic Church needed miracles to affirm the existence of God, for Protestants the Word was sufficient. He quoted the Gospel of Matthew: "Blessed are the peacemakers for they shall be called the Children of God."

Dr. Schweitzer spoke with wonder in his voice: "These words of Jesus are the real miracles to me." Before he followed Mlle. Mathilde and Nurse Ali Silver out of the room, he sat at the piano and played a well-known song, inviting everyone to sing along. Casually, his hands glided into some of his own compositions.

When this nightly ritual ended, Louise was shown to her rudimentary private room. There was no electric light, no running water. Just a portable kerosene lamp, a tiny washbasin and a jug of water. A chair, a table, a small closet. It was like being on a train except each room was separated only by a thin plywood wall. One could easily converse with the person next door through the walls. On the front and back, there were no walls at all, only screens fine enough to keep out the mosquitoes.

Lying in the pitch-black night, listening to the buzzing of insects and the high-pitched calls of monkeys amid the sweet aromas of the forest, she was astonished to discover the symphony of natural sounds and smells was a prelude to the strains of J.S. Bach that were played by the great organist Dr. Schweitzer himself in his nearby house. If he ever missed a note, he would meticulously replay the entire piece until it was re-mastered on the specially built pedal piano-organ that had been given to him in 1913. It had been stored in a zinc-lined case and delivered in a dug-out canoe.

This unexpected concert at the end of her unintended quest connected her to memories of her childhood. Before her father's death, she would sit happily under her mother's piano for hours, listening to her mother play, daydreaming of one day becoming a doctor.

Louise recalled reading how Dr. Schweitzer had temporarily rejected music as bourgeois when he first set up the hospital and was living in what was really a revamped chicken coop. In those conditions, classical music seemed somehow out of place. But after treating some two thousand patients in nine months, he had gradually returned to music, dedicating himself to interpretations of Bach, César Franck and Max Reger in the evenings.

Rising the next morning, Louise naturally felt obliged to make herself useful. Unlike some medical visitors, she was not appalled by the apparent squalor in the hospital compound. She agreed it was prudent to avoid large, European-styled hospital wards in accordance with Schweitzer's view that anxiety could kill. Therefore, allowing the patient to stay alongside their own large families, as well as their goats and dogs and chickens, made medical sense.

Non-emergency treatment of patients was not permitted until the patients felt themselves settled. Healthy members of the family were expected to help with the garden or laundry, or with building maintenance and, of course, with child care. Visiting journalists who were taken aback by non-hygienic conditions failed to realize that a community environment was helpful in minimizing the strain for everyone when a death occurred. Family members were present to perform required rituals and provide emotional support.

As someone partial to the teachings of St. Paul, Dr. Schweitzer, a vegetarian, had a somewhat Eastern view of life. Louise soon discovered his proviso that all life was to be revered included even the lives of rodents and mosquitoes. She saw that Schweitzer really did feed a nest of benign ants that lived in the floorboard of his room. For years after every evening meal, he would take small pieces of fish back to his room and place them beside the kerosene lamp on his table for the ants. Immediately, the ants would come crawling up the table leg, walking in a straight line over his mass of papers to carry away the tiny chunks of food. He would approve of their progress with delight. His reverence for life arose from the gift of a Bible at age eight. Soon thereafter he took the commandment "Thou shalt not kill" to mean he ought to affirm kinship with all living beings.

Louise recalled that some outsiders had claimed Dr. Schweitzer could be aloof and even dictatorial, but she did not see any sign of that. She remembered what the manager of the hotel had said, that Dr. Schweitzer treated everyone with respect, and that appeared to be true. Visitors were not given any highly restrictive instructions, even though they were obviously an inconvenience.

She learned he paid his staff well. He financed their transportation to and from the hospital, as well as their vacations, and he did not resent their inevitable decisions to leave when they'd had enough of the rudimentary lodgings in one of the most stifling climates on the planet. Everyone came voluntarily and they left voluntarily.

The main problem Louise had with Lambaréné was, strange as it may sound, with the turkey. In order to visit the latrine, it was impossible not to cross the yard and follow a narrow path toward the river that was guarded by a very large and very aggressive turkey. For some inexplicable reason, this obstreperous bird had singled her out as an adversary, or prey, and became unusually fierce whenever she approached. She soon tried holding off her visits to the outhouse until dark, hoping the turkey would not be there, but somehow it had developed a sixth sense about her whereabouts.

The others laughed at her discomfort, amused by the attacks, but there was nothing humorous about these confrontations as far as she was concerned. As soon as she had managed to get past the bird, it would give chase, stretching out its neck and pecking at her as she ran. One day, Schweitzer happened to witness this phenomenon. Much to her disappointment, he also took her predicament lightly. "Why is this turkey always chasing after *me*?" she cried, exasperated. He only chuckled. "Well, young lady, I suppose he enjoys pinching such lovely legs."

An old African nearby was also watching her distress. Without much hesitation he picked up a long stick and hurried towards her attacker, as if to strike it, in much the same instinctive manner that a man might respond to a snake.

"*Que fais-tu!*" shouted Dr. Schweitzer. She had never heard him use such a thunderous, commanding voice. Evidently his reverence for life extended even to belligerent turkeys. The man immediately threw himself to the ground, prostrating himself before the feet of the great doctor, not unlike some Muslim praying towards Mecca, begging for his forgiveness. This event lasted for only a few seconds but she found it very disturbing.

"*Eh, bien*," Schweitzer said, giving the man permission to rise, and then was on his way, as if little had happened. When she confided the details of this encounter to Anne-Lise, the head children's nurse, it was explained to her that many of the older Africans believed Schweitzer was a supernatural being, beyond human. Otherwise, how was it he could continue to function so well, for so long?

Life expectancy in Equatorial Africa was nowhere near age ninety. The older a person became, the more that person became venerable. The older Africans feared the wrath of Schweitzer in much the same way as they were wary of offending an ancestral spirit. He loomed large as both a benevolent and frightening figure because many assumed he could be immortal. And, after decades at Lambaréné, Schweitzer knew this. Some critics had suggested he had developed into an all-powerful, God-like being, someone who could not be contradicted, but she soon saw how Schweitzer repeatedly used the power of his personality to lift spirits, providing hope and confidence, sometimes with only a brief appearance.

Mostly Schweitzer avoided meeting people when not in public. It was almost impossible for anyone to strike up a private conversation with him. He had books and letters to write. But by the fifth day, when Louise was scheduled to leave—having learned to extract teeth—he asked to see her privately. This was a tremendous honour, and everyone was envious of her. When she was invited to his room, some of the staff were perplexed. Men sometimes went there on occasion, but a young woman?

Louise did not feel privileged. In fact, she dreaded what he was going to say to her. As much as she craved to go off and have a restful journey on a freighter, beyond the borders of any country, she understood that some children would have to die unnecessarily if she left. She knew full well that an epidemic of measles had brought scores of sick children to Lambaréné, and that her previous experience of treating measles in the tropics had been of great assistance in combatting the disease. In fact, she had helped patients with measles almost as soon as she had arrived. She had isolated those with the virus because it is so easily spread through the air, and she had helped to calm their fever with the easily available acetaminophen. Forming a smooth working relationship with Nurse Anne-Lise, Louise had taught the sobbing mothers of sick children how to cool down the feverish bodies with a wet cloth. Often a stethoscope was unnecessary. She could place her hands flat on a child's burning chest and feel the roughness of breathing inside.

As soon as she entered Schweitzer's tiny quarters, she was astonished to see books piled every which way, batches of letters and papers heaped in bundles, personal belongings strewn about. It was a shambles. A few faded photos and African straw mats decorated the wall above his unkempt bed and his famous miniature organ. There was barely room for one person to move, let alone two.

She squeezed her way to the only chair. He was not the least bit interested in her response to the clutter. For him, it wasn't chaos. Moreover, in the same way that he planned his evening lectures, he had an agenda for their meeting.

"This is the first time that someone from Norway has come," he began. They reminisced about the torches held aloft at the Oslo City Hall, his lecture at the university, the hymn and the extreme generosity of the Norwegian people. "And now I must appeal to Norwegian generosity again," he said.

The anger she felt surprised her. She looked away. A feeling of inertia followed. She knew what was coming. "You have experience in tropical medicine and we have an outbreak of measles," he said softly. He was not inviting her into his private world to give her compliments and send her on her way with a sentimental handshake or hug. "I would be greatly obliged if you would stay at least until another physician arrives."

Louise knew that it might take months until another doctor could arrive. She was already feeling exhausted and spiritually weakened by her experience in the Congo and the tropical heat of Lambaréné. She would be trapped with the others, part of the old man's regime. The sleepy town of Lambaréné afforded no reprieve, not a vestige of Western entertainment.

Except for one small generator for the operating room, there was no electricity because the old man didn't want the beauty of the tropical night disturbed by the noise of generators.

She did not know whether he could sense her reticence because she was looking into her lap. "I know what it's like to be a young physician alone with oneself in a strange place," he said. "People who have never been to Africa can easily criticize us and judge us. They don't know what Africa gives us in return. They don't get to see the drama of life and death played out here with such beauty, the way the struggle for survival here is fought with such courage. Africa makes modern man small and humble before the Creator."

It was like receiving the telegram all over again. She had not been able to refuse the Red Cross. And here, face to face with greatness, she knew she could not live with herself for the rest of her days if she refused Albert Schweitzer. "You are young. Some members of my staff have considerable experience. You could learn from them. And I daresay there is a good spirit of cooperation here."

Now he was pleading. She had to make him stop. A flood of energy rushed through her body as she relented and made the inevitable choice. She took his hand and said she would very much like to stay. His old eyes sparkled. He leaned forward and looked at her intensely, as if she were an apparition that had descended from heaven. "Can you please tell me," he said, "how it is that a specialist in tropical medicine just happened to step ashore in a canoe right in front of my hospital? In a time of dire need?"

What happened next was even stranger. She found herself talking non-stop about herself, confiding hopes, dreams and insecurities. Would she ever have a family of her own? Would she even want one? She had kept her emotions so tightly locked away, it felt almost unseemly to let them free in a rush.

Louise was not religious in any conventional sense, but here she was using the wise patriarch as a father confessor. How irresistible it was to open up to this sympathetic listener. Thoughts and words spilled from her that she had no idea she was harbouring.

Eventually Dr. Schweitzer rose, with effort, and moved forward to touch her cheek as he passed. This blessing, this communion of friendship, was just the beginning. With some concern for his age, she watched as he crouched down on his knees and hauled out a dusty case from beneath his bed. From inside this chest he took a bundle wrapped in old cloth. Clutching it to his chest, he struggled to his feet and went to his desk, pushing aside stacks of paper. "In memory of our conversation today," he said, pulling aside the cloth, "I want to give you this."

Although his gift of appreciation was not exactly the Ark of the Covenant, the care that he took unveiling the metal tools in the bundle showed these were precious belongings. Splendid and archaic, these were his complete set of dental instruments, probably more than forty years old, first brought to Lambaréné before the Great War. She hoped she would never have to use them. They were rusty. But, of course, they were in reference to the first words she'd said to him.

"Please do not show them to anyone here," he said. "I don't want any jealousy among my staff." Already there was some slight recognition that she had become favoured by him, so she was careful not to upset Mlle. Mathilde in particular. She went back to her quarters and hid the dental tools in her suitcase. The two of them had a secret.

❧

ALTHOUGH SHE FELT continually shy near Dr. Schweitzer, and often preferred to remain on the periphery when crowds gathered round him, their relationship grew steadily, largely unnoticed by others. Soon, when the weekly bag of mail arrived, she was invited by Mlle. Mathilde to answer nearly all of the letters from the Scandinavian countries. It did not take long before she was also accorded the challenge of answering his letters from English- and German-speaking countries, as well.

As an ardent letter writer herself, Louise soon proved herself invaluable at Lambaréné day and night. She would often consult with him about the content of the letters. If they had not been together for a day or two, he would jest, in passing, "Don't you have a letter you'd better discuss with me?" He never resented being interrupted by her questions, and she was careful, as his youngest assistant, never to ask for any favours. The only persons who knew about her frequents visits to discuss letter writing with him were Nurse Ali and Mlle. Mathilde.

Louise came to understand how much personal questions surprised and embarrassed him. She grew to know him as a shy and humble person who genuinely preferred the undemanding company of his pet animals and the tranquillity of his private quarters. He began to greatly enjoy her often humorous stories about being a bush doctor in Tanganyika.

One day he asked, "Were you never afraid in the bush by yourself?"

"I'm not afraid of death," she said, "so why else should I have been afraid?" she responded. As soon as she spoke, she knew her answer had been glib.

"Afraid of hurting someone's feelings," he said, "afraid of misunderstanding a person, of unwittingly causing harm; afraid of not being able to pay back a debt; afraid of forgetting a promise, or not fulfilling a responsibility; afraid of not living up to a friend's expectations; afraid of failing a patient. . . ."

"That is a different sort of fear," she said, but she felt embarrassed.

Albert Schweitzer entered into a lengthy dissertation in which he explained his Reverence for Life philosophy:

"The anxiety I am talking about has to do with personal guilt. A conscientious human being, especially a physician, ought to feel guilty. Don't you know that? A guilty conscience is necessary to keep the mind alert. I dare say that one is always guilty, for, by making the decision to save a life, one's action will often hurt other lives.

"The debts one heaps upon oneself by one's actions, and especially through one's mistakes, are hard to pay back and they create the feeling of guilt. Therefore, one cannot be indifferent to the results of one's actions. Only nature is indifferent. Others say nature is cruel, but I say, no, nature is indifferent. But I refuse to be part of that indifference.

"In my younger days, when I travelled up and down the Ogowe

River, I would sit for hours, looking at the tropical forest on either side of the riverbanks. The ever-changing sight of the lush vegetation oppressed me. I saw how plants and trees choke and crush each other to reach the sun.

"'Who cares?' I once thought in a gloomy mood, 'whether that tree over there will grow up or whether it will succumb and become rotting underbrush? It just happens. Some die so that others might live, just as it occurs in the animal world and in our lives, too, for that matter. All life wants to survive. All living creatures become part of the powerful interplay of procreation, survival and death.'

"But do we also have to feel indifferent toward other living beings? Even animals will sometimes give their own life to protect and save the lives of their young. That kind of self-sacrifice demands our admiration and respect.

"'Reverence for life,' I thought. Suddenly I felt great joy, for this was an answer to the problem of how to deal with the indifference of nature. Reverence for all life, any kind of life, because the will to live is part of the force that preserves life on earth. This is a distinctly human thought, born out of protest against nature's arbitrariness. It makes man more than just a living being sharing the will to live with all life—it makes him Homo sapiens.

"And if man takes another step and fills reverence for life with love and the will to protect other living creatures, then he becomes an ethical human being who, through his action, elevates life onto a higher plane of existence.

"So, guilt, the pain of guilt, forces one to reflect, to think to the last consequence what it implies to be a human among all other beings. Reverence for life has given me an answer. It is an ethical and moral truth, if you will, but a truth anyway—and that has meant more to me than all the philosophical and religious theories in the whole world."

Feeling it could be time to change to a lighter subject, Louise admired a beautiful grass mat that was hanging on the wall of his room. "Where did that come from?" she asked. He explained it was made by the wife of one of his patients who told him all her thankful thoughts were woven into the pattern. The women on the Ogowe, he explained, took pride in making the most complicated patterns and they travelled far down the river to find the right kind of grass. "I have never seen another one quite like this," he concluded.

Their talks would continue. He understood and soothed her worries that arose from being a doctor. She would go back to her room and record his words in her diary:

> We physicians are constantly confronted with people suffering pain. Our wish to take away this pain becomes an obsession. Nothing is more rewarding for us than when a patient stops moaning and says, "Doctor, the pain is gone, nothing hurts anymore!" And yet, it is not always in our power to take away the pain. Our remedies sometimes fail, especially in patients with chronic illnesses or in those who are terminally ill. Then we must have the courage to share the pain: the patient with his body and we with our hearts. If we can stand this pain, then our patient can, too. Holding together as brothers and sisters, we can help the sufferer to give up the attitude of protesting against fate.

> We, as physicians, can stand in awe and recognize the essence of true humanness: the triumph of spirit over matter. Then we understand the words from the Sermon on the Mount: "*Selig sind die, die da Leid tragen, denn sie waren getröstet werden.*" Blessed are those who endure pain for they shall be comforted. With that in mind, we shall find the strength to go along with our patient and to bring him comfort for the last, difficult stretch of the road. The love and respect we feel for our fellow sufferer is the love of Jesus as I understand Him, and that, for me, is the essence of Christianity.

> If only the idea of Reverence for Life and the true spirit of Christianity could be merged into one great philosophy, an ethic so simple that everybody could understand it—then it

would give birth to a new attitude and my life's work would not have been in vain.

⤙

THE MEASLES EPIDEMIC subsided some weeks later. The isolation of those infected with the virus had helped enormously. Those who had been suffering from ear infections or other such infections as a result of contracting measles had been treated with penicillin, of which they had a good supply.

Now that she was not quite so busy, Louise had time to get to know the other staff members. Initially, she had rarely had dealings with Dr. Takahashi, one of the three other permanent physicians. He spent most of his time at the nearby leper colony, looking after approximately two hundred quarantined patients.

More intriguing was Dr. Friedman, a taciturn, serious middle-aged Jew who was so withdrawn that he hardly spoke to anyone other than Dr. Schweitzer. He was one of the very few people who were known to be welcome at Schweitzer's private quarters on an ongoing basis.

In the consultation room, the sad-eyed Dr. Friedman had his table close to hers. She remained intimidated by him but gradually, since they had both trained as doctors in Germany, they found common grounds for conversation. Without being obtrusive, Dr. Friedman looked out for her and gave her much-appreciated advice when she was troubled by difficult cases. Still, she kept her distance.

Dr. Friedman had taken over care of the mentally ill at Lambaréné after Schweitzer had withdrawn from that specialty. He was always taking copious notes when Schweitzer spoke in the evenings. During philosophical discussions that ensued, he was the only person who was sufficiently confident to challenge the great man's views.

Dr. Friedman was prone to outbursts, and then pearls of sweat would appear on his forehead. There was a fanatical intensity to his eyes when he became angered. Once, after a shouting incident at his examination table, during a break, she ventured to approach him with an ironic remark. "You're not very happy today, are you?" She immediately regretted opening her mouth. With a swiftness born of rage, he rolled up his sleeve. The blue tattoo marks on his skin were all numbers. "All my family members, every last one of them except me, were killed in the gas chambers."

Shame prevented her from speaking. He confided his story to her in a voice only slightly louder than a whisper. Liberated from the death camp, he had lost everything, including God and joy. He was bitter and restless. As a last resort, he had visited Lambaréné and had remained living alongside Dr. Schweitzer ever since. He said it was the only place he felt at home.

"He took me in as if I were his son," he said. "He gave me back a sense of worth by entrusting me with the care of the most miserably suffering patients of all—the mentally ill. When one of them improves, I feel my life is worthwhile. When I fail, I fall back into dark brooding. But I know that Dr. Schweitzer is always there to help me find reasons to live again."

Mostly, however, Louise worked with Dr. Müller, the surgeon. Along with her duties overseeing the children, she was expected at times to assist him in the operating room built on poles, high above the ground. The ordeal of standing for hours with a face guard, a head cover, in heavy gowns, in the sweltering humidity, even in the early morning hours, was almost more than she could bear. Some staff members nearly did collapse.

The most common operation was for treatment of hernias. Africans, for reasons the staff did not yet understand, were more prone to twisted bowels, or incarcerated hernias, than other people. When lifting a heavy burden, African men were abnormally prone to having parts of the small bowel herniate. Sometimes the herniated bowel part became twisted, and gangrene could set in quickly. If not treated promptly in a hospital, the unfortunate victim would die in agony. Time-consuming operations for incarcerated hernias or bowel resections were performed nearly every week.

The prolonged surgery Louise dreaded the most was for the removal of overgrown tissue on the leg of a patient who was suffering from elephantiasis. This hideous condition was caused by the bite of a fly that enabled a thin worm, the filaria parasite, to lodge itself in the lymphatic vessels of the lower extremities. In order to remove the superfluous tissue, it could take several hours for Dr. Müller to lift off the skin from the afflicted area, cut out the fibrous material, painstakingly litigate all the blood vessels and finally rejoin the skin. It was always amazing to see how the leg returned to normal.

During this procedure, Louise's task was not only to hand him his surgical instruments but to hold up the heavy leg in the oppressive heat. It took all her willpower not to faint. The duty nurse had to constantly wipe the faces of Dr. Müller and Louise to prevent their perspiration from dripping into the operating field. When offered a cold drink, they had to carefully twist their heads backwards, without moving their hands, in order to sip from a cup held off to the side.

Once, during another operation, a lizard, overcome by ether vapors, dropped from the ceiling into an open abdomen. The surgeon wordlessly took the forceps, fished out the inert lizard and tossed it over his shoulder. Antibiotic powder was sprinkled into the cavity and the patient survived the procedure with no ill effects.

Some of their improvisations would never be sanctioned in a European hospital. For example, when Dr. Müller opened the abdomen of a young woman with a ruptured extra-uterine pregnancy, blood gushed so effusively that a blood transfusion was urgently required. None of her relatives was near. Louise pointed out that there were several pints of the woman's own blood in the abdominal cavity, so why not try returning it to her? With the aid of some anticoagulants and a strainer, she devised an "auto-transfusion," whereby the scooped blood from her sterile abdomen was infused into a vein in her arm. The patient recovered without complications.

Among the staff, Louise became closest to the nurse Anne-Lise who spent the better part of her evenings looking after the sick children. While the other doctors were relaxing, the nurses would carry kerosene lamps among the campfires. Smoke burned in their eyes as they stepped cautiously amid the pots and pans. Louise often joined

Anne-Lise in her rounds. People were sleeping everywhere, in or under beds, or on boards covered by grass mats. Anne-Lise could always distinguish the sleeping children who were patients. She joked with families and gave them encouraging instructions for the night. The people responded with friendliness and gratitude. After doing these rounds, Anne-Lise and Louise walked up the hill to their small sleeping compartments, seeing the brilliant stars and the moon through the gently swaying branches of the palm trees amid the sounds of a tropical night. They didn't need to talk much.

FROM TIME TO TIME there would be visiting doctors at Lambaréné. Among these visiting doctors, Anne-Lise and Louise dreaded the presence of an elderly visiting professor of pediatrics. Humourless and aloof, he could not stop criticizing the lack of hygiene in their ward. He could not comprehend that worm-infested, malaria-ridden and malnourished children of the tropics, often suffering from high fever, or diarrhea, could quickly succumb to heat collapse, dehydration, pneumonia or heart failure.

The visitor expected European standards and practices. He was shocked when the nurses injected fluids into the peritoneum during emergencies. He was even more shocked when Louise transfused her own universal donor blood directly into the jugular vein of an unconscious, anemic child gasping from lack of oxygen. Louise and the nurses knew from experience that such a child would often fall peacefully asleep after receiving a small amount of fresh blood.

They learned it was expedient to divert the attention of the pediatrics professor by keeping him occupied with less urgent cases. One day, Anne-Lise asked Louise to see a beautiful little girl, about four years old, with intelligent dark eyes and a cherubic smile, who had been given an aspirin by the professor to combat a burning fever. This child was exhibiting the heaving respiration common to someone with pneumonia. Louise placed her stethoscope over the lungs and heard the tell-tale crepitations. The child would have little chance of survival unless intensive treatment began immediately. Louise and Anne-Lise gave her penicillin and supportive measures. They showed the parents how to keep her cool during intense heat,

Three days later, the professor saw Anne-Lise giving the girl her penicillin injection. Furious, he ordered the treatment stopped. By using antibiotics too frequently, he argued, they would be jeopardizing penicillin's efficiency—because bacteria would become resistant to it. An aspirin was sufficient. Louise protested, but it was impossible for him to comprehend that this child would quite likely never come into contact with western medicine again. He believed Anne-Lise and Louise were inexperienced and were allowing their sympathetic natures to over-prescribe antibiotics.

The family lived far away. Because the girl was very special to them, they had undertaken a long and arduous journey, paddling days and nights to get help from Dr. Schweitzer. The girl's health had been improving with the injections, so very reluctantly Anne-Lise and Louise agreed to placate the intimidating senior physician by letting him resume treatment of the case. This mollifying decision to accede to what he considered to be the standards and practices of modern, European medicine would prove fatal.

Days later, the distraught parents knocked on Anne-Lise's door. Their beautiful child had relapsed. She was burning hot and breathing with great difficulty. The professor was not available. They immediately reinstated antibiotic treatment and watched for signs of improvement, which did not come. Anne-Lise placed the little girl in an aerosol tent the next morning for some relief, but the poor child was at the point of choking. Louise consulted with Dr. Müller, asking if they ought to consider opening her airways with a tracheotomy.

The all-knowing professor had no explanation for what was happening. The child's temperature was so extremely high that even the ubiquitous worms, the ascarids, began to leave her body, creeping out of her mouth and nostrils. The doting parents pleaded with the medical staff to save the life of their daughter whose eyes were wide open and glazed. The little girl was even thrashing her arms about in a desperate effort to get air. They could all see how even the abdominal and neck muscles were sucking as hard as possible to breathe.

They grabbed the child from the arms of her crying mother and rushed her to the operating room for Dr. Müller. Her eyes had a pleading expression as she watched the doctors in gowns preparing the surgical instruments. She lay as still as a sacrificial lamb to enable him to open her windpipe. Dr. Müller sliced open her throat, exposing her windpipe, cutting through the cartilaginous rings of the trachea, the windpipe. The child took a few deep breaths. The surgeon inserted a metal cannula into the new opening and arranged a bandage around the child's neck. Relief showed on her face as her lungs were filled at last.

Unable to speak, the courageous little girl grabbed the hands of the adults in gratitude. It was an extraordinary gesture from such a tiny person. The adults had to hide their tears when the parents were fetched. With much difficulty the girl stretched out her arms, and her lips silently mouthed the word Mama. All the air went out through the tracheal opening so no sound could pass from her lips.

The parents looked with fresh alarm at the piece of metal sticking out of their perfect child's throat. As much as the doctors tried to explain the situation, everyone felt guilty and sad, rather than relieved. The parents were horrified. Dr. Schweitzer's helpers had violated their child. As days passed and the child's strength did not return, the little girl harboured no ill feelings, but the parents became increasingly unfriendly towards Anne-Lise and Louise. With a courageous smile, the little child learned to drink by plugging the tracheal opening. Anne-Lise and Louise arranged a room for her and her parents close to their quarters, so they could watch her better during the night.

The all-knowing professor had completely lost interest and had never asked to see the child again. He did not even ask about her welfare. Firm in his belief that the principles of modern school medicine must always be rigidly upheld even in the remotest jungle, he left Africa saying nothing. Meanwhile the father and mother remained steadfastly hopeful and sad, never leaving the girl alone. The father would collect wood and buy food for meals and the mother would make a small fire and cook outside the open door, so that their daughter could take part in everyday life. When one was sleeping, the other would be awake at the bedside. They remained deeply disturbed because their daughter could not talk to them. "It is not the head of our child anymore," they said reproachfully.

Every day they asked Anne-Lise and Louise to remove "that thing sticking out of her throat." But as it became increasingly clear that the brave little girl was not going to survive, the parents' attitude changed. The parents, who had been so deeply dutiful and caring, became more like helpless children themselves. The dying girl, in contrast, appeared to be filled with love and compassion for her parents, as if she wanted to transfer her strength and courage to them.

When she died, Anne-Lise and Louise sat immobilized with grief. The piercing cries of sorrow from the mother were chilling. Suddenly, the father threw himself upon the body of his dead child and, with trembling hands, he ripped out the hated cannula from his daughter's throat. He wrapped their daughter's dead body in a blanket. He would not allow anyone to take back the bandages that were needed at the hospital. Hatred flashed in his eyes. Anne-Lise and Louise had to leave the room.

After this ordeal, Anne-Lise and Louise could hardly eat and could barely muster enough strength to carry on their daily work. They would sit together for hours, reliving the events, asking themselves if anything could have been done differently.

Dr. Schweitzer became aware of their misery and helped them overcome their futile ruminations. He spoke frankly about his own experiences of despair. To show them they were not alone with their feelings, that such moments were part of being a healer, he read to them several passages from his early diary, published as *On the Edge of the Primeval Forest*:

> With this continual drive and impatience of the waiting sick,
> I often get so worried and nervous that I hardly know where

I am and what I am doing. At times I am so depressed that I can hardly summon up the energy to work.

In my own life, anxiety, trouble and sorrow have allotted to me at times in such abundant measures that had my nerves not been so strong, I must have broken down under the weight. Heavy is the burden of fatigue and responsibility which has lain upon me without a break for years. I have not much of my life for myself, not even the hours I should have liked to devote to my wife and child.

Not long after the girl had died, Dr. Schweitzer called Anne-Lise and Louise to see a boy in acute respiratory distress. He was the only son of Fulani merchants who peddled their goods up and down the Ogowe River. About eight years old, the boy had experienced a fever for several days. When it worsened, they had steered to Lambaréné. That morning, when the boy began gasping for air, they had hurried to ask Dr. Schweitzer to save the boy.

Here was another much-beloved child, with the same symptoms of choking they had witnessed in the little girl. When Dr. Schweitzer asked their opinion as to how to treat the boy, they naturally expressed their apprehension about proceeding with a tracheotomy.

He agreed to first try antibiotics, but when there was no improvement and the situation was dire, he ordered a tracheotomy to be performed. He was philosophical. "When we have done all we can," he said. "It is not in our hands whether the patient survives or succumbs."

This time the boy lived with the help of the tracheotomy. But even after Dr. Müller closed the tracheotomy opening, the boy did not dare to try to speak for a long time. One day, after more time had passed, Dr. Schweitzer, together with the parents, Anne-Lise and Louise, all stood around his bed and assured the boy that he would certainly talk again. The boy started to cry. There was his voice! He stood up in bed, stretched out his arms and said in a hoarse voice, "Mama, I am fine!"

Laughing with joy, the parents caught him in their arms, hugging him fiercely. Anne-Lise and Louise looked at each other, thinking of the other child. Then the friendly eyes of old Dr. Schweitzer met theirs; he smiled and nodded his head. Louise felt a flow of goodness and love surging towards her. The heavy feeling lifted from her heart, and she was filled with new strength. Albert Schweitzer had known the trials they had been through. Anne-Lise and Louise both understood they had his full approval and support while looking after all the sick and suffering children.

DR. SCHWEITZER'S commonsensical dictum that staff must not leave the hospital grounds after dark was well known, and Louise usually followed it. But on one occasion she found herself intrigued by the growing excitement among the African staff about a forthcoming gathering to be held in a distant village. Curious, she pestered Gustave, her African helper, until he finally told her about an impending feast at which a famous medicine man would appear. "Come and see for yourself," he said finally. Knowing any such expedition at night would be completely forbidden, she asked Eric, the camp carpenter, a volunteer worker who did not belong to the hospital staff, if he might also be interested. Regarding himself as not being tied by the rules of the hospital, he happily accepted her proposal for some adventure. "We could take my canoe," he said.

Gustave provided a makeshift map to help them reach the gathering. The village, he said, could be found on a tributary of the Ogowe. It all seemed straightforward. To start out they had to slip under Schweitzer's window at night while he was working. It was then not far to the water's edge where Eric had hidden his canoe in the long grass. Once they had found the canoe, he unlocked the chain and they set off. They paddled beyond the lights of Lambaréné into the darkness of the river and the uncanny-seeming forest. But eventually, even with the map, they found themselves lost. Eric stopped paddling and asked if they should go back.

They brought their canoe along the shore and, in the ensuing silence, they could hear faint drumming ahead and decided they could continue. Eventually they saw the reflections of many bonfires on the water, and they headed towards the fire. Once there, they beached the canoe and walked up to the assembled throng. At first, they hoped to be able to blend into the gathering, but they soon realized that would not be possible since their pale skin and clothing made them conspicuous. They caught sight of Gustave among the dancers, but he was intent on ignoring them completely. Or was he in such an altered state of rapture that he was simply oblivious?

Louise had been counting on Gustave to act as a go-between, to introduce them. She had no way of knowing if Gustave had mentioned their possible visit or not. Even in the dark, she could feel the unfriendly looks in their direction. Bewildered, she was considering retreat until someone brought them two lawn chairs. Now they felt obliged to sit down and stay. They were offered a greenish drink, probably some sort of palm wine. Hallucinogenic plant extracts were often added to beverages for festive occasions, so she took the risk of declining for them both. With Gustave still not making himself available to translate, their refusal to participate caused some consternation. Fortunately, someone brought over a half bottle of red wine and two cups. Everyone relaxed when they drank the wine.

Children gathered round them with their typical curiosity. Eric's natural inclination was to reach out and touch them as a display of friendliness, but she warned him against doing so. If one of them fell down, started to cry or suffered some mishap, he could be accused of evil influence. The pace of the trance-like dancing and monotonous drumming increased until a group of men suddenly began clattering sticks together, with a rapidly increasing staccato rhythm. Then the music and dancing stopped abruptly and soon the general level of excitement led to the appearance of a bizarre, tall man dressed in straw, complete with a straw mask concealing his head and face.

The eerie, gyrating figure appeared to be vibrating as he slowly walked round the circle and then appeared to stalk her, like some creature that was poised to strike. Everyone grew tense, not knowing what might happen next. Instinctively, she knew she must not show fear. Louise reached out her hand. When her fingers touched the extended hand of the medicine man, she could have sworn there was an electric spark. He jerked away his hand, violently, and shrieked. Or rather, a wild bird sound emanated from the mouth of the straw mask. The figure turned away and soon disappeared into the surrounding darkness.

Looking around at the crowd after the incident, Louise and Eric could not tell if the attitude of the gathering was hostile or perplexed. Could it even be possible they feared her? Soon they all went into a frenzy and danced convulsively. Louise and Eric dared not move. Suddenly the women and children were all sent scurrying to their huts. Some of the men were shouting in hostile voices.

At this point she nearly wished she had allowed Eric to bring a gun. Firearms were strictly forbidden at Lambaréné but he had one for emergencies. Once a young American had visited Lambaréné while travelling solo through equatorial Africa, confident in his abilities to manage because he carried a gun. Dr. Schweitzer had pleaded with him to leave his gun behind before he went further upriver. If the Africans saw a gun, he told the American, they would fear his intentions. News reached them a few weeks later: the cavalier explorer had been killed. Dr. Schweitzer had blamed himself for a long time afterwards for permitting the young man's foolhardy behaviour.

Now the masked straw man had reappeared. The men formed a tight circle around him. Their faces were turned inward. She saw their glistening backs as they sang a rousing song, making undulating movements, enacting some ritual that was seemingly kept secret from the women. It was all a prelude for the men to disperse, leaving the medicine man hovering over an emaciated young man who was clearly ill and was wailing, apparently in great pain. When the straw-masked man came towards him, the victim or patient, whichever he was, trembled, crying out in some kind of agony that could have been spiritual or physical.

The medicine man repeatedly approached and hovered over the young man until finally he reached forward and touched him. The cries suddenly ceased and the young man lay still, as if he were dead. Louise guessed he had fainted. For the first time, they were now directly asked to leave. Oddly, however, even though they were petrified with fear, they remained with stone faces, as if they belonged at the ceremony. This unwillingness to obey was possibly interpreted as an indication that she and Eric might possess some unknown powers. The limp body of the poor young man was carried into a large, makeshift compound created by high walls of straw. Louise could not see what happened during the incantations that followed, but soon they distinguished the protesting cries of a child.

Sure enough, a small boy came running out of the compound, pursued by both men and women. They caught him and forced him to wear the same kind of straw costume worn by the medicine man. The boy stopped crying and proceeded to precisely re-enact the same dance, whirling to the same rapid beating of sticks. As he did so, everyone burst into laughter, as if relieved, clapping their hands with pleasure. Louise wonderer what sort of ceremony they had just witnessed. Was it to save the ill child? Or did it have something to do with village taboos. She would never discover what it was they had just seen.

At this juncture, Louise heard a voice speaking French behind them, from the darkness. It might have been Gustave but she wasn't sure. "You better leave now," she was told.

This time, intuitively, she decided to heed the advice. They hurried back to the river. At first it was difficult to distinguish Eric's particular canoe from the others. Neither spoke a word until they had safely found the canoe, climbed in and disappeared around a bend in the river—at which time a far worse danger arose. They were drifting into a grunting herd of hippos.

A mauling by hippos was a common cause of death. They could hear loud snorting and splashing on both sides of the little canoe. At any moment she expected to see white teeth shining in a gaping, open mouth. They dared not paddle for fear of striking one of the ferocious hippos. By comparison, a man dancing in a straw costume would have been far, far preferable. By the time Eric decided it might be safe to paddle again, she was spent and barely able to help. Every noise in the jungle made her jump. When her hair was caught in an overhanging branch, at first she thought it could be a snake. When the canoe bumped into something solid, she was sure it was a crocodile. "Just a tree stump," Eric whispered. He had no way of knowing for certain.

Eventually by dim moonlight, they made it out of the tributary and back into the wider waters of the familiar Ogowe. They needed only to follow the shoreline to reach the hospital landing. When they arrived, they could see that everyone else was asleep. The light was out in Dr. Schweitzer's window. They had made it back safely, unscathed and undetected.

For the first time ever, Gustave was late for work the following morning. He seemed unchanged and was as collected and polite as ever. In his gentle face there was no indication he had danced for hours like a man possessed the night before. He did not mention the village feast at all, not a word of it, and she obliged him by not referring to it either. She would never know if he had recognized that she was there for much of the ceremonies or not.

Strangely, however, word had somehow spread within the staff entourage. Judging by their stares and stern faces, most of her co-workers knew she had knowingly and recklessly broken the rules. Had Eric told someone? That seemed unlikely. So whose voice was it that advised them to leave the ceremony, and in French? Everyone expected Dr. Schweitzer to appear and deliver a firm reprimand. She feared a public shaming from him almost as intensely as she had dreaded the gaping mouth of a hippopotamus.

"Did you have an interesting evening?" he asked, when he appeared at the breakfast table. "Interesting, yes," she replied. "But not enjoyable." And nothing more was said.

IN TANGANYIKA, everywhere Louise went she had been called *Mama Mganga*, and she had told herself she liked the name. But it meant for months she never heard her own name. Sometimes when she saw African families together at the end of the day, usually people of all ages, from infants to the elderly, clustered around a little fire, she experienced bouts of loneliness. She would be forced to admit she required the intimacy and comfort of a companion.

In the convivial and sophisticated atmosphere of Lambaréné, where it was standard procedure for the staff to make a fuss over birthdays, she atypically decided to enjoy the attention that would be bestowed on her for her birthday with a ceremonial feast, as was the custom. In her bed, at 7:30 in the morning, she listened with pleasure to the faint footsteps and hushed voices of those who had gathered outside her room to sing the song that Dr. Schweitzer had introduced for birthdays, usually performed at lunch. The vocal arrangements he had orchestrated were unusually sophisticated and she could clearly distinguish his voice of harmony in a high register. "*Harre meine Seele*" (Trust patiently, my soul).

At the last verse of the song she hurriedly made the bed and was ready when Dr. Schweitzer was the first person to enter. Her hand disappeared in his two hands. Then she received a cold, perfunctory kiss from Mlle. Mathilde and came back to her senses. It was a formal ceremony. Everyone was expected to offer congratulations. He insisted on it.

Gifts were piled at her place at breakfast. Eric had made her a beautifully carved chessboard. There were local wood carvings, a new stethoscope and a book from Dr. Schweitzer with a personal dedication. But inwardly she was disappointed. She knew the traditional gift for valued, long-term members of the staff was always a painted piece of cloth. She wondered if they had forgotten to give her one.

The Africans knew it was her day. Some of the mothers with their sick children wished her *un joyeux anniversaire*. Some silently squeezed her hand. Others tapped her on the shoulder. Or brought her a cooked banana. Or an egg. Gustave embarrassed her when he quietly placed a small object in her hand, whispering in her ear, hoping she would enjoy good fortune. It was a carved image of a pregnant woman. Red-faced, she thanked Gustave for the fetish and quickly put it in her pocket.

She was embarrassed again at lunch when Dr. Schweitzer gave a birthday speech openly praising her in front of her colleagues, thanking her for having agreed to stay. "We have all learned to appreciate the Lady from the North, "at work and at leisure time when her charms and social skills are especially welcome."

Beet-red, she waited for the traditional birthday song to be sung for a second time. She assumed Dr. Schweitzer would go the dining room piano, as he usually did for birthdays, but this did not occur. Was this because he had heard the morning version of it?

Disappointed, she asked Anne-Lise later in the day why it hadn't occurred. Anne-Lise suggested it was likely because she was not officially part of the permanent staff and was therefore not deemed entitled to the full ceremony. This would also explain why she had not received the painted cloth either. "It is Nurse Ali and Mlle. Mathilde who decide such things," said Anne-Lise, regretfully.

It was never considered appropriate for the staff to complain about the conditions at Lambaréné, such as the oppressive heat, the isolation or the arduous hours. It would have been childish to say anything about a birthday celebration. But she struggled in vain to regain her spirits. It was shameful to be disconsolate over the slight. She fought back tears. Hadn't she worked just as hard as any of the other doctors? Hadn't Dr. Schweitzer said as much?

Everyone at Lambaréné knew the birthday procedure, and there were few secrets among the staff. Her disappointment could not be adequately hidden. That accounted for what happened next. All the staff stopped whatever it was they were doing and listened as a group of Africans, mostly women and children, formed their own choir and were approaching singing the birthday song for her, evidently aware it had not been sung at lunch. Her face lifted with pride. Nurse Ali and Mlle. Mathilde looked embarrassed.

Dr. Schweitzer nodded in support. He ordered cookies and chocolate to be brought and distributed them to the children. Their little hands stretched eagerly for the treats; mothers draped in their best garments, with babies in their arms, beamed with pleasure. The Africans had succeeded in making La Doctoresse happy again. "Few of us can match their skill and sensitivity in human relationships," Dr. Schweitzer said, with unfettered admiration. "This is the best compliment you have received today." And with those words of praise, Louise found herself well pleased with her birthday.

SOON AFTER HER BIRTHDAY, Dr. Schweitzer asked Louise to visit a Swiss family who had been living for years in a primeval forest where the husband operated a timber business. Four babies of this family had been delivered at Dr. Schweitzer's hospital between 1948 and 1953. He wanted to know how they were doing in the solitude of the forest. The family made only short annual trips to their Swiss home country, but recently had not contacted Dr. Schweitzer as they usually did upon their return.

To reach the remote forest homestead of this family, Louise had to travel in a small and uncomfortable riverboat through dark lagoons that endlessly wound around giant trees looking like huge columns stretching upwards to reach the sunlight. The lagoons finally widened to small lakes. Footprints on the beaches were left by the wild animals that came to drink there. The dark still waters, mirroring the huge trees, could lead one into a dreamy state.

At the end of the waterways, she had to walk about ten kilometres through the forest to reach a small savannah. There, close to the edge of the dark and forbidding tropical forest, she found the lonely homestead where the Swiss family had been living for many years. The head of the family was a headstrong man, a clever mechanic who was much too involved in his timber business to spend much time with his four children whose upbringing he left to his friendly, somewhat naive, much younger wife. It was she who told Louise the bizarre story of Silvio, their youngest son, a strange child who caused his mother much anxiety and frustration.

Silvio's birth at Dr. Schweitzer's hospital in Lambaréné had been complicated: a Caesarian section had to be performed. The newborn child had rarely cried and had shown little or no interest in his surroundings, so much so that his mother had feared he was not normal. But Silvio appeared to develop well physically. He began to exhibit strange behaviour only as he became older. He never played and hardly ever talked with his brothers.

Silvio would mostly sit by himself, and he became lively only when his mother took him for walks in the forest. There he showed an interest in the plants and flowers, and especially in trees. During these walks, Silvio would suddenly stop at a tall tree, throw his head back and stare up the trunk until his whole body trembled, seemingly overcome with emotion. At his mother's calling his name, he tore himself away from the tree, ran to her and clasped both arms around her with closed eyes, as if he felt dizzy and was afraid of collapsing. In vain, his mother had tried to interest him in other things but he seemed to have fallen under the spell of the forest. He thought about and talked only about the forest and its trees. He would play with his brothers only when they went together into the forest.

Before long, Silvio started to climb trees, even the very tall ones, and became an expert tree climber. He amazed the local Africans with his ability at such a young age. Against the stern warnings of his parents, Silvio continued to climb the tallest trees he could find. When they forbade him to climb such tall trees, he became hostile, refused to eat and cried until his mother, for the sake of peace, allowed him to climb smaller trees at the edge of the forest where she could watch over him. Silvio would spend all of his days there.

One day, with a slight feeling of horror, the mother saw that Silvio's feet were different from those of other children: the big toe stood wide apart from the other toes. Silvio used that in climbing;

he grasped branches with toes like fingers on a hand. Sometimes he appeared to his mother as if he were a being from another world. But he was a good-looking child with a fine face and big eyes.

Usually Silvio kept his eyes half-closed but when standing under a tree in the forest, he opened them wide and stared with fascination at the leaves glittering brightly in the sunlight and at the fruits. Soon, the boy knew the names of the trees, their fruits and blossoms and the season of their appearance. Silvio hardly ever talked with his father, except when his father spoke about trees. Then Silvio looked at him and listened with keen attention. Otherwise, Silvio remained ill-humoured with his father.

The parents were helpless in how to deal with the behaviour of their son. When the mother gave in to his strange requests in order to preserve the domestic peace, the boy's peculiarity became rather grotesque. Only during the family's walks in the forest did Silvio jump with excitement. He would then climb trees to fetch blossoms and fruits for his mother. At these times, he would suddenly embrace his mother in silent anxiety.

When all the children were school age, the parents decided to return for some time to Switzerland. Above all else, Silvio's mother wanted Silvio to be examined by a child psychologist to obtain expert advice on his development and upbringing. In Europe, Silvio showed no interest in all the new things in the cities that excited his brothers; only when he saw a tree or flowering bush did his face light up. His mother heard him mutter, "So, there are also trees growing here."

When his mother took Silvio to the psychologist, her son was in a bad mood and tried to resist entering the office until he saw a blooming lilac tree in the garden of a house near the entrance. He appeared enchanted by the lilac bush and wanted to break off a branch. When his mother did not allow him to do this and explained that the trees and bushes in Europe belonged to the owners of the garden, Silvio became angry and cried noisily until the lady of the house came out. Upon the embarrassed mother's explanation that the boy wanted to break off a branch from the lilac bush, the lady made Silvio happy and cooperative by generously presenting him with a lilac branch.

After numerous tests, the child psychologist stated that Silvio appeared to be a normal and age-adequate child. His mother was disappointed; she assumed that a psychologist in Europe unfamiliar with the situation in the African forest had arrived at the wrong conclusion. Silvio had been so happy with the lilac tree that he had cooperated with the doctor.

Silvio was inattentive and failed at the school in Europe, only listening to the teacher when the topic was nature and plants. And, while in Switzerland, he became miserable and emaciated because of his longing for the African forest. His parents found a private teacher for the instruction of their children and took a flight back to Gabon. Silvio trembled with impatient excitement; anxiously he asked his mother whether the forest might have forgotten about him.

Upon arrival at the family's homestead, he stared wide-eyed at the edge of the forest. Then he threw himself on the ground. Sobbing, he cried, "Mother, mother I don't ever want to leave here. I must live here in the forest or else I must die." Silvio's mother tried to calm him by reassuring him that he could certainly stay. She began to add that at some time in the future he might want to return to Europe. "Never, never!" cried Silvio.

When the rainy season arrived, Silvio had to stay in the house as everybody else did. He became irritable and hostile. He finally built himself a small hut of branches at the forest edge and, after many scenes of tearful pleading, he was allowed to stay there at times. In his school lessons, he performed poorly, especially in mathematics, until his teacher used trees instead of numbers. Silvio was able to calculate with trees, write about trees and make beautiful drawings of trees. These were not childlike images but trees according to their real nature and type. He achieved an expertise in tree drawing that rivalled many an adult artist.

At the dinner table, Silvio's parents often discussed the future of their children. They would one day have to return to Europe for further education. Silvio could perhaps train to become a forester, then he could stay in Europe and be around trees. But Silvio shook his head and insisted he wanted to stay near his African forest his whole life. His father angrily called this impossible as Silvio had to learn a profession.

One day, Silvio's mother found him at a strange occupation by which he was so spellbound that he did not hear her coming. Silvio was tearing small trees out of the ground and throwing them away. Then he tore branches off bigger trees and trampled angrily on them. When his mother asked in astonishment why he was doing such a thing, he muttered, "One has to overcome the trees."

In the days before the next great rainy season, Silvio often stood quite still by the window and looked over to the tropical forest. Once he let his head drop and said with an infinitely sad voice, "I don't want to live any longer. In the rainy season I am not allowed to stay in the forest. I want to build a house with a hole in the ceiling, plant a tree and let it grow through the hole. Then I could stay under the tree during the rainy season."

His mother had to laugh about Silvio's idea and did not notice the deeply sad mood of the boy when he could look at the forest only through a window. As a nine-year-old boy, he still often ran to his mother to embrace her anxiously, crying all the while, as he had also done in his earlier years.

After the end of the rainy season, the family went again for a walk in the forest. Silvio ran around wildly until he saw an unusually tall tree with red fruit. The other children wondered whether one could fetch these but their mother told them, "Leave them alone; it is far too dangerous to climb this high tree."

Silvio looked with burning eyes to the red fruits glittering high up in the sunlight. The next morning, Silvio entreated his mother to let him fetch the fruits from the tree. His mother was busy and distracted by her work, and not remembering which tree Silvio spoke of, she agreed. She insisted, however, that he take a younger brother and the African houseboy along.

After quite a while, the younger brother came running home

terrified with the news that Silvio had fallen from the tall tree and looked dead. Shortly after, the houseboy arrived carrying Silvio in his arms and placed him on his bed. Trembling with fear, Silvio's mother looked at her son, who failed to answer her, only uttering low moans. His right leg appeared to be shortened but she could see no wound and no blood was evident.

His mother sent for her husband. They stood helplessly beside their unconscious child, waiting for the regular plane to arrive at the local airport. This would be the fastest way to get medical attention. They were afraid to move him. Finally, after some hours the plane landed. They carefully carried him to the plane. She nearly fainted when she noticed with horror that the boy's pelvis was shattered.

At the hospital, the parents had to wait outside while their child was examined. Soon the doctor came out and said with sympathy that the boy had been dead for hours, a death caused by internal bleeding. The doctor assured the parents that Silvio had been unconscious and had not been feeling pain.

Louise, once again, visited the family at Dr. Schweitzer's request. Both of the parents spoke about Silvio. The mother showed her a collection of Silvio's drawings. The mature skill with which Silvio drew trees and flowers of the tropical forest was astonishing and moving. On one drawing of a tall tree, Silvio had used an exaggerated perspective to emphasize its majesty. On another drawing of a lovely tree with beautiful flowers he wrote, "Mother is so dear." The most impressive drawing depicted a threatening tree, all red, in which a boy with a flower stood high up in the tree on a branch that was about to break—a foreshadowing of his death. Silvio's mother had adorned his grave at the edge of the forest with his favourite flowers and plants.

Louise visited this family several more times. Eventually Silvio's mother said, timidly, "You have already heard so much about our son Silvio that you must be tired of these stories." Louise assured her that was not so. Encouraged, the mother confided that she loved to talk about him; it made her feel as if he was still alive. "When I go back to Europe, it will be hard to leave him here alone," she said, with tears in her eyes. "But at least Silvio's wish never to leave his beloved forest has been granted."

～

THERE WAS A REGULAR mail service at Lambaréné, which made it easy for Louise to correspond with the outside world. She wrote most frequently to her mother, but it was impossible to convey to her, or to anyone, how vivid and intense events could be. She only mentioned strange cases such as Silvio in passing. Details about her special relationship with Dr. Schweitzer were inappropriate. Her mother was worried about her, of course. Most upsetting to Louise were her mother's comments about the possibility of marriage for Louise and children of her own. She feared that her daughter might be missing out on the richness of family life. Try as she might, Louise could not dismiss her mother's concerns.

Although claustrophobic, Lambaréné could often seem like a satisfying world unto itself, hermetically sealed. The outside world appeared as an uncontrollable and unpredictable force, akin to foul weather. This feeling was increased when she received a surprise and mostly unwelcome visitor. This was Richard, her pilot from Matadi. Although Richard had shown some romantic intentions in Matadi, Louise had not encouraged him. The only time Richard had kissed her, and it was on the cheek, was when he was leaving her aboard the Dutch ship in Pointe-Noire. After that, he had apparently thought often about her and had convinced himself that she was attracted to him.

Somehow he had learned of her whereabouts and decided to pay her an impromptu visit, arriving on the same commercial flight she had taken from Pointe-Noire. At first, Louise was happy enough to see him again because she had genuinely liked the man, but she became distressed to discover that he was assuming there was something romantic between them. The other problem was that she discovered once Richard was no longer *her* pilot, he had very little to say. When not flying and talking about flying, he turned out to be a bore.

Their situation soon became a keenly felt embarrassment. Richard failed to understand that she did not love him, could not love him, and yet she could not help feeling both responsible for and irritated by his presence. She finally had a long talk with him, explaining that she valued his friendship but that she did not feel as he seemed to. It took a number of days for her words to sink in, but finally he decided that he would have to accept her decision, and he left on a returning flight to Pointe-Noire.

LOUISE'S DECISION WAS made much easier as Richard's arrival corresponded with an ongoing drama concerning an unusually tall woman from a remote village, and this caused her to throw herself into caring for the woman. Over several weeks, everyone at Lambaréné had grown to like this young and gentle woman who was strangely incapacitated for weeks by extreme fatigue. There were no symptoms of a grave illness and yet it appeared as if she were slowly dying.

The loud sobbing of her grief-stricken relatives added to their feeling of helplessness and disappointment. Blood-chemistry tests were abnormal in a peculiar way but the unknown illness proved to be fatal before the staff had the time to investigate. To make matters worse, the friendly patient had thanked everyone warmly for their efforts to save her life; then she had closed her eyes, never to open them again. It didn't happen often but sometimes when things went wrong unexpectedly, the Africans suspected the staff had not really wanted to help. The scorn of the mourning relatives was becoming intense. Albert Schweitzer joined Louise at the bedside and, seeing everyone's distress, he tried to ease the shared feeling of failure. He said he had never seen such a case.

Louise and the other staff members discussed the case further until Dr. Schweitzer decided an autopsy was unavoidable. He had good connections with a medical laboratory in Europe, where he could send tissue samples for analysis. Even though tissues were often too damaged to render any positive results after such a long journey, he said it had to be tried. It would take hours of skilful negotiation with the reluctant relatives to get permission for the autopsy; and who was going to take on the unpleasant task of performing it? He himself felt too weak to undertake it this time.

Louise looked at the strained and fatigued faces around the bedside. "I will do it," she said. There was silence. Dr. Schweitzer looked at her searchingly. "You are the youngest among us," he said. "To perform an autopsy here in the tropics is not the same as doing it in the morgue of a European hospital. Are you sure you have the strength to do it?" She recalled the pathology theatre at the university in Zurich where her professor used to demonstrate autopsy techniques and where she herself had become proficient in doing them, and felt confident she would be able to do it. With a certain pride in her own abilities, she assured him that she was prepared. The others were relieved that Louise had volunteered and that they did not have to be involved. It was with relief that they returned to their daily duties.

Dr. Schweitzer asked his trusted African helper, Joseph, to assist her because he had assisted Dr. Schweitzer in performing autopsies before. It would take the whole day and part of the next before the relatives allowed the autopsy to be performed, and only after finally accepting some strong persuasion from Dr. Schweitzer himself. An autopsy, in the opinion of the deceased's relatives, would be a repulsive violation of the dead.

Once she was actually confronted with the task, Louise was hardpressed to believe otherwise herself. Even though she had accepted the task willingly, she knew that she had always found it was a frightening experience to touch a corpse. It would be even more unsettling to operate on one in Africa. But she knew that the situation challenged her to confront her fears; she was determined to carry on. The corpse was brought to a small hut that had been specially built for this purpose at a safe distance from the hospital.

The relatives and friends of the deceased gathered outside the hut as soon as Joseph and Louise arrived in the early afternoon. Women were sobbing, children were crying. The men muttered unfriendly words aimed at her as she passed through the emotional crowd.

The body had already been placed on a narrow metal table. Bottles of formaldehyde for the organ samples, a pair of surgical gloves, a scalpel, and a few other surgical instruments were ready for her. The distended corpse of the obese woman towered like a mountain in front of her eyes. Her hands began to shake as she approached the table and put on the gloves. Sweat trickled down her back, but she forced herself to pick up the scalpel. With the wailing crowd outside, and the vivid image of the living patient still in her mind, the autopsy was made a more formidable task when she realized Joseph appeared as troubled by the noise of the crowd as she was. Holding the scalpel firmly, she pressed it against the skin and drew the classic incision line from the chin, over the chest around the umbilicus, and down the abdomen to the pubic region.

In the sweltering heat of the tropical sun, decay had already set in. As soon as she opened the abdomen, a well of stinking fluid gushed out and a horrendous stench filled the little room. This putrid wave hit her like a solid thing and filled her with a sudden panic. Half-dazed, she put her hands inside the open abdomen. At first, she was unable to recognize any of the organs. Her whole being protested against what she had to do. Her work was with living human beings—to prevent death. Now here was death in its putrefying manifestation. Once a life was gone, she should not be involved. Fear gripped her heart at the smell of death and her instinct was to run away. A cold sweat burned in her eyes.

A new wave of panic seized her when some of the foul liquid seeped into her glove. She knew that if she had the slightest lesion on that hand, it might be lethal. But she had to continue. She could not possibly quit now. Had she not declared in front of Albert Schweitzer and the others that she could manage this?

The sun was shining mercilessly on the tin roof of the windowless little hut, making the heat unbearable. A wave of nausea turned her stomach. Almost ready to give up, she went to the door. But when she heard the cries of the people outside, she hesitated. What would they think and what might they do if she opened the door and they could see the woman's mutilated body, cut open like that? They would feel that she had murdered the patient all over again.

Nothing had gone really wrong so far, but if she did not hurry up, the suffocating heat and stench would certainly make her faint, and then everything would go wrong. She tried to pull herself together to think clearly, to plan her actions, but panic gripped her fiercely. She felt she was drifting into a dream-like state.

She had lost the scalpel among the intestines. She knew she had to retrieve it and quickly. Her will-power had to overcome her fear. Her mind had become a slave-driver and her will must become her whip; her hands would be the slaves. Her movements became deliberately slow as the slave-driver angrily urged the slaves to search for the missing scalpel. There was no necessity to do a full autopsy, the slave-driver decided; she needed only a small piece of the liver, the kidney, the heart and the lungs.

The slave-driver was obeyed and the liver was found: there it was! Now she ordered her hands to cut off a piece and to put the bloody tissue into one of the bottles with formaldehyde. Mechanically her hands returned into the cavity. The fumbling slaves were whipped around mercilessly in the dark until they hit upon something hard: a kidney. They were ordered to cut it free so they could get hold of the particular part needed for the sample. That, too, landed safely in a bottle.

The piece of lung tissue required created no problems. She did not seem to hear, see, or smell anything at all. The room did not seem to exist anymore. The slave-driver lifted the whip. What about the heart? A few courageous cuts and it could be lifted from the bloody cavity. She stared at the magnificent organ: how strange it was to hold a human heart in one's hands! She, too, had a heart and she could feel it throbbing right down to the tips of her fingers. Yesterday, this cold and silent heart now in her hands had been warm and beating, giving life to a lovely, young woman. This strange ceremony set her thinking: *Forgive me, sister, for touching your heart. I have to molest it for the sake of* . . . but she could no longer finish the thought.

Somehow her mind commanded her hands to cut into this architectural masterpiece. Like the marble columns of a gothic cathedral, the tendon cords arched into the bloody cavity: *Sister, I open your heart with reverence.* She saw the strong bundles of muscles boldly modelling the hollow of the chambers. In splendid harmony, they twined together, forming the apex of the heart, lending strength and endurance to the pump that must never stop as long as life is to remain in the body.

A deep sigh and a cough from her helper Joseph brought her back from her almost unconscious musings to reality. Quickly placing a piece of the heart into the waiting formaldehyde, she stepped aside. The heat and the stench hit her again with full force. She gasped and made a sign that the autopsy was finished and that he should take over. It was his job to sew up the body. To her dismay, she watched as he simply dropped the heart into the abdomen and the kidney into the chest. Surely the Creator would forgive their human shortcomings and the relatives would never know. She waited impatiently for Joseph to finish; it seemed an eternity before he had stitched up the body, washed, and wrapped it in a blanket.

As soon as her full concentration and willpower were not needed anymore, her strength drained away. With one last effort, she pulled off the slimy gloves. Then everything blackened before her eyes; she had to hold onto Joseph to remain standing. He quickly opened the door and the fresh air from outside helped her muster enough strength to face the reproachful countenances of the relatives. Then she and Joseph walked away from the brutal ceremony.

A cool breeze gently caressed her burning face. Never before had the air had a scent so sweet. She distinguished the aroma of the grass, the flowers and the trees. She took a few deep breaths to chase away the stench of death from every last corner of her lungs. How immensely rich was the air between heaven and earth.

Thoroughly washed and cleaned up, but still shaky and pale, she found herself again amidst the life of Lambaréné, with all its vitality and beauty. She appeared late for the evening meal. Dr. Schweitzer looked at her across the table. "Are you feeling all right?" His voice sounded worried. "Did it turn out well?"

She looked at her plate. "I managed" was all she could say. She lifted her head and met the old doctor's knowing eyes unflinchingly. At that moment, she knew Dr. Schweitzer's concern for her and her knowledge of that perfect beauty of the human heart that she had just held in her hand would help her overcome the horror of death and decay. And her life would go on.

The day after, when she returned to her room, she found an oblong parcel on her table. It was clearly meant as a gift. There was no card. When she unwrapped it, she found the beautiful grass mat that had been Dr. Schweitzer's prized possession. Her heart was filled with joy and pride. She knew she would keep that mat on her wall no matter where she lived, for the rest of her life. When their eyes met over dinner that evening, they both smiled. A silent understanding was better than words.

DURING HER STAY, among the hundreds of visitors who came to Lambaréné to see the great doctor, far too many had disrupted life with their cameras. Everyone who worked with Dr. Schweitzer was appalled by tourists who saw fit to take photographs of people in pain. Because of this general aversion to cameras, Louise never saw fit to ask anyone to take a photo of her alongside Dr. Schweitzer.

One group in particular stood out most favourably from the hordes of gawkers and that was a number of Finnish ladies. As members of an Albert Schweitzer club, they had saved money for years in order to charter a plane from Scandinavia to Lambaréné. These ladies wandered happily around, half-dazed by the heat, always respectful and amazed.

In their midst they had a paralyzed lady in a wheelchair, which they all took turns pushing so as to let her see and touch and smell all the beautiful trees on the way. The lady in the wheelchair was a nurse who had contracted poliomyelitis while nursing patients with that disease. Her friends made sure Dr. Schweitzer heard about it, and the peak experience of their day came when the old doctor gallantly kissed her hand, sincerely expressing his respect for her.

The invalid nurse as well as some of the more courageous ladies accepted an invitation to stay for supper while the others returned to their hotel in Lambaréné village. Dr. Schweitzer was animated by these friendly ladies from the North. At the dinner table, the ladies became quite timid, however, as they nervously tried to keep an interesting conversation going with the hero of their dreams. When they finally ran out of topics, Dr. Schweitzer said invitingly: "Are there any questions you would like to ask me?"

One of the ladies, moving restlessly on her chair, asked: "What is going to happen to Lambaréné when you are . . . I mean when you are no more?" This was a question which undoubtedly was on many of their minds. But to put it bluntly to his face! A short silence followed: everybody looked embarrassed. The poor lady, realizing the impact her question had made, slowly turned red. Dr. Schweitzer smiled and said, "I intend to live until I am about a hundred years old, so there is still lots of time before we have to worry about that." Everybody laughed, including Dr. Schweitzer, and the lady, who by now had tears in her eyes, found the time to recover. It was the typical Albert Schweitzer way of handling an embarrassing situation.

The Finnish ladies found out that Louise, too, was Scandinavian, and so they gathered around her and asked if there was anything they could do to please Dr. Schweitzer before they left. "What if we sing a song for him?" suggested the nurse in the wheelchair. Louise still had a cherished memory of the old Norwegian hymn that was sung in Oslo when he had received his Nobel Prize. The Finnish ladies knew this hymn, "Wonderful Is the Earth," which was sung all over Scandinavia. With the invalid nurse alongside, they assembled after dinner in the dark outside Dr. Schweitzer's residence, and sang the hymn to him under his window. Of course, he recognized it, and he came out on the porch to listen.

"Thank you, you have made me very happy," he told them. And they could hear that he was truly moved. Soon after, they rolled the nurse in the wheelchair down the path to the river. There they lifted their frail friend into the boat and seated her comfortably. While their boat sailed down the river, they again intoned the hymn. Louise translated it into English for the rest of the staff:

Wonderful is the Earth,
Mighty is God's heaven,
Beautiful the pilgrimage of the souls.
Through the fair realms on the earth
To Paradise we walk in song.
Ages shall come,
Ages shall pass,
Kin shall follow the path of kins;
Never ceases the heavenly tones
In the soul's joyful pilgrim-song!
Angels first sang it
To the shepherds on the field;
From soul to soul in joy it passed:
Peace over Earth! Humans rejoice.
A saviour for all time is born!

It sounded beautiful in the tropical night. Dr. Schweitzer reached for Louise's hand and said, "I'm glad you are still here." They remained that way, hand in hand, listening to the sweet voices coming over the water as the boat disappeared around a bend of the river, until the melody eventually faded away into darkness. Both knew that her own departure was imminent.

Dr. Schweitzer insisted on corresponding with a Dutch shipping company to make the arrangements for her to be picked up at Port-Gentil, at the mouth of the Ogowe River. From there, she would be taken by a Dutch freighter to Dar es Salaam, a journey that would take several weeks. He bought her a ticket for a first-class cabin on the Dutch ship and paid her well for her time at Lambaréné. When she insisted it was too much, he said, "You deserve it." When soon after the new physician from Europe arrived as her replacement, Louise felt much happier about having to leave, knowing that Dr. Schweitzer had the help he needed.

On the morning of her departure, Dr. Schweitzer told her how much everyone had appreciated her medical skills, her youthfulness and happy temperament. She was deeply moved and on the verge of tears. "If you continue to work diligently," he said, "you will become an even more successful healer."

Everyone accompanied her to the landing as she boarded the riverboat. Some boys shouted from high in the trees; others paddled little canoes alongside the ferry as it sluggishly turned back into the current of the slow-moving river. Louise turned and saw Dr. Albert Schweitzer waving on the riverbank, easily distinguishable with his tropical hat. She knew she would likely never see him again and yet she felt fortified. Before coming to Lambaréné she had assumed an ideal physician was someone who knew best what medicines to prescribe and how to make close contact with the patient. Now, after working in Tanganyika, in the Congo, and in Lambaréné, it was abundantly clear to her how much illness and unhappiness arose from mental problems. The realm of psychiatry beckoned.

CHAPTER 6

Tanzania & Moon Madness

WHEN LOUISE RETURNED to Europe via Dar es Salaam in 1962, she had only the money that Dr. Schweitzer had paid her but she also had a great deal of determination. She was resolved to return to her work on epilepsy, and she knew that even a small amount of recognition and support from the medical establishment could radically improve the lives of countless thousands who suffered from epilepsy throughout East Africa.

First, Louise felt obliged to take the bark sample from the Mahenge medicine man to Manfred Bleuler, her professor in Zurich. He agreed to have it analysed for her but that would take some time. As chief of the university psychiatric hospital in Zurich, Bleuler offered her a position at the Klinik Burghölzli. He also agreed to supervise her doctoral thesis about the medical, psychological and social repercussions of *kifafa*.

With Bleuler's assistance, Louise spoke at various scientific congresses about epilepsy in Africa and, to her dismay, she discovered that epilepsy was low on the list of priorities for governments and international agencies. She grew to realize that epilepsy was "a stepchild of medicine tossed between the specialties of neurology and psychiatry." Unable to persuade charitable organizations to provide any funding for her treatment program, she was grateful when Bleuler sympathetically arranged for her to have a meeting about *kifafa* at the World Health Organization (WHO) in Geneva.

Louise ascended the steps of the Palais des Nations with great excitement, knowing a productive meeting could relieve millions from misery. She felt as if her entire life was about to make perfect sense. Her confidence was immediately destroyed, however, when she was invited to sit at a large green table in an oddly darkened conference room, and she discovered there would be only one other person at the so-called "meeting." This was an elderly gentleman in charge of Mental Health for the World Health Organization. In the dim light from a desk lamp, this man seemed to be hiding behind his pair of dark glasses, inscrutable, devoid of courtesy.

Without any niceties or preamble, without any curiosity expressed about her stint with Dr. Schweitzer, she was told to speak. The more this old man remained hidden in the shadows, without even a token *harrumph*, the more his obdurate silence bordered on disdain. He did not move or interrupt to ask questions. He mostly just waited for her to finish, having clearly made up his mind about the fate of this meeting before she arrived. Once she had finished with her proposal, he finally spoke: "Are you a specialist in neurology or psychiatry?" She had to reply honestly.

"Well then, young lady," he said, clearly annoyed, "neither Professor Bleuler's recommendations nor your beautiful eyes will help you in this matter." As far as he was concerned, the important point was that he remain impervious to her female wiles. Frustrated and humiliated, she wanted to blurt out: *We are not discussing me! What about all the epileptics in the meantime?* But any outburst would only be characterized and dismissed as a weakness of her gender. "I suggest you come back to us when you are a specialist and have made a name for yourself. Maybe then we could consider lending you the umbrella of the WHO," the old man said disdainfully.

As she ran down the steps of the Palais des Nations, her disappointment changed to anger. She vowed she would never again allow anyone to dismiss her that way. She recalled the incident when, years ago, her school teacher had told her she would never become a doctor and she had felt the same anger. At the same time, she realized that although she was able to state the facts of her situation effectively, she now knew that fundraising was not merely a matter of putting words and numbers on paper; it entailed personal politics and networking. As a start, Professor Bleuler contacted Swiss pharmaceutical companies to have them donate medication and funds for the epileptics. For the rest of her life, Louise would continue to fundraise, but she would also continue to send several thousand dollars of personal funds annually to her clinic, as well as sending gifts of money to staff for Christmas and other holidays.

Professor Bleuler arranged for Louise to be a resident psychiatrist-in-training at the Swiss Institute for Epileptics in Zurich headed by his friend, Dr. Landolt, an international authority on epilepsy. Here she would write her thesis on epilepsy. Professor Bleuler's fatherly concern also extended to her private life. Bleuler tactfully suggested that Louise might be sacrificing her private life if she invested too much time in Africa. He warned her not to drift into a situation she had not really planned for. This could have serious consequences for the remainder of her life. Translation: her zeal was admirable, but she was risking not getting married and having a family.

Working with Dr. Landolt at the Zurich University Clinic was an adjustment. In contrast to the open spaces and bright sunshine of Africa, the old hospital with its long corridors and locked doors seemed oppressive. Staff physicians still lived in the Klinik Burghölzli just as Professor Bleuler and his father before him had done. Bleuler's "home" was in the main building, and most of the residents in psychiatry had their rooms next to his suite. They were all expected to make ward rounds before and after the regular work hours, and the physician on call had to go through the whole hospital in the late evening before retiring for the night. She recalled her feelings about the hospital in comparison to her African clinic:

When I wandered through the dark corridors at night, hearing shrieks and moans, as the orderly with the bundle of heavy keys unlocked one door after the other, I tried to ease the tension I felt by thinking of my friends in Africa. How this place would have frightened them! They would have thought that the whole hospital was full of menacing spirits.

She could well imagine that many of her African patients in such an inhospitable building would have reacted with violent behaviour.

THROUGHOUT THIS TIME, Louise kept in constant contact with her clinic at Mahenge, and whenever it ran out of funds, she would send part of her salary to the nurse in charge. Grateful students at the outlying schools that she had visited wrote plaintive letters, asking not to be forgotten. A schoolboy named Mawanja asked for her picture, and wrote to her: "I cherish to read a letter from a person while being in possession of that person's picture."

Some patients with epilepsy wrote to tell her about their progress, trying all the while to replicate highly formal English: "I must try to identify to you my movements because of these tablets with the very precious treatments which must make me remain always thankful to you for carefully managing to care for my disease. Yours cordially, Amani."

Others tried to appeal to her by emphasizing humility: "Dear doctor of mine, I am sure you won't remember me if you only read this letter, but I will remind you that on the day before you left Mahenge for Europe, there were two young men who came to your office for a farewell. The young men asked for your address, which you kindly handed to them. They also asked you to find girl friends for them in your country, whose request you kindly accepted. I'm one of those young men." Despite the awkward phrasing in most of these letters, the earnestness of these appeals was unmistakeable.

When Louise sought the permission of the bishop of Mahenge,

himself a member of the Wapogoro tribe, to write about the health problems faced by his tribe, he graciously replied:

Dear Doctor Louise,

I am glad to hear that you are going to write a book about the Wapogoro and their *kifafas*. I think you can write about the poverty of Wapogoro, their beliefs about *kifafa*, and their attitude towards those who have *kifafa*. Nobody will be offended if it is done in a manner which does not show that you intend to despise them for these weaknesses. . . . You may state the fact about their poverty, and also about their beliefs about *kifafa*, and their attitude towards those who have *kifafa*. But then it would be good to point out that the cause of all these lies in the lack of facilities for improving their standard of living, and lack of education about the causes of illness. Such a book will be all right, and I hope and believe every reasonable Wapogoro will be delighted to read it. . . . Wishing you good success, I pray that God will bless your endeavour. Yours sincerely, Bishop of Mahenge.

LOUISE COMPLETED HER thesis under Dr. Landolt, and was soon able to leave the psychiatric hospital and commence work at the Swiss Institute for Epileptics where she was deeply moved by the epileptics who lived in houses surrounded by fields and gardens. The patients' medical conditions could be monitored with an electro-cardiograph as they worked together on the farm and took care of the animals. Here was a model for what she hoped to achieve for the Wapogoro.

Months after Louise had brought back the bark for analysis, a professor of pharmacology at the University of Zurich invited her to a meeting with a representative of the pharmaceutical laboratories where the specimen had been analyzed. There was good news and bad news. The medicine man was right. The bark was found to have anticonvulsive properties in tests. A decoction of the bark had been administered to rats and it had diminished induced convulsions. Unfortunately, the amount of bark material remaining was insufficient for further experiments. As much as a thousand pounds of the bark would be needed for conclusive analysis. Would Louise be willing to leave her position at the Klinik Burghölzli to undertake a prolonged expedition to gather more of the bark material?

Although the pharmaceutical company was willing to pay for all her expenses, the news rendered Louise speechless. The first time she had gone to Tanganyika, it had been an adventure; everything was new to her. But now she was anxious and full of doubts about what she would find there in a colony that was in the process of achieving its independence.

Certainly an all-expenses-paid journey was tempting, but realistically how could she get hold of a thousand pounds of the bark? And who would help her? Would the medicine man, if she could find him, be willing to collect such an amount? And would the people of the area take offence at such a commercial undertaking? The knowledge of medicinal herbs belonged to the whole tribe. What would happen if they demanded monetary compensation?

The pharmaceutical company also didn't realize that she would be obliged to treat a great many people once word spread that she had returned. It would be impossible to travel inconspicuously. New patients would swell the number of patients attending the clinic. The bare-bones clinic was barely able to handle current demands.

But her greatest fear was not about work; it was loneliness. The truth was more complicated than she was able to admit. There had been times in Africa when she had wept bitter tears, feeling bereft and isolated, longing to hear someone speak her real name. Once she had stayed in her room all evening and through the night so that the moon could not shine upon a lonely person.

Louise felt herself caught in a quagmire of doubt. She could not admit to anyone that returning to that inner cell of loneliness was more intimidating than Africa. Of course, she *must* do what was right. Her deep apprehension struck her as shamefully selfish. And yet she was increasingly feeling she belonged at the Klinik Burghölzli. She was part of a functional, professional family there.

It was at this juncture, as she was sitting at her desk and gazing somewhat forlornly out the window, that an energetic male colleague at the institute—an Austrian psychiatrist who fancied himself a bit of a lady's man—interrupted her confusion with an invitation. By any chance, would she be at all interested in driving out to the old Schloss Rapperswil built in the 13th century?

This man named Jilek said he had just dropped by her office on the way to pick up some books. She wanted to believe that was true. Jilek said he was a photographer. That was the reason he gave for visiting the restored castle.

Even though he had tried flirting with her several times before from a distance, and she had always succeeded in ignoring him, this time his direct offer of congenial company struck her as genuine and harmless. It was such a lovely evening. She told herself that this, after all, was what normal people did.

Off they went for a summer drive. They had never seen one another outside of the hospital. Previously, he had struck her as a somewhat vain person but obviously bright and self-assured. She now told herself she mustn't be so judgemental. Just because someone is charming, does that person have to have improper intentions? And the roadway alongside the lake was unquestionably beautiful.

Certainly the afternoon drive was far healthier than moping and feeling sorry for herself. He liked to talk, and she was a good listener. She was happy to be entertained. They eventually stopped at a bridge that traversed the lake at a narrow point, which afforded a marvellous view of Schloss Rapperswil.

Her companion brought out his tripod and camera and proceeded to carry his equipment over his shoulder to the middle of the bridge where there was a lookout with flowers and benches. People were taking their early evening stroll on the bridge, mostly couples.

Louise saw that the best perspective for a photo of the castle was from a bench occupied by a young couple with their arms around one another. Without a hint of apology or embarrassment, her compan-ion placed his tripod right in front of them. The young lovers objected to this incursion and said something in Italian, but Louise's colleague was not the least bit taken aback. He made a small joke in Italian, a remark that made everyone laugh. The couple was now complicit with his objective. They agreed to appear in his photo, which would include the picturesque castle glowingly mirrored in the calm waters during the sunset.

Louise stood at the railing, watching from a distance, but feeling part of the picture being taken. This man had a way of getting what he wanted. The magnificent sky with its gold-rimmed clouds on a warm evening, with the songs of birds, filled her with contentment. On the way back to Zurich, she found herself unburdening her wor-ries about Africa and the difficult decision she was trying to make. He was sympathetic.

After he dropped Louise at her apartment, her loneliness returned and she took it as a sign that perhaps she was not meant to go. As Dr. Bleuler had pointed out, she wasn't getting any younger.

Nevertheless, on the day she had to give an answer to the Swiss pharmaceutical company, Louise knew she would not be able to live with herself, let alone anyone else, if she did not take this opportunity to continue what she had started in Africa.

Just as she was leaving the Institute for her appointment, Jilek, her photographer colleague, appeared. "Would you like me to go with you?" he asked. At first she thought he was referring to her appoint-ment. "To Africa," he added.

Her brother Cato had had that same light-hearted, devil-may-care approach when he suggested riding their bikes to the Arctic Circle.

Jilek pointed out that he had some years of experience in neurol-ogy and psychiatry. He could help her at the clinic. She looked at him in astonishment. He had absolutely no idea of what he was propos-ing. But someone who was willing to share the responsibility of the journey, someone with whom she could consult when facing difficult patients, well, that struck her as entirely a good thing. Her voice was trembling with disbelief. "You really want to come with me? To Africa?" Jilek grinned, amused, in a carefree way that seemed to indicate it would be as simple as driving to Rapperswil.

She rushed off to her meeting with a sudden joy in her heart. It took Louise an hour before she realized she had just decided to travel to Africa with a man—and she didn't know his first name.

Wolfgang Georg Jilek was born on November 25, 1930, in Tetschen (or Decin), in the north of what is now the Czech Republic, an area still known as Bohemia. His first language was German; his family's national identity was Austrian.

Wolfgang's family had a long and proud history in medicine. In the 1860s, Dr. August Jilek had lived at Castello Miramare, near Trieste, as the personal physician of Archduke Maximilian, the ill-fated emperor of Mexico. Another Dr. Jilek had sailed around the world on the frigate *Novara* as a physician in the Imperial Austrian Navy. As a boy, Wolfgang had discovered the memoirs of that naval physician in his grandfather's library, and those accounts of his adventures triggered a lifelong fascination with heraldic emblems. After he had become a psychiatrist, he would publish many articles on symbols and their psychological effects.

Wolfgang's family had lost their Sudetenland home in 1944. At about the same time, his father had been interned in Russian POW camps, and Wolfgang had been forced to lead an itinerant existence in central Europe as a refugee during and after the war, along with his mother and brother.

Forced to take odd jobs as a teenager, Wolfgang finally gained his medical degree in 1954. In Vienna he developed his interests in history, medicine, psychoanalysis, Adlerian psychology and a method of German psychology that had been developed by Wilhelm Wundt in the 19th century called *Völkerpsychologie*.

Wolfgang had been inclined to specialize in neurology until he met his lifelong mentor and friend, Victor Frankl, now famous for his book about Auschwitz. His encounters with Frankl in 1954 led him to logotherapy, a psychotherapeutic approach that he would later apply in his work with diverse ethnic and cultural minorities.

In the 1950s, Jilek went to Zurich for three years, where he trained in psychiatry and epileptology under Manfred Bleuler at the Klinik Burghölzli, and under H. Landolt at the Swiss Institute for Epilepsy. It was here that the happy meeting took place with Louise.

WHEN LOUISE AND WOLFGANG arrived in Dar es Salaam in 1963 for what was to be a three-month stay, it was during the worst rainy season she had ever experienced. In spite of the downpours, she received a wonderful welcome at Kwiro, with the *kifafa* patients giving them a big feast with dancing and singing. Because they were not married, they were given separate sleeping quarters, and because they were staying at the mission, they also ate separately. Wolfgang had the privilege of dining with the Fathers in the refectory while she had to eat alone in her room, waiting for the lights to go out in the refectory, at which time Wolfgang would come and briefly say goodnight and report on his conversations before returning to his room at the Fathers' house.

In keeping with her three-month plan, the medicine man took them on trips into the mountains to gather the barks and roots he used in the treatment of *kifafa*. He explained the names and properties of trees and herbs so well that they were able to identify the collected specimens botanically. The mission at Kwiro allowed them to dry the various plants they collected in the attic above the schoolgirls' dormitory. The girls reacted with apprehension, fearing the medicine man's powers. One night when the pungent smell of the *nefuzi* roots sifted down into their dormitory, they fled in panic. The medicine man had to be summoned to reassure them before they would agree to go back to bed.

Working together from morning until after sunset, Louise and Wolfgang went foraging with the medicine man. After they thought they had collected enough bark and herbs, they turned to reorganizing the *kifafa* clinic. The plan was to leave the clinic in the charge of a Swiss Catholic nun from Kasita with three trained Wapogoro girls to help care for the patients and their families. As news of her reappearance spread, the number of patients receiving regular treatment swelled to over two hundred.

After several months, it became clear that transporting their cache of dried plants and bark to the coast was going to be a major undertaking. The sacks had to be carried over flooded fields, canoed across swift rivers and driven on pothole-ridden roads, then tightly packed into the back of a Land Rover for transit to Dar es Salaam. Most of the material had to be dried again when they reached the coast, so they gained permission to spread their cargo on the sunbaked roof of the Archbishop's house.

At the docks, Louise and Wolfgang were relieved when they managed to get their cargo safely through customs onto to a freighter and on its way to Switzerland. Unfortunately, the couple's efforts to contribute to the development of a new antiepileptic agent out of the traditional African pharmacopeia would prove to be in vain. Once the laboratories in Switzerland set about isolating the effective ingredients, it turned out that the processes would be uneconomical for commercial manufacturing.

Working side-by-side, operating as a team of two, nonetheless proved to be a successful elixir for trust. Their growing intimacy was finally consummated in a Dar es Salaam hotel room. Wolfgang had previous experience; she had not, and the experience was not as romantic as she had hoped. Louise was expecting Wolfgang to be doting and to say lovely things. Instead, she woke in the morning and discovered he had already dressed and gone out. While she had been expecting loving words and reassuring caresses, he had opted to take his camera to the beach to take photos.

She got up, dressed and walked to the beach where she saw him from a distance, immersed in his photographic pursuits. An old Indian man who was nearby saw distress in her face and struck up a conversation. His kindness was such that she soon found herself confessing her disappointment to a complete stranger. Because she was on the verge of tears, the old man took it upon himself to go and have a few wise words with Wolfgang. Although Louise would never see the old Indian man again, she would never forget his intervention.

Soon after, Wolfgang proposed to her. She accepted. With no friends or relatives to share the news, Louise took Wolfgang to be introduced to her friend, Archbishop Maranta. She had already told Wolfgang about her earlier private tour of Tanganyika in the Archbishop's car. When she showed Archbishop Maranta their engagement rings, the Archbishop's face became animated, and he was intensely curious about their relationship. "Wolfgang's reaction to all this made me wonder," she recalled, "if he worried that we had been infatuated with each other." Decades later, her recollections of courtship would be terse: "We had a few relaxing days before we left East Africa. I thoroughly enjoyed them and had no objections when my friend took me to an Indian jeweller to choose our engagement rings."

Some months later in 1963, the couple had two marriages: one in Oslo and one in Vienna. When they were married in Oslo, a telegram was delivered from Archbishop Maranta with wishes for a long and happy life. He thanked them for having helped so many people suffering from epilepsy in Mahenge. "I will give you a ceremony in my church in Dar es Salaam," he wrote. He died twelve years later without ever seeing them again.

Soon after she was married, Louise's legal name was recorded in her passport as Louise Mathilde Jilek. After their immigration to Canada, she would switch this to Louise Mathilde Jilek-Aall. This final change of name was not because they thought the man's name should come first, but they believed the addition of her original surname, Aall, served to further differentiate them when they commenced jointly publishing academic articles.

CHAPTER 7

Home Life & Psychiatry

BEFORE THEIR TRIP TO TANGANYIKA, Wolfgang and Louise had both written independently to Dr. Eric Wittkower at McGill University in Montreal expressing their interest in his new discipline called transcultural psychiatry. The newlyweds now agreed to a joint plan to take post-graduate studies under Wittkower. They had no intention of becoming Canadian citizens. It was a Canadian immigration official, impressed by their credentials and personalities, who urged them to apply for citizenship when they were seeking only a student visa.

Even when they learned they would have to retake all their general medical examinations in order to practise as doctors in Canada, the couple decided to proceed. They were intrigued by the prospect of living in an emerging multicultural society.

In Montreal, they commenced their association with the newly founded Section of Transcultural Psychiatric Studies pioneered by Wittkower and his associate, Henry B.M. Murphy. In order to do so, Wolfgang had to forfeit his Austrian citizenship (re-awarded to him by the Austrian government in 1997 on the basis of his scientific achievements and publications).

After passing her specialist exams at McGill, Louise received her specialist certification and soon after Fellowship in the Royal College of Physicians. The couple then remained in Quebec for approximately a year doing neuropsychiatric research at the Institut de Recherche Psychiatrique in Joliette, northeast of Montreal. In 1965 to 1966, they were on the first Canadian team to investigate and describe the psychotropic effects of carbamazepine, an anticonvulsant now used to prevent and control seizures under the trade name Tegretol. Early research indicated that carbamazepine could have positive effects on seizure activity and on certain behaviour disturbances arising from convulsive disorders.

During a vacation, they rented a car and drove across the country to the West Coast where they connected with Edward Margetts, Director of Mental Health in B.C., who knew about them as a result of his own medical experiences in Africa. Edward Lambert Margetts (1920–2004) was a Canadian psychiatrist who had graduated from McGill in 1944. He had served as the medical superintendent of Mathari Mental Hospital in Nairobi, Kenya, from 1955 until 1959. He would later publish *The Medicine Man—and Woman—East Africa* in 1985 about his experiences in Kenya.

It was Margetts who suggested they might wish to develop a new psychiatric practice in the Upper Fraser Valley area, east of Vancouver, where hitherto there had never been any permanent psychiatrists. There they would be able to implement their transcultural psychiatric treatment methods.

From 1966 to 1975, Louise and Wolfgang were the only psychiatrists in the Upper Fraser Valley for a cultural mosaic that included Dutch Reformed Christians, Germanic Mennonites, Russian Doukhobors and Coast Salish people.

It was the First Nations people who became the main focus of their ethno-psychiatric investigations. Through personal acquaintances with First Nations ritualists, the couple were able to observe ceremonial dances, potlatches and healing procedures among the Coast Salish and other First Nations along the Pacific Coast from Washington State to Alaska.

"As their physician friends," Wolfgang wrote, "we witnessed the revival of the Salish Winter Spirit Ceremony in the Indigenous renaissance of the 1960s and '70s in North America" (Jilek 1978). "We reported on its therapeutic benefits, in particular for young Indigenous people, victims of what I described as anomic depression characterized by loss of traditional norms, cultural identity confusion, and relative deprivation" (Jilek 1974).

The first of their many significant publications from this realm, entitled "Transcultural Psychotherapy with Salish Indians," was presented at the 5th World Congress of Psychiatry in Mexico City in 1971. As the couple extended their work to the northern region of the Northwest Coast, their work became familiar to Claude Lévi-Strauss and other anthropologists.

In the early 1970s, Pierre Maranda, a professor at the University of British Columbia, invited Claude Lévi-Strauss to come to Vancouver where Lévi-Strauss gave some lectures and chaired some seminars with professors and graduate students. At the time, Lévi-Strauss was internationally recognized as the leading figure in post-World War II ethnology. Born in Belgium in 1908, he rejected the notion that Western civilization was either privileged or unique in such books as *Tristes Tropiques*, *The Raw and the Cooked*, *The Savage Mind* and *Totemism*.

Louise and Wolfgang discussed their mutual interests in shamanic ceremonialism with Lévi-Strauss at their home and also escorted him to visit some of their First Nations contacts. For at least thirty years, Lévi-Strauss had conducted research into North and South American Indian tribes, including considerable studies of masks in the Pacific Northwest. Originally published in French in 1945, Lévi-Strauss' *The Way of the Masks*, translated by Sylvia Modelski, became a standard reference work for anthropology related to British Columbia.

To help Lévi-Strauss continue his analysis of coastal Indigenous mythology, Louise and Wolfgang arranged for him to meet a Salish chief and key informant at their home, as well as elder ritualists at a Salish spirit dance ceremonial. Levi-Strauss subsequently cited and credited them as "grands connaisseurs de la culture salish" in *The Way of The Masks* (*La voie des masques*) (1979, p. 52).

Discussions with Lévi-Strauss about his interests in shamanism were influential in guiding Wolfgang to publish his work pertaining to British Columbia, *Indian Healing: Shamanic Ceremonialism in the Pacific Northwest Today* (Hancock House, 1982, 2004). This was a transcription of his anthropology thesis that he completed at the University of British Columbia. Long-time teacher and colleague, Manfred Bleuler, who also visited their home, provided a foreword to Wolfgang's ground-breaking but now dated book.

When Bleuler came to visit, Louise and Wolfgang made a trip with him along the Northwest Coast to meet Indigenous elders, among them the old Salish shaman Isidor Tom.

Expanding social relations with Indigenous communities led to the couple's friendship with British Columbia's most renowned Indigenous artist, Bill Reid, who first met his wife Martine, from France, at their home. She had made her first visit to British Columbia in the company of a French anthropologist.

In 1969 Louise commenced her own studies in anthropology and sociology at the University of British Columbia, earning her Master of Arts degree in 1972. By 1975 she had branched out to become an assistant professor in the Department of Psychiatry at the University of British Columbia.

Further contacts with Indigenous elders along the B.C. coast were made possible through UBC Psychiatric Outreach consultations. The couple also volunteered for the State of Alaska Alcohol Prevention Project among North Alaskan Inuit at Nome and St. Lawrence Island. They learned more about Arctic populations through participation in Circumpolar Health Congresses, befriending a cultural psychiatrist in Siberia named Caesar Petrovich Korolenko in the process.

Travelling further abroad, in 1976, they observed and helped treat a *koro* epidemic in Thailand and met Wolfgang Pfeiffer, in Indonesia, who was well known for his research in that country. A subsequent collegial association with Wolfgang Pfeiffer would open many doors for Wolfgang Jilek in Java, Sumatra and Bali in the 1980s. In Malaysia, their friend Wolfgang Krahl facilitated Wolfgang's recording of the Hindu trance rituals *thaipusam* and *mariamman,* and of devotees undergoing sacrificial ordeals.

Louise and Wolfgang twice toured South America for information on traditional therapies. They examined the alcohol-deconditioning by curanderos of the Colorado Indians in Ecuador and reunited with McGill colleague Lydia Aguirre Perales at the First World Congress of Folk Medicine in 1979, in Peru, while also visiting an ayahuasca healing centre in the Amazon. They witnessed shamanic rituals of the Ayoreos in the Chaco bush in Paraguay and later took part in events organized by Latin American colleagues in Bolivia by M. Hollweg, in Brazil by M. de Noronha and in Mexico by S.J. Villaseñor Bayardo.

Meanwhile the couple's anthropological and medical associations with Indigenous clients and friends on the West Coast resulted in a wide range of publications pertaining to the Pacific Northwest in scholarly journals.

A listing of these publications can be found under "Research & Scientific Papers" near the end of the volume.

In 1979, Louise published her first book, *Call Mama Doctor: Notes from Africa* with Hancock House. It was later translated and published in Japan, China and Hungary. It was dedicated to her mother, Dr. Lily Weiser-Aall, "who inspired my interest in anthropology and in folk medicine."

After her sister Ingrid provided some critical responses to Louise's writing, Louise expressed both gratitude and embarrassment to her sister in 1982. She wrote: "I think I know my own limitations and I am unable to leap out of my own skin—a skin that I feel is rather rigid and anxious. I have never been a person of great expression; writing does not flow easily for me. I am rather shy regarding my own person, have never had great self-esteem. My way is to be the observer rather than the maker. I like to heal and improve the quality of life for others. I have seldom been concerned about my own feelings or life-situation. There is like a quiet happiness inside of me, which gives me the strength to help others; therefore I have never thought much about myself."

NO MATTER HOW IMPORTANT their life in science was, it may well be that the most important event of their lives in Canada was not professional. Having determined that she was unable to conceive, Louise asked Wolfgang if they could adopt a child. He agreed to do so on the condition that they did not adopt a boy.

From a visitor to their home, they had learned about the plight of street orphans in Bogota, Colombia. During a ten-year period known as La Violencia, it was common for soldiers and renegades to attack farms in the mountains. They would kill the farmers and their wives while looting their homes. Survivors or other villagers would sometimes rescue small children who were spared and deliver them to the capital, dropping them off on the streets to fend for themselves.

The proliferation of these street children, who became beggars and thieves in Bogota, prompted one couple to start a privately run orphanage, providing shelter to some of the most needy and miserable cases. When these children were rehabilitated, the couple would seek homes for them with good families.

In June of 1978, Louise decided to visit this orphanage and volunteer her services as a physician. In this way she was able to assess the facility and the children. After several weeks, she urged Wolfgang to join her. One girl in particular had galvanized her interest because of her gentle temperament. Better still, it was clear that they would not be taking her away from her family as there were no traceable relatives following the death of her parents. Nobody knew how long she had been in Bogota. She was likely between ages three and four. She was generally friendly and cheerful but also clearly recovering from trauma. After a series of interviews and investigations, Louise and Wolfgang received approval for formal adoption. The girl herself was happy to be adopted by her new parents.

They chose to call her Martica. Louise and Wolfgang brought her to Canada in early 1979 where she learned to speak English quickly, but remained apprehensive and timid if somebody became angry or quarrelsome. This would not prevent her from developing a close bond with her mother and, once she was a little older, to travel extensively with her parents, particularly in East Asia.

One of their first trips abroad as a family came when Louise and Wolfgang visited Mao's China with a group of Canadian doctors invited to examine herbal medicine, acupuncture anesthesia and "barefoot doctors." With the help of Chinese colleagues, they examined victims of an another epidemic of *koro* in South China.

While Martica was too young to take much interest in their research in China, this all changed when she matured. After her schooling was finished, Martica gained her credentials as a registered nurse and assisted her mother on several trips to Tanzania where she proved particularly adept as a videographer. She and her mother also co-authored a research paper in 1997 called "Psychological Study of Epilepsy in Africa," in the journal, *Social Science and Medicine.*

Martica also helped her mother when Louise was stabbed twice in the chest during a mugging in Dar es Salaam near the end of one of their trips. Louise later recalled the incident:

> We were in the big hotel where many tourists stayed in order to get a special bus to the airport the next morning. It was a very hot evening so Martica and I went out for some fresh air in the street. But the street was empty and we soon decided to return to the hotel. Suddenly we heard running feet. A few young men came out of the shadows. One of them grabbed my purse but foolishly I refused to let go. Then someone stabbed me twice in the chest and I fell onto the pavement.
>
> Sensing danger, I shouted to Martica to not move, and I let go of my purse. The men grabbed the purse and then they all ran away. I lay still and I tried to determine how badly wounded I was. There was quite a bit of bleeding because

the two stabs had penetrated the breast but fortunately the knife had only struck two of my ribs. One of my collar bones was also broken but I felt it was not too dangerous. Martica helped me up and she began to cry. Mostly I tried to calm her down. It was not so bad but my blouse was red with blood.

At the hotel the tourists stood around with shocked faces. I remember Martica brought me some water. We then went to our rooms and I changed the bloody blouse. Soon after, we both went to the police and then took a taxi to the Aga Khan Hospital. I got a few stiches, a bandage and an X-ray. There was no damage to the lungs, so that made everybody happy. It turned out the surgeon who treated me had done some research in the Ulanga District about the incredibly high rate of epilepsy in the Highlands, especially in Mahenge. It became an interesting conversation for both of us.

After a few days I felt that I was slowly recovering. I did not feel anger towards the men, but instead felt a bit embarrassed that we had gone out on the street after dark. I had only thirty dollars in the purse and no important papers. As the wound was still very painful, we stayed in a game park until the next plane arrived about a week later. I wanted Martica to have some relaxation and fun. Martica returned with me to Africa a few times after that, but she was nervous about being in Dar. The purse was gone but it was easy for me to get a new one in Oslo, a better one, which I still have.

In 2005, during another visit to Mahenge, Martica made an important contribution to her mother's research by recording instances of the "head nodding" syndrome in the region. Later, Martica left the field of nursing and moved away to pursue writing and art. She has never been inclined to visit Colombia where she was born.

CHAPTER 8

The Work Continues

IN 1971, WHEN THE World Health Organization selected the new republic of Tanzania to participate in an initiative to establish mental health centres in developing countries, Louise was contacted and asked if she wished to relocate her clinic to Mahenge's hospital. It seemed at first to be a good plan, and so in 1972 the epilepsy clinic was officially placed under the auspices of the newly established Mental Health Centre of the Government Hospital at Mahenge to be staffed with one psychiatric nurse, who was designated to treat patients with either mental illness or epilepsy.

As it turned out, the move did not do as much for the epilepsy clinic as Louise had hoped it would. Only a small space was allocated for the clinic, so in fact the relocation was not a great improvement. She heard stories that the Government Hospital remained primitive, with no electricity and not much equipment. People used to report that they avoided going to the hospital because they were afraid of dying there. As she had expected, the new Mental Health Centre was inundated with an increasing number of epilepsy patients while the number of psychiatric patients remained small. Although basic medications were supposed to be supplied by the Tanzanian government,

Louise found it was necessary to supply the clinic's patients with medication through the help of her friend, Al Elliott, of the pharmaceutical company Elliott-Marion of Canada.

Although the lone nurse who had attended WHO-sponsored training courses for mentally ill patients had little training in the care of epilepsy patients, she cooperated in keeping the patients' files and reporting to Louise about the cases, as well as organizing supplies. Eventually, Louise's persistence gave rise to a semblance of progress: the epilepsy operations were accorded a dilapidated room within a warehouse outside the main hospital building.

At the Epilepsy International Symposium held in Vancouver in 1978, Louise's presentation with Wolfgang on *kifafa* and the factors accounting for its relatively high prevalence met with some renewed interest. This rekindled her hopes for the realization of a comprehensive treatment program for all sufferers from epilepsy in Africa.

In time, WHO staff at the new facility in Mahenge confirmed that an unexpectedly high percentage of patients suffered from epilepsy. The Danish International Development Agency (DANIDA) also came to that conclusion when surveying the effectiveness of the new mental health centres throughout Tanzania.

As a result of these WHO/DANIDA overviews, Louise's work at her clinic at Mahenge was "rediscovered" by Tanzania's two neurologists at the University of Dar es Salaam, Dr. Henry Rwiza and Dr. William Matuja.

Dr. Henry Rwiza had trained with Dr. Meinardi in Heemstede, who, as director of Epileptology at the Instituut voor Epilepsiebestrijding, in the Netherlands, had made Rwiza aware of Louise's little-known early scientific publications. In the summer of 1989, with the help of funds from the Netherlands, Dr. Rwiza undertook an epidemiological survey, incorporating significant information and data on convulsive disorders from the Mahenge clinic in the Ulanga District.

This "Rwiza survey" re-confirmed a predominant range of afflictions in most Ulanga District villages from eight to twenty epileptic patients per thousand. He also recorded in the same survey that some Wapogoro villages in the Mahenge Mountains had a remarkable prevalence rate of forty per thousand.

⌒

AS A RESULT OF the new research into epilepsy in Tanzania, and the rediscovery of Louise's earlier work at her clinic, she was invited in 1990 to head up a Tanzanian team, which would include Dr. Rwiza, to lay the groundwork for a more extensive Ulanga District field study into the etiology and clinical characteristics of *kifafa*. As she thought back to her earlier days in Mahenge, she realized with a shock that it would be almost thirty years since she had last been in Africa. This 1990 trip to Africa would be only the first of a number of such trips as she continued her research into *kifafa*.

During the week preceding her 1990 flight back to Tanzania, Louise did two interviews: one with the leading newspaper in Vancouver, and another with a radio station, and each time it distressed her to hear her own voice talking about herself. It felt too much like advertising. And she knew she was not good in interviews, especially when one was required to present oneself as cheerful and upbeat.

"You are going on a real expedition—and you are the leader!" someone had said to her gleefully. It was true, and she felt proud and excited. But she was already worried about how much support she might be able to gain from the many new people on the ground. For instance there was a new bishop, Bishop Iteka, someone she had never met. She had bought a gift for him, a beautiful candle in a candleholder, and she had decided she would look for a similar sort of gift during her stopover in Amsterdam for Father Mhasi, the new Father Superior in Mahenge.

Her medical colleagues in Vancouver said goodbye to her as if they were envious of her making an enjoyable escape from academic work, as if laying the groundwork for a detailed examination of the causes of *kifafa* might be some sort of holiday. On her way to the airport, Louise reminded herself that that she did not have to worry about Martica, that she would be leaving her daughter in good hands.

Wolfgang and Martica had developed their own relationship over the years, and she knew, at heart, he was a kind man. It might even be good for them to fend for themselves.

As the Vancouver airport terminal came into view, the simple act of feeling her passport in her hand filled her with exuberance. On the tarmac, as the pilot waited for permission to take-off, Louise wrote the date in her otherwise blank journal. Tuesday, January 16, 1990. It was beautiful and cold when she landed in Amsterdam. At a Dutch epilepsy clinic, she met a physician who had once met Dr. Rwiza at an epilepsy conference. Louise was glad to hear he was a gentle person, not at all pushy.

Finally, on a Thursday, she saw the sun rise in all its glory over Africa. Looking down from the plane's window, she saw majestic Mount Kilimanjaro with its rounded dome below. Her fellow passengers were mostly tourists bound for Serengeti safaris, "roughing it" for an astronomical price in order to take photos. She already knew she would see more wildlife for one-quarter of the cost in the less-visited national parks at Mikumi or Ruaha.

At the Dar airport, a large African with sunglasses was holding a sign saying "Dr. Jilek." She happily pointed at herself and smiled. This was Dr. Rwiza. He talked to a customs official and easily arranged for her baggage to be hurried through without being checked. At first, his English was hard to follow, but finally she understood that he was simply telling her that his car was waiting. By asking him polite questions, she soon learned that he and his wife had six children, and that he was by no means living a luxurious life. He earned $70 per month. His wife earned $30 per month as a nurse. She supplemented the family income by making and selling ice cream.

By North American standards, her hotel room at the Oyster Bay Hotel was cheap, only $31 per night with breakfast, but she would have preferred somewhere less ostentatious. When she told Dr. Rwiza where she was staying while on the way to the hospital, he replied that he had never heard of it. Clearly it was not a hotel that he and his friends could afford to stay at. When they arrived and went into the

Muhimbili Hospital, where Dr. Rwiza worked as one of the country's foremost physicians, Louise thought the building looked more like an abandoned factory. It seemed that crowds of people were seated everywhere, sick and bandaged, in casts, or on improvised chairs, waiting for treatment. Far too many people had a resigned, pleading, sick look. The air was uncomfortably sticky and everyone seemed to be sweating profusely.

Everywhere they went, people approached Dr. Rwiza and asked him for something. It was impossible to maintain a conversation with him over the din. Finally, they went to his office where the walls were filthy, especially around the doors. Files were stored in cartons. Louise found the overall atmosphere to be oppressively grim, but Dr. Rwiza seemed impervious to it all. When they were taken to the Dean of Medicine's office to meet him, she saw that at least it had a comfortable feeling. When the Dean entered and saw her, he appeared incredulous. "Are *you* the same doctor who wrote about *kifafa* in Mahenge?" he asked. "I expected to meet a grey-haired old lady!" Laughter lifted everyone's spirits. But in fact little was done about their new research project on *kifafa*.

A few days later, Dr. Matuja, her other main medical expert, arrived at her hotel to fetch her in his car to take her to St. Joseph's Cathedral to meet the Bishop. As they drove along, she was able to compare Dar es Salaam, past and present. Mostly the homes and schools were terribly rundown; only the sturdy, German-built structures held sway. Cars were old, clanky, battered. There were a lot more of them and the government had not kept pace. The city had only a few traffic lights, and the streets were choked with cars and full of potholes. Dust mingled with exhaust so it was often hard to breathe and there were large heaps of garbage everywhere.

She noticed that the streets were crowded with boys and men doing nothing, just waiting. For what? Crippled polio victims crawled in the dirt. Women walked slowly, as if asleep. It struck her that these women were dressed in old cast-off European clothes. Only a few were still wearing the traditional *kangas*. Louise saw a few old men outside on the sidewalks, still treading their old Singer sewing machines. She asked Dr. Matuja why she did not see any Indian families outside, having picnics with their families, as had been the custom thirty years ago. "Now the people are too afraid of robberies," he said.

When they arrived at the cathedral, and were made to wait to see the Bishop, nobody came and offered them a glass of water or a drink, as had been the custom in the past. Such discourtesy would have been unthinkable in the old days. When Bishop Iteka deigned to appear, refreshed after his afternoon shower and nap, he was polite and seemingly interested but again no refreshment was offered. Louise was close to fainting in the heat, but she could not bring herself to ask for anything. The Bishop said he had heard of her and they briefly discussed her research before the Bishop indicated that he must leave.

On the surface, not much appeared to have been accomplished by the visit, but they knew it was necessary to ask permission of the Bishop in order to do anything new, such as the research she wanted to do on *kifafa*. If her work went well, the church or the government officials could take credit, but there would be limited support until success was certain. At least the Bishop had offered some assistance with transport. That could be viewed as a victory of sorts. Afterward, she and Dr. Matuja laughed about their dry mouths.

It was clearly time to set out on a tour of the surrounding hospitals to learn what had been done with the epilepsy patients in the time she had been away. On the following Saturday, she was picked up in a Land Rover from the hospital, along with Dr. Rwiza, at half-past eight, much later than planned. They would be travelling in the heat of the day.

They stopped only briefly at Morogoro to pick up Sister Regina, a nurse. By this time it was already so hot that Dr. Rwiza feared Louise was going to faint. Fortunately, someone had brought some biscuits and that seemed to help, dry as they were.

Passing through Mikumi National Park around 3 p.m., she saw countless elephants, giraffes, impalas, baboons and zebras. These creatures no longer existed in any appreciable numbers beyond the parks. The road from Mikumi was as bad as ever, possibly worse, but she was smiling the whole way because she remembered everything. At least in the countryside, everything was wonderfully the same. She hoped that Dar es Salaam was an aberration. They endured a full day on the road, without any stop for food, until they arrived at Ifakara at 8 p.m. Ifakara was where she had been sent by Geigy many years earlier to experiment on drugs to counteract amoebic dysentery. Waking up on Sunday morning, she felt cheerful and expectant. At the church and at the Father's House at Ifakara, she recognized some of the priests and required fewer introductions. She enjoyed telling them about how they were setting out on the initial leg of her plan for research into epilepsy.

The next morning they left again in the Land Rover and ascended into the mountains where they finally reached Mahenge. She thought the town looked dirtier and more crowded than before. Or had she just imagined it was better before? No, there was no doubt that the little Mahenge hospital was severely rundown. Worse, the adjunct epilepsy clinic was a ramshackle mess. She was relieved to learn there was no room to stay at the dirty guest houses. She suggested driving to nearby Kwiro, where her clinic had originated, but it, too, was like a bad dream. Everything appeared shabby, rundown. All the nuns were Africans; the lone Capuchin priest didn't know her either.

Fortunately, the Bishop had preceded them that very morning and had instructed the Father Superior, who was African, to give them rooms in the Father's big building at Kwiro. Perhaps she had under-estimated this Bishop? Perhaps her research project was going to be taken seriously? That was what she cared about most. They were given lots of clear water to drink and fed a fine lunch that lifted her spirits.

Now, the main hurdle was establishing her credibility as an expedition leader. Things had greatly changed in Tanzania and she was clearly out of touch. Surely Dr. Rwiza could see she was ill at ease. That afternoon, as she sipped her tea in a roadside restaurant, next to a smelly tire garage, Dr. Rwiza told her that the epilepsy clinic had never been properly taken over by the government, as she had been led to believe. Most of her patients had just scattered. She did her best to hide her irritation. Dr. Rwiza had waited all this time to let her know of the rundown conditions. Some of the epileptic patients had tried to come to the Mahenge hospital for their phenobarbital, but no medications were available. What had happened to the funding she had sent? Dr. Rwiza had no idea.

At the Kwiro hospital itself, they waited half an hour for someone to find a key to open the mental health nursing office—to no avail. Father Superior told her that the only person he knew who had been affiliated with her clinic, and who had worked directly with the *kifafa* patients, was Sister Anastasia, who now owned and operated her own orphanage. Louise remembered her well and decided that they must go immediately and search her out.

At first, Louise mistrusted the instructions to find the orphanage because the road was so bad. It was an overgrown track and it appeared no vehicle had used it for years. When they finally came upon a gaily painted house, with flowers in pots, it came as a surprise to her. Eventually an elderly woman appeared with an alarmed expression, as if she were apprehensive about being inspected by someone from the government. Who else could possibly want to pay her a visit?

But as soon as Louise opened the door of the Land Rover and stood before her, Sister Anastasia was delighted and gave her a big hug. Tears of recognition and relief rolled down her cheeks. The aged nun ushered them inside. On the bare floors they saw about twenty-five sad-looking and silent children, ranging in ages from infants to about six years old. Sister Anastasia explained she had barely enough money to buy milk for the babies. The Father at Kwiro had helped for a time in supplying milk, but after Brother Mathias left, there was nobody who knew how to look after the cows.

All the orphans looked thin and undernourished. None of them moved or babbled happily as normal children would. Some of them had swollen feet. Others had swollen bellies. Clearly, they were close to starving. Louise took out 200 shillings and gave them immediately to Sister Anastasia. She said she wished she could give more.

Sister Regina gave a few shillings. Dr. Rwiza had tears in his eyes. Even with a doctor's salary he did not earn enough to offer anything. Sister Anastasia praised God and laughed. The depth of her gratitude disturbed all three visitors. In the end it was a good visit but there was clearly no information to be gained about what had happened with the epileptic patients.

Afterwards, at the Sunday-night dinner table, Father Superior asked her if she had noticed much progress in thirty years. Remembering how Kwiro had once been a happy place, festooned with flowers, she crafted a diplomatic response. "It's much the same as I remember it," she said. On Monday, as they prepared to set out, it was apparent that their government car needed to have a tire replaced. They were able to obtain a different government vehicle but this one needed diesel. They went to the government garage for fuel but everyone just stood around, seemingly for no reason. Dr. Rwiza whispered to her, "If you have a government car and you want it repaired, just forget it. When you take it to them, they will tell you your parts are broken and they do not have any spare parts. Then while you are waiting, they will take out the parts and hide them or perhaps sell them. A few days later you will pay to have the same parts put back in."

As it turned out, however, they were not made to wait unduly, and they were able to fill up with diesel. On Tuesday they drove on to the Ulanga Plain towards Ngombe for a short visit to a small health centre. When they arrived at the building, Dr. Rwiza looked at a few files but found little of interest. They then drove to Chirombola where, in another small dispensary, he was able to find files for seventeen patients with *kifafa*. The orderly stood at his shoulder, sweating and nervous, but he had kept the records well. It was much more promising, and they left in high spirits as they drove to Ruaha, a mission station south of Mahenge.

Ruaha was in fact their chief destination. There they were expecting to find Sister Sieglinda, who had written to Louise saying she had looked after 140 people with epilepsy. Once they arrived, there was a lengthy delay, and then a sullen dresser appeared and told them Sister

Sieglinda had left two years ago. The dresser could not tell them anything about epileptic patients, and he didn't know where Sister Sieglinda had gone. The dresser also didn't know how Sister Sieglinda had obtained medications for *kifafa*. A Swiss Capuchin Father appeared but he, too, had no information even though he had arrived in Ruaha sixteen years ago. He had never heard of Louise.

She spoke to this Father in German, mentioning it was midday and that they hoped to find some lunch. He replied in English, "I'm sorry, lunch has already been served." Nevertheless, with a little persuasion, some bread and tea were found to tide them over. They left Ruaha to return to Kwiro only to discover the road was blocked because a truck had skidded at a turn and was now lying on its side. They would have to wait for at least two hours in the blazing sun. In the middle of the repair work, all the men sat down to eat. A tractor pulling a load of stones could not pass either. It was a traffic jam in the middle of nowhere.

After considerable negotiations, it was agreed that the driver of the tractor would allow the men with the truck to unload most of his stones to build a firm track for the extraction of the stranded truck. By the time everyone was allowed to again be on their way, Louise welcomed the thunder and lightning in the mountains where the air was much cooler.

By the end of the day they had successfully commandeered files for about fifty more epilepsy patients—and so the research had commenced. The following morning, Sister Regina was ill and thought it might be her malaria again. Louise provided medication and suggested she should not accompany them any further. Sister Regina, however, insisted on being included. After a delay replacing a tire, they were rewarded when they reached Igota. A mental health worker in the dispensary there knew nine people with epilepsy and could provide files for all of them. Dr. Rwiza was joining with Louise to examine the files closely for accuracy, when suddenly a wet splash of bat droppings fell on his glasses. Without missing a beat, he said, "There is a local saying that bat shit always brings good luck." Louise didn't know if he was joking or not, but his equanimity impressed her.

The health-care worker at the next health station had not kept thorough records, and so it was a wasted visit. When their driver suddenly announced that he must go to Ifakara for diesel as there was not enough fuel to return to Dar, it was decided Sister Regina would go with him to ensure he came back. Louise and Dr. Rwiza proceeded to visit various people in the outlying areas, searching for more patients, but without success. She felt foolish constantly having to fan herself in the extreme heat. She could not remember ever doing so in the 1960s. Even when they returned to the health centre, she could not cool off.

When Sister Regina returned with the driver and car, she brought back three dried fish with freshly baked bread for a feast. There was even fresh tea for Louise and warm beer for the men. They felt emboldened to visit two more of the outlying clinics, driving all the way to Mtimbira, several hours away in the Ulanga district. At Mtimbira, Louise dreaded the notion of staying in the pokey, hot hotel overnight. Their clothes were already drenched in sweat. Fortunately, there were not enough rooms. Only four were vacant, not five. Dr. Rwiza suggested asking the mission if they had a room for Dr. Jilek—as he still called her—and they all agreed that was a good plan. The Father at the mission happily consented to offer her a clean room. She knew she would be fed at the mission. Even better, there was a shower.

That evening was like old times. She sat around talking with the Father, who had been accommodating and friendly, and a Swiss Brother who looked like someone out of a Raphael painting. There was also another young man whose name she did not catch. They were all drinking bottles of Fanta pop. Louise and the congenial priests talked well into the night. Afterwards, they all went outside and looked at the stars.

On Thursday morning, Louise treated herself to another shower and attended a church service. The congregation was sparse. Where were all the mothers with their little babies on their backs? Only one woman sang. Later, when she joined up with Dr. Rwiza, he told her that the hotel had been rife with mosquitoes. She changed the subject, suggesting that children were better dressed than she remembered. His response surprised her. "That one nice dress will be all they have," he said. "There's practically no money here because there are so few jobs. The good thing about that is that there are hardly any alcoholics. There is no beer or other alcohol available except for what the people make for themselves. They make it from bamboo juice."

The team then visited another small clinic where the nursing assistants had not made any effort to find out why the patients had stopped coming for their monthly appointments. The staff had also failed to understand the importance of maintaining records for research purposes. Nerves were frazzled. Dr. Rwiza grew impatient. At one point he turned to Sister Regina, accusingly, "You should have supervised the helpers." Sister Regina was indignant: "It is so far away. I have no transportation."

When Dr. Rwiza went to talk to the village elders, someone gave him a live chicken. Should they keep it in the trunk, where it might suffocate? It became a problem because the gift could not be refused. Later that afternoon, en route to the Lupiro mission, the car became stuck in the mud. When they got out to have a look, they found that the car had careened sideways and was half in the ditch. Who was at fault? The careless driver? Or the leader of the expedition who knew full well it was dangerous to drive as night was approaching and when little could be done if a mishap occurred on the road?

Fortunately, the driver was able to put the car into four-wheel drive and slowly extricate it from the mud. But then he was unable to get the vehicle out of four-wheel drive. Consequently, he claimed that they had to drive very slowly the rest of the way. At Lupiro, where Dr. Rwiza admitted for the first time that he, too, was exhausted, they discovered there was no accommodation. Louise hastily devised a plan to proceed to Igota, and they set off on the bumpy road that she thought she remembered was the right one.

Eventually she recognized that they were on the right road to the mission. The Father's house was new but the church appeared to be much the same. And there was her old dispensary! And there was the place where she used to sleep! Igota was the first place where she had branched out on her own, the first place she was independent after Ifakara, before she had treated the epilepsy patients at Kwiro. She felt she was finally returning to the very place where her relationship with Africa had taken hold.

The African Father welcomed them and said the Bishop was expected to arrive soon. But when the Bishop did not arrive, as predicted, it was decided that the others should drive to the Kifuko River so they would not miss the last ferry to Ifakara, a place where they knew the men could sleep comfortably before making their way back to Dar. Or should they try to intercept the Bishop at some point? If every day was going to be this frustrating, Louise worried her nerves would be too frayed to continue. Ultimately, she decided to resist her impractical temptation to stay in Igota, even though this detour felt like the homecoming she craved, and instead proceed with the others back to Ifakara.

The driver was nervous about proceeding in the dark so they would have to drive painfully slowly. But this way, if they left Ifakara early the following morning, Dr. Rwiza would be able to reach his family in Dar es Salaam as quickly as possible. Not long after she was reconciled to this approach, the headlights of their car illuminated a white vehicle coming towards them. The Bishop! Louise was much relieved to find him courteous when they urged him to stop. The Bishop obligingly suggested Louise and Sister Regina could transfer their belongings to his vehicle and travel with him; the men could proceed to catch the last ferry across the river in order to reach Ifakara by midnight.

Everyone quickly agreed to re-gift the chicken to the Bishop as an acknowledgement of his generosity. Once underway, Louise found that the Bishop's driver went much faster than their previous driver. She noticed, however, that it was difficult to have any conversation with the Bishop as he was sitting in the front seat. Moreover, he did not seem to be feeling well. Later, the Father at Igota told her the

Bishop had only recently returned from a two-month stay in England for his health; he had nearly died from a combination of diabetes and alcoholism.

The next thirteen days, based at Kwiro, were very much easier for Louise. When she was not making more field trips, she spent countless happy hours in her comfortable room in the Father's house, preparing the medical records for the *kifafa* patients that they had discovered on the trip. She did not resent the paperwork. On the contrary, such careful reckoning was the primary reason for her trip. Her aim was nothing less than to determine once and for all why the rate of epilepsy in eastern Tanzania, in the Mahenge Mountains and the Ulanga Plain, was ten times higher than the world norm.

Father Mhasi at Kwiro was appreciative of her hard work. It was an honour for him, he said, to play host to a North American doctor who was also a psychiatrist. He had never known a real psychiatrist before. When he told her that he found the people of Mahenge were lazy, she made no comment, knowing he was speaking from a European viewpoint. "There are times when I want to take a whip and force them to work," he said. To this sort of threat, she thought it better just to nod. In his defence, she remembered that unlike many of the Fathers, he was quite industrious, growing vegetables and keeping cows and goats.

The most extraordinary member of the compound was the Dutch Father, Theogonius, a self-appointed archivist. When she went to him to learn if the diocese had any records regarding epilepsy, he told her how difficult it was to bring some order to the mess he had inherited. He confided that the African priests had no appreciation for his work. For starters, they could not read German—as he could. "When I think of all the letters and documents that have been thrown out over the decades . . . ," he said. It was so appalling he could not finish the sentence. "Nowadays the Africans would prefer to falsify history, but when you properly compile the records, it's astounding how much work those early Capuchin Fathers did." She nodded. That much was true.

Wolfgang Jilek (left) accompanied Louise upon her return to Mahenge in 1963.
After Tanganyika had become independent, Tanganyika and Zanzibar
were united to create Tanzania in 1964.

Maasai men were intimidating as medical patients, usually demanding to be
treated before everyone else who was already waiting. An encounter
at the roadside was not to be welcomed either.

During his travels around the world, Wolfgang Jilek took many photographs
including this one in the Ulanga District of Tanzania.

This medicine man helped Louise gather bark that was dried on Archbishop Maranta's rooftop before it was tested for medicinal benefits in Switzerland.

With their Norwegian and Austrian mothers beside them, Louise and Wolfgang were first married in Vienna, with a follow-up ceremony in Oslo.

Having re-written their medical exams for accreditation in Canada in 1964, Louise and Wolfgang received their diplomas as transcultural psychiatrists at McGill University. Also, in Quebec, Louise published the first scientific paper in medical history to identify the "head nodding" syndrome that occurs in children who later develop epileptic seizures.

Louise with her daughter Martica Jilek, who soon became
an experienced world traveller with her parents.

Family friends included Holocaust survivor and author Victor Frankl (left).

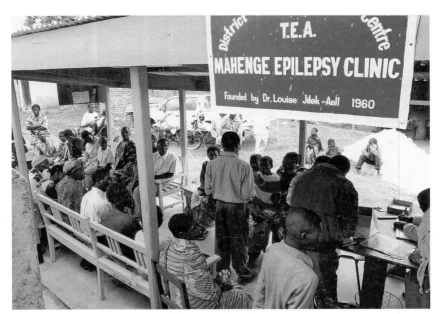

Louise first treated people with epilepsy in 1959, in the nearby Kwiro Mission, before opening this permanent clinic at Mahenge in 1960. Photo from 2003.

Father Placid Kindata has been instrumental in helping to oversee rehabilitation programs whereby patients with epilepsy hope to become self-supporting agricultural workers.

Fundraiser Nancy Morrison (right) with Nurse Kibiriti and Louise in 2009.

Earth to Earth

Africa, dark and mysterious mother of man.
The rain is the tears of her pain.
It was meant to give life to plants, and to flowers perfume.
and now it has to wash away the stench of death
as thousands of children, women and men
flee through the forest for shelter and food in vain,
as they sink into her warm and muddy embrace
and their wounded and tired limbs find rest
and peace spreads into their troubled minds.
They hear mother's voice whisper in the rain:
From Earth did thou come
and to Earth shall thou return again.

—Louise Aall

Louise and Wolfgang, at home in Tsawwassen, British Columbia, in 2016.

Father Placid instructs agricultural workers in the rehabilitation program at the Kasita parish during a visit to Tanzania by biographer Alan Twigg in 2017.

Medison Manyuka, Pius Magwira and Theresia Mlungamo worked within the rehabilitation program for people with epilepsy at Kasita Seminary in 2016.

Nurse Kibiriti, novice priest Peter Mlimakifu, fundraiser Ken Morrison (Provision Group) and Dr. Dan Bhwana, the new clinic director, in 2018.

ALAN TWIGG

JULIANA SHINNICK

With the help of Louise's clinic, hope abides for the people of Mahenge.

Father Theogonius was not able to find any references to cases of *kifafa* in his archives but he did discover that Sister Valentina had died at Kwiro in 1967. After that, he assumed the treatment of epilepsy patients would likely have deteriorated. He believed that African nuns and dispensary workers simply did not wish to care for chronically ill patients, especially for those with leprosy or epilepsy. When she failed to nod in agreement, to prove his point, he told her that when the Baldegg Sisters had left their leprosy and epilepsy colony at Ifakara in order to return to Europe for six months, all the African nuns had refused to treat the patients. The mission at Ifakara had had to ask a retired Swiss nun to help out until the Baldegg Sisters returned.

This time it was easier for Louise to nod than say nothing. Years in Africa had taught her an instinctive diplomacy. Her silence seemed to embolden Father Theogonius. He stood and walked in circles as he talked. He was self-fixated, almost comical, but he did possess an undeniable historical perspective. "The mission went through difficult times in the seventies," he said. "That's when many of the Africans wanted us all to leave. Many missionaries became so discouraged they did go. But now the government has asked us to take over the schools again."

Once, when she went over to the Bishop's house, and there didn't seem to be anyone around, she heard someone mumbling from one of the rooms. The door was open. She could hear someone moving around and counting gleefully: "56-57-58. . . ." It turned out to be Father Theogonius holding a fly-swatter. He proudly showed her a container holding 60 cockroaches. "Look, I've got 60 of them! Our chicken loves them." He also had a system of traps, and when he tried to drown the captured roaches in a bucket of water, some refused to die so he had to crush them. The cockroaches were his particular enemies because they liked to munch on his precious storehouse of papers and books.

Their meals in Kwiro were generally solemn affairs. Little was said at the table with the priests. Louise always took care not to take too much food. The drab menu never varied: a heap of rice and a sauce with very little meat, followed by bananas afterwards. Often there would be little left for latecomers.

Louise had been given two people to help her put the files in order at Kwiro. Nurse Calista requested 1,000 shillings per week. The other assistant, Mr. Kaaya, said he had a salary so he didn't need to be paid. She decided to pay him anyway, just to be fair. Nurse Calista advised her that Mama Choma probably knew the most about epilepsy patients, so naturally Louise asked why Mama Choma had not been assigned to work with her. It turned out that Mama Choma was the new name for a nun formerly called Sister Anunciata. Nobody wanted to explain to Louise why this was so, although it did not take long to deduce that Sister Anunciata had become pregnant and had to leave the order.

Louise also heard that the last priest at Luhombero, Father Damian, had been a thief. Rumour had it that he had stolen almost everything when he left after many years—the furniture, the sheets, everything—but having visited that parish thirty years before, Louise was less hasty to condemn Father Damian. Priests in faraway and poor parishes had almost no income and had to cope with depression and loneliness. Perhaps this Father Damian *was* a bit of a rascal, but she had visited remote priests and could appreciate their underlying despair and bitterness.

Nurse Calista escorted her to one new dispensary, where she was pleased to meet a nun who knew about her work. Just as quickly Louise was disheartened when the old nun told her they no longer treated epilepsy. "The people cannot understand why no more medicine was sent," she said. "Many died. Some people think that Mama Doctor probably forgot about them because she got married." In fact, she had worked continuously to coordinate the medical supply line. It sickened her to know that some of her former patients could have felt a sense of betrayal.

So many people had disappeared or died unnecessarily! With Dr. Rwiza, Louise had managed to gather documentation for only some two hundred former patients. For those she knew or whose names she recognized, she placed a little tick on the upper right-hand corner of their cards. It wouldn't mean anything to anyone else who sifted through the two hundred or so cards but she felt the little tick added humanity to the numbers: August Bondero, Maria Habedi, Josefina Marazina, Natalie Lukas, Emanuel Petri, and so it went on.

She was thrilled to meet Emanuel Petri and see that he had completely recovered from his epilepsy—so much so that he had been able to marry a girl from a non-*kifafa* family. They had four healthy children. When he saw her, he exclaimed, as if seeing an angel, "*Mama Yangu, nina furaha sana, mimi mzima kabisa, asante mama* (My mother, I am so very glad, I am so happy, thank you, Mama)." He was so overcome with gratitude he did not know how to contain himself. He looked at first as if he were going to embrace her, but then it was clear that he did not dare do so. Instead, he seized her hand in both of his and would not let go. His shining eyes sparkled with moisture and he continued to say, "Mama Yangu." She pointed to a chair. He sat there but he would not let go of her hand for a long time.

Justa Sirili had also made a full recovery. She had nine children who were all well. But Louise's heart fell when she saw Edward Mahengo. Sitting in rags, he looked deeply depressed. He told her in a low voice that he suffered an attack every day. He did not have any burns because he knew when an attack was coming: his heart started to beat faster. But during an attack he was continually hurting himself, writhing on the ground with nobody to help him. After each attack he had a bad headache. Everyone said he was very industrious, working hard every day, planting, but he remained an outcast.

Knowing Edward's health and living situation had remained the same for decades was all the more reason to one day start a rehabilitation program for patients, who could be gainfully employed. In the interim, she could only give Edward some money to buy a few new clothes. She had no access to medicine on this trip.

It pained her to hear accusations from some of the nuns that African nurses and dressers were stealing medicines, as well as syringes and mosquito nets. "When a box of medicines comes to the Mahenge

Hospital," she was told by one hospital worker, in a whisper, "it is all gone in a few days. It cannot possibly be used up in that time because I do the distribution." Selling medicines on the black market was inevitable when an African physician was being paid so little.

Many doctors had to work in their own fields to supply their families with sufficient food. After his holiday, one surgeon returned to work only to be unable to operate because his hands were so blistered from farming. Another was accidentally killed by lightning while working in his field. Or so she was told. As stealing spread, there was growing resentment towards the strictness of the European nuns and priests who forbade it.

One of the priests, Brother Edwin, told Louise—speaking in German so nobody else could understand—that he feared the Baldegg Sisters in Ifakara might soon have to leave for their own safety. Brother Edwin told her about Old Father Coelestin who had been murdered in Ifakara the year before. Father Coelestin was one of the first missionaries to come to Ifakara. "Some friends of his had been visiting from Switzerland," Brother Edwin said. "We had all been drinking beer and joking until late at night. After he went to sleep, men broke through his window. They slashed him on the head with machetes.

"They were looking for something to steal in his house. They couldn't find any money so they took his old typewriter. When I went to him in the morning as usual, he was half-conscious with his face covered in blood. We took him to the hospital. People were crying because they loved him so much. Although his skull had been cut open and he seemed to be recovering, the wound became infected at the hospital and he died. The men who had attacked him were arrested, but they had to be set free because there were no witnesses."

Some days later, Bishop Iteka paid a personal visit to Mama Doctor to thank her sincerely for giving him a donation, a gift of money with no strings attached. "I will write you a receipt," he promised. "I will help with your project as much as I can." She gratefully accepted his offer to use the services of his driver, Peter Epondawill, to take her to Tabora and other villages.

⌒

THE MORE LOUISE PERSISTED with her investigations with Nurse Calista and Mama Choma, who had finally been assigned to her, the more she was forced to realize the extent to which the scourge of epilepsy had been superseded by the scourge of HIV and AIDS. It was not an easy subject to discuss. When Sister Maria-Paula made fun of a cleaning woman at the hospital who was wearing two pairs of gloves, Louise was obliged to interject. "You cannot be too cautious when you are handling an AIDS patient," she explained.

Both the nuns and the African people in general believed the disease had emanated from laboratory experiments in the United States, either from some virus or experiments that had gone wrong. It was believed that young, rural Tanzanians were especially susceptible because they had less immunity. There were pamphlets that warned people not to have anything to do with foreigners, especially tourists. In fact, it is now generally accepted that the HIV virus spread from Africa, from chimpanzees in the Congo.

Few people came for testing, so anytime there was a severe accident, it led to the serious risk on the part of the nurses of contracting HIV from a patient's blood. One physician told her that the number of cases of AIDS was rising, and yet most of the hospital staff were thoughtless when handling possibly infected objects. The physician feared that expat doctors like himself would increasingly decide not to come to East Africa— or else decide to cut short their stays, as he planned to do—due to the danger of contracting HIV.

⌒

A HAPPY MOMENT FOR Louise occurred when she had left Kwiro to cash some traveller's cheques at the bank in Mahenge, and she no longer had to think of either *kifafa* or AIDS. The bank was in one of the old German buildings. The young bank manager was very nervous, not sure how to manage the conversion of currencies. For twenty minutes Louise waited for assistants to tally the figures. Then the manager called on another female assistant to check over the calculations with an automated counting device. When she determined that the first figures were incorrect, the bank director began sweating nervously. Meanwhile Louise did her best to appear good-hearted and relaxed, as if this was all normal. Any sign of bristling impatience would only succeed in prolonging the drama.

"I think I remember you," the bank manager finally said. The man was about forty years old. Perhaps he was confusing her with some other woman. "Were you the lady doctor who came to our school at Ruaha many years ago?" Indeed. She had stayed for weeks at a mission school near Igota during a major outbreak of schistosomiasis, one of the most common parasitic diseases in Africa, which affects the liver, kidneys and bladder.

It was one of the most stressful situations she had ever faced because, while treating boys for schistosomiasis, they came to her dispensary in increasing numbers complaining of nausea, headaches and "pain all over." The whites of their eyes had taken on a yellowish colour. It looked to her as though the boys were suffering from infectious hepatitis. The fate of the entire school population had been in her hands. It was the most frightening and prolonged crisis she had ever faced—alone—throughout her medical career.

"I was in grade one," the bank manager continued. There was a gentler tone to his voice now. "My goodness," she said, smiling, as the banking transaction was quickly resolved. "You certainly didn't know then that one day you would grow up and be a bank manager!" "No, that is very true," he said with a proud smile. She had the money in her hand at last. With difficulty she rose from her straight-backed chair. He followed her politely to the door. "I hope you will come and see us again," he said. It was such moments that made it all seem worthwhile to Louise.

Before leaving the Ulanga district, Louise arranged for a feast at Mama Choma's place. She went to the market and bought smoked fish and chickens. With a borrowed camera she took two photos of some of the people selling vegetables, and several people became very angry. Accustomed to taking photos of her patients for scientific reasons, she had forgotten she was in a public place.

The feast was a success but the incident in the market was upsetting her somewhat, and Louise decided to go for a final walk in the moonlight. When one of the senior nuns, Sister Maria-Paula, asked if she could join her, Louise was not anticipating that the Sister would open her heart to her.

"Now that we are old and ugly," said Sister Maria-Paula as they were walking in the coolness of the night, "people don't want us anymore. All the years and strength we gave to help these people don't seem to count for much. Nobody remembers. Now we are just a bunch of frightened old women.

"We have nobody to talk to. Father seldom comes to ask us how we are doing, not since Father Coelestin was murdered. We are too afraid to protest when people steal the medicines. We fear for our lives because we have not much protection. When patients die because we have no medicines, and we know their lives could have been saved, we feel so terribly guilty. And now one of my dearest young helpers, a young African nurse, has killed herself because she was pregnant from one of our African priests. He denied he was the father. I had warned the girl that this was likely to happen.

"Excuse me for talking so much. I have nobody to talk to and I feel so depressed. Please tell me, Doctor, do you think I should give up and tell the superiors that I am sick and must be sent home?" Louise hesitated. She knew how difficult it could be for these independent nuns to return to conventional service in Europe where they must suddenly accept subordination in a home monastery. How many, she wondered, might look back on Africa with nostalgia and longing?

Louise inquired after her health. Learning it was fine, she spoke slowly, asking the Sister to remember that in Europe it had taken many, many centuries before present-day Western values and practices could take hold, and that here in Africa the work was just beginning. The seeds she had sown with her relentless work and sweat, and sometimes tears, could not be underestimated.

Asking herself what Dr. Schweitzer would have told the Sister, Louise suggested hesitantly: "You can be content knowing you have brought the message of compassion and love to Africa." Louise could see that Sister Maria-Paula left relieved. Nevertheless, Louise inherited her unease. Would there be someone someday to comfort her in the same way? Her love affair with Africa was a lifelong commitment—a passion—and she had to wonder if, like Sister Maria-Paula, it would be the most important relationship she would ever have. It was certainly the longest.

As suggested by Wolfgang in a letter, to culminate her visit, Louise invited the major medical professionals in Dar es Salaam to bring their wives to a dinner, at her expense, at the Oyster Bay Hotel. The ladies were beautifully dressed and laughed among themselves about getting a whole chicken each for dinner. The men became high-spirited. The Dean of Medicine admitted he had once served a prison term for earning some extra money treating private patients. Despite the recent death of a friend, Dr. Matuja overcame his low spirits, even though he was terribly worried that he now felt obliged to help look after his friend's family financially.

At the head table, Louise was seated beside Dr. Rwiza's wife. Facing her was Dr. Rwiza and the Dean of Medicine. Someone told a story about a colleague who was keeping a cow to earn a little extra. He was paying a man a few shillings to look after it. The man took a bucket to wash the cow with insecticide. The phone rang. The man ran to take the call. The cow was thirsty. The cow drank the suds. By the time the colleague visited his cow, it had died. The colleague was so distressed he could not work for three days. The colleague fired the man. They all laughed. Everyone was cheered to hear this story. Nobody died except a cow!

Strategically, the dinner was a success. The Dean promised Dr. Rwiza he could have computer access to tabulate the findings of their collective research, and her work could continue. Once more, she had overcome the odds and endured paltry meals, exhausting heat, stressful journeys and primitive accommodations. She had allowed the Fathers to feel they were in control, whenever necessary. Now, with the data on epileptic patients, Louise could proceed with a major application to do further international research to fulfill her professional and moral goals.

As everyone thanked her for their splendid meal, Louise couldn't escape the feeling that the banquet at the needlessly posh hotel only made the sufferings of others seem more acute. As the evening drew to a close, and most of the guests had left, Louise excused herself and found a balcony that afforded a clear view of the Indian Ocean. As she listened to the beckoning lull of the eternal waves and smelled the salty sea air, it struck her, in a moment of sadness, that she had not given herself an opportunity to go for a swim in the Indian Ocean.

With all this work on epilepsy, it is amazing that at this time she was able to write and have published her second book, *Working with Dr. Schweitzer: Sharing his Reverence for Life* (1990). It was based on her journal and drawings that she had made in 1961 while working with Dr. Schweitzer. It was once again published by Hancock House. The publisher no longer has the volume in print but it can be found second-hand on Amazon.ca from third-party sellers.

IT IS INTERESTING TO RECALL that Louise's clinic—first at Kwiro, then at Kasita, then permanently at Mahenge—remains the only such facility in East Africa. After touring the Ulanga District in January and February of 1990, Louise went on to coordinate epilepsy treatments for approximately 400 patients who were supplied phenobarbital or phenytoin. Without her direct subsidization of money for the medicines, the clinic could not function effectively, so in December of 1990, she appealed to the Vancouver Neurological Centre at Vancouver General Hospital for help. She wrote: "Because the Tanzanian Ministry of Health is not yet prepared to make adequate budgetary provision for the treatment of these patients, and, of course, the poverty-stricken people themselves are unable to pay for the medicines, we will have to rely on donations for some time to come." Only a small grant was forthcoming from the Vancouver hospital at the time.

She later persuaded her African colleagues, chiefly Dr. Matuja, to co-found with her the Tanzania Epilepsy Association as an official organization both to accept donations and to supervise distribution of donated medications. Under her guidance, the Mahenge Epilepsy Society was formed as a branch of the Tanzania Epilepsy Association.

With her files, Louise could now supply documentation to verify that about 75 percent of some two hundred patients who had received regular treatments over a ten-year period had become free of seizures or had improved greatly, mainly due to the provision of phenobarbital. Also in 1990, a World Health Organization publication called "Initiative of Support to People with Epilepsy" mirrored her earlier findings: "It has also been shown repeatedly that phenobarbital alone — a low cost drug — can satisfactorily control seizures in about 75 percent of the cases. In the remaining cases alternative drugs will have to be used."

Following her consultations with Dr. Rwiza and others, Louise submitted a proposal to the International Development Research Centre (IDRC) in Ottawa to combine researchers from the University of British Columbia and the University of Dar es Salaam to undertake field trips during 1991 to 1994 to investigate the etiology and clinical characteristics and high prevalence of convulsive disorders among the rural people in the Ulanga District. In August of 1991, she received news that almost $300,000 would be made available over a three-year period. This research work would formally include the first internationally sanctioned investigation of the "head nodding" syndrome that Louise had first witnessed in 1959 and had identified in medical journals in 1964 and 1965.

Unfortunately, this IDRC grant was approved primarily to encourage the ability of developing countries to improve their own medical and technological knowledge. Limited funds could be allocated for Canadian research at the University of British Columbia, so research to validate Louise's groundwork would be stymied. Her finding that the infestation of the filaria worm, *Onchocerca volvulus*, was much higher in those people suffering from epilepsy than in healthy people in the same region — and thus was a cause of the epilepsy — would remain unproven as a result.

In 1992, Louise remained worried about the ever-problematic need to secure a steady supply of anticonvulsive medication. When she contacted Dr. Bertelote, senior Medical Officer, Division of Mental Health, at the World Health Organization in Geneva, he advised her he could help her purchase antiepileptic drugs through WHO at reduced prices. She had hoped to introduce the use of carbamazepine but there was no follow through. Once more she was disappointed by the WHO administration.

⤳

DURING ANOTHER FIELD TRIP in July to September of 1994, Louise decided to undertake a comparative study of health and treatment standards in the district of Ruaha. In this region, west of Mahenge, where the prevalence of epilepsy was very high, she was able to gather comparative statistical and observational evidence that validated her earlier progress at Mahenge. Louise was able to prove that conditions in Ruaha were just as bad for epilepsy patients as they had been when she had come to the Mahenge area some thirty-five years earlier. On the strength of her interviews and data, Louise concluded, "Most people suffering from epilepsy in Ruaha appear to have given up any hope of receiving effective treatment and have resigned themselves to an outcast existence in society."

Tanzania had become socially progressive soon after it peacefully gained nationhood under the direction of Julius Nyerere, who was the dominant anti-colonial leader from 1961 to 1985, but subsequent Tanzanian governments were not able to provide significant health-care funding in outlying areas such as the Ruaha region.

It had fallen to the churches, mainly the Roman Catholic, to run the only health-care facilities in remote areas, usually charging patients for a significant part of the medication costs. Given that earning an income was almost impossible for people with epilepsy in Africa, few patients could pay for the medications and could not therefore undertake long-term treatment. Moreover, the church workers had not provided any systemic health education to counteract traditional beliefs and superstitions. Understaffed church dispensary personnel also frequently changed in the Morogoro region, so lack of continuity further degraded treatment, lowering the confidence of the patients in the process.

In 1994, the government of Tanzania dispensed with its socialist policy of providing free medication at its government-run hospitals and, instead, introduced a "cost-sharing" program with small dispensaries. This more variegated system appeared at first to be more advantageous to some epilepsy patients who could obtain their anti-convulsants from a nearby pharmacy instead of from Mahenge—but only if they could earn enough money for their medicine. Even if a patient could acquire medications, they needed counselling.

As a physician who had also become a psychiatrist, Louise remained convinced that mental health problems—such as low self-esteem born of poverty and superstition—had also to be addressed. Persons with epilepsy had to be healed in mind, body and spirit. But where to start?

Louise attempted to engage the psychiatric community with her concerns and discoveries by attending conventions and publishing in scientific journals. It was not uncommon for her almost exclusively male colleagues to dismiss her as an over-emotional female, a situation that was similar to her painful experience in her twenties when her appeal was rejected by a World Health Official in Geneva. As always, Louise encountered the widespread prejudice that epilepsy was a hybrid problem, neither entirely mental (psychiatric) nor entirely physical (conventional medicine).

Who was this zealous woman with the hard-to-pronounce name who was evidently setting the bar as high as possible for the benefit of mostly illiterate Africans? In the interior of some country most people had barely heard of? Her medical resolve to generate maximum success for her patients was considered radical. She was either making them all look bad with her high ideals or else one could dismiss her as a bit of a crackpot. Academically, she amounted to a bit of a nuisance.

She nonetheless kept reiterating her platform of five principles for the socio-cultural rehabilitation of epileptic patients in East Africa:

- Make the patient and the patient's family appreciate the "biomedical" nature of the illness.
- Motivate the patient to take medication consistently for years to come.
- Encourage family members to also participate in a consistent program of treatment.
- Find ways to rehabilitate the patient's self-respect to reduce their plight as outcasts.
- Take educational measures to counteract deep-seated prejudices about epilepsy.

In paper after paper in scholarly journals, Louise clearly stated that epileptic seizures in Africa were generally believed to be caused by witchcraft, daemons or an ancestral spirit taking revenge for some taboo-breaking within the family. Families had to hide their ashamed and humiliated epileptic members because it was generally believed a convulsing person's saliva and urine and any other bodily excretions were contagious. Such articles could appear as much anthropological as they were medical.

In order to seek recognition and support for her Mahenge Clinic from colleagues in Asia, Europe and North America, she kept publishing in journals such as *The Pakistan Journal of Clinical Psychiatry* in which she outlined her methodology:

Each and every patient receives a card with the date of the next monthly visit to the clinic; patients have to take the medicine bottle and show the nurse they have used up their monthly supply whereupon it is refilled for another month.

Each time the nurse makes sure that the patient or else the

responsible family members know how the medicine is to be used, and they understand the possible side-effects and the dangers of not taking the medication regularly.

If a patient was not able to keep his or her appointment at the clinic, one of the nurses' helpers, or possibly a nurse, would be despatched to find out why the patient has failed to appear and bring that patient the monthly medication supply. Such home visits were highly prized and appreciated. They improved social status and self-esteem. They proved to the family that someone cared about them a great deal.

⁓

LOUISE RETURNED TO Mahenge once again, in July and August of 2003, in order to present a much-prized, new motorbike, as well as to continue her work on *kifafa*. This motorbike would enable the male nurse at Mahenge, fifty-year-old Edward Mzurikwao, to make home visits to many of the more than one thousand out-patients who were receiving their medications from the clinic. The Rotary Club of Canada had sent funds to the Rotary Club in Dar es Salaam for the purchase of the bike in Tanzania.

Accompanied by family friend Flight Captain Michael Wilson and his teenage son, Mitchell, Louise arrived in the capital to discover the local Rotary Club had failed to purchase the motorbike. To cover up what appeared to be misappropriation of funds, she and Michael Wilson, as a representative of the Canadian Rotary Club, had to quickly purchase a new motorbike for the nurse in order to present it to the Deputy Minister of Health for Tanzania and the chairman of the Tanzania Epilepsy Association.

Next, a promised car and driver failed to materialize for her party to proceed to Mahenge, so she would be required to make the gruelling journey by bus on mostly unpaved roads. A plane flight to Ifakara was beyond her budget, and she believed the small airlines that serviced the interior of Tanzania were unsafe. Tanzanian buses are usually crowded, without a washroom, and they frequently break down, but she and her party bought their tickets for the bumpy, bone-rattling, two-day bus ride.

After she was met by Father Abdon Mkope in Ifakara, Louise arrived in Mahenge only to discover the new guest quarters at Kasita Seminary had yet to be completed. She and her party were taken instead to sleep at the Capuchin Monastery in Mahenge—a facility that was unaccustomed to having women on the premises. They would have to travel back and forth to the Kasita Seminary for meals, but she was used to improvising. Such inconveniences did not match her earlier difficulties as a bush doctor.

It was only when she finally visited her outpatient clinic at the German-built Mahenge Hospital that she became distraught. She had known that her clinic had been moved so as to be part of the hospital complex, but now she discovered that a dividing wall to create a small room for epilepsy consultations had been removed in order to accommodate more hospital patients due to overcrowding. Nobody had forewarned her that the room which had been designated for the epilepsy clinic had been completely taken over by the hospital.

Her next rude awakening was the news that the headquarters for her clinic had been transferred to a former storeroom. Already full of hospital equipment, this dilapidated space afforded room only for a small table and two chairs. The door was a metal sheet that could not be closed. The only window was a hole in the wall. Patients had to wait outside, with nowhere to sit, in the pouring rain or the hot sun.

"Naturally I felt angry," she recalls, "but who am I to judge? Obviously, the hospital did not hold the people with epilepsy in high esteem—much like everyone else." It was a call to action. Captain Wilson had practical skills and Father Abdon knew everyone in Mahenge for materials and labour, so she had the storage room emptied and the walls stripped bare. For the next three weeks they set to work repairing the roof, adding a proper ceiling and a new window with iron bars and mosquito netting, a new cupboard, a book shelf, a new meeting table, a new examination table. They also framed in a new door that could be locked. The interior walls were painted blue and white to give the area a restful feeling.

Outside, they levelled the waiting area, made a large and slightly elevated platform out of stones and cement, and built a roof over it. Benches were added so people could sit out of the sun. A local sign-maker added a blue and white sign that declared: "District Mental Health Office, MAHENGE EPILEPSY CLINIC, founded by Dr. Louise Jilek-Aall in 1960." She had first treated people with epilepsy in 1959.

When some patients looked at the new sign and muttered, "We never knew a doctor by that name," Louise was bemused. However, once she introduced herself, they were incredulous. Buoyed by these rebuilding efforts, Louise did something that was astonishing to al-most everyone in Mahenge. She remembered how successful her two dinners had been on her previous visit, and she decided to organize a feast for the epileptic patients. After much effort, the gathering and the dinner were a huge success. Although one of the diners experi-enced a grand mal seizure, this was something the gathering could in-corporate with relative ease. Nobody else at the occasion would ever have thought to sponsor such a party. Some guests lingered around the epilepsy centre for days, still buoyed by the novelty of the event.

⁓

TWO YEARS LATER in the summer of 2005, she once again returned to Mahenge, this time with her daughter and an international team of researchers to work on the research project "A Collaborative Study on Onchocerciasis and Epilepsy." This team included Professor E. Schmutzhard (Austria), an expert in tropical neurology, Dr. Andrea Winkler (Germany), a neurologist with experience in East Africa, and Louise's trusted co-researcher from Dar es Salaam, Dr. Matuja, who succeeded in gaining government funding for two additional hospital nurses to assist at the epilepsy clinic.

This research team was able to gather extensive data and take blood, CSF (cerebral spinal fluid) and skin samples back to Europe for laboratory testing. As well, during this work Louise was finally able to take some children with "head nodding" syndrome to the Aga Khan Hospital in Dar es Salaam for electro-encephalographic and magnetic resonance studies. These tests confirmed the presence of an epileptic disorder in the children who exhibited the same symptoms and behaviour she had first described in 1959.

Louise increased her resolve to initiate a rehabilitation program at the epilepsy clinic. She initially talked with two Fathers at Kasita who wanted to start a reforestation project—Father Abdon Mkope and Father Komba—and who needed workers for their vegetable gardens. She asked if they would be willing to hire some recovering epilepsy patients if she would pay some of their salaries.

This initiative began in a promising manner, but soon ran afoul of complications, mainly because the well-meaning administrators tended to treat the epilepsy workers differently from other workers. It was not that they treated them badly but that they were more lenient with them. The epilepsy workers often worked only a few hours and had many rest periods. The other workers did not like this, there was jealousy, and some of the epilepsy workers began to believe they were "very special."

On the other hand, when the epilepsy workers realized that they usually received a lower salary than the other workers (because they had worked fewer hours), they thought it was unjust and they sometimes chose to believe they were being discriminated against. Some quit and returned to begging.

After assessing the program for some time, Louise finally decided in August of 2009 that the entire project should be placed under the supervision of Father Placid Kindata with the help of Nurse Mzuri Kwao. Father Placid, who understood agriculture, would become her most integral "on the ground" collaborator for almost ten years, sometimes working alongside the patients.

With Father Placid in charge, ten patients called "clients" were paid and treated the same as other workers as much as possible. This rehabilitation project, which started as a pilot project for a year, was deemed worth of continuance and has been maintained. When a client dropped out of the project, another one was added because there was money allotted for twelve months. Questionnaires were prepared, and Father Placid was able to communicate the results to Louise through emails.

The first ten patients that Father Placid monitored in the rehabilitation program were Salama Kapelewe (19 years old, dropped out due to "health problems"), Siwema Mahabusi (20 years old), Alnorda Matale (30 years old), Agata Magwira (30 years old), Solana Goha (age unknown), Notkeria Mpinduli (49 years old, left without explanation), Theresia Mlungamo (dropped out due to pregnancy; did not want to come back), Gisila Ulanda, Laurent Chidowi and Pius J. Magwira.

Other groundbreaking patients in the first year included Aindra Matase, Anzelmina Fanyakazi, Fatia Ali Maokola, Medson Manyuka, Simon Shilaga and Siwena Mahabusi.

Louise and Wolfgang would continuously be associated with this employment program as financial donors, along with liaison from Ken Morrison of Provision Group. Father Placid's sensitivity, along with his optimistic outlook and his considerable farming expertise, were equally vital for continuity and productivity. It helped, too, that he had expertise as a qualified accountant.

⌒

EPILEPSY CONTINUES TO be the most common neurological disorder throughout sub-Saharan Africa. According to a 2009 article co-published by Louise and Andrea Winkler in the *African Journal of Traditional, Complementary and Alternative Medicines,* of the approximately twelve million people with epilepsy in sub-Saharan Africa, 90 percent did not receive adequate medical treatment.

After conducting a survey in northern Tanzania, researchers for a study cited in the same AJTCAM article found that 44.3 percent of the people they interviewed were still convinced that epilepsy could be treated successfully with traditional healing methods such as herbal medicine, spiritual healing, scarifications and spitting. As well, 34 percent thought that Christian prayers could cure the cause of, or treat the symptoms of, epilepsy.

Since the early 1990s, Louise has relied upon her integral liaison with Dr. William Matuja, a university professor under enormous pressure as one of the country's few neurologists. Despite being overworked, Matuja has consistently made requests to the Government of Tanzania to supply nurses and medicine for her clinic.

Unable to travel by airplane any longer, Louise was also grateful for the work performed by Yohana Mahenda Ng'wigulu, head nurse of the Mahenge Epilepsy Clinic, who took over soon after the death of Edward Mzurikwao, who had held the position for decades and is remembered for his devotion to his patients.

More recently, the facility has been managed by the tireless Nurse Grace Kibiriti in collaboration with Dr. Dan Bhwana, a doctor from Tanzania's National Institute for Medical Research.

Similarly, she feels indebted to Father Achilles Ndege, formerly rector of Kasita Seminary, and to Father Filbert Mhasi, who became rector at Kasita Seminary in 2010. For supervision of rehabilitation programs involving agriculture, Father Charles Kuandika has also been essential and diligent.

Louise remains ever-hopeful that the Tanzanian government will eventually give the people of Mahenge a much-needed Centre for Rehabilitation for Recovering Epileptics. Meanwhile, rehabilitation projects have been largely financed by donations from Louise and Canadian supporters. Ken and Nancy Morrison have made repeated visits to Mahenge and have spearheaded remarkable educational projects in Ifakara, including an ambitious construction project for a new dental college in Ifakara and a dormitory for female students.

Work programs were temporarily in jeopardy after the bishop for the Mahenge region transferred Father Placid to the village of Luhombero, but plans to reinvigorate the program resumed in 2019 after fundraisers in Canada, with assistance from the readers of the literary publication, *BC BookWorld*, resolved the transportation problems of Father Placid. Julianna Shinnick, an American who has overcome epilepsy herself, was also an important supporter.

Most importantly, the timely arrival in 2018 of Dr. Dan Bhwana to take over management of both the Mahenge hospital and Louise's epilepsy clinic invigorated both facilities.

~

DAN BHWANA WAS BORN on July 16, 1990, in Misungwi, Mwanza, in Tanzania. His mother had a nursing certificate but her salary was insufficient to cover daily living expenses.

"I grew up in a challenging environment," he says. "My mother could not get married because my father, who was a doctor at the district hospital, had another woman by the time he met my mother."

Bhwana's mother maintained a small vegetable garden and worked hard to support her children, wanting them to have a better life. At the age of eight, as the self-described "third child and second son" of his mother, Bhwana was taught to read and write by Madame Mary Nyanda at Mitindo primary school. A diligent student, he dreamt of becoming a medical doctor, like his father, in order to help others and also to relieve his mother of her "poor social economic status."

After seven years, Bhwana graduated to Ikizu Secondary School. Four years later, with exemplary marks, he was selected for two years of advanced studies at Kibaha Secondary School. High marks in his entrance exams enabled him in 2011 to attend Muhimbili University of Health and Allied Sciences—regarded as the foremost medical school in Tanzania.

"I first learned about Dr. Louise Jilek-Aall," he says, "when I was in third-year medical school. I came to know more when I joined the multi-disciplinary approach team to control Onchocerciasis, the ailment commonly known as river blindness, caused by the parasitic worm *Onchocerca volvulus*. It is also associated with epilepsy in the Mahenge area."

Under the direction of Dr. Matuja, Bhwana first joined a research project, based in Mahenge, that was being conducted by Tanzania's National Institute for Medical Research (NIMR) in collaboration with the University of Antwerp in Belgium. While posted at the Mahenge Epilepsy Clinic, Bhwana has continued to work as a research scientist and project clinician, reviewing some of the literature and records at the clinic which had originated from Louise's work. He hopes to obtain a PhD specializing in epilepsy.

"During my training in neurology," he writes, "I also managed to investigate a family with genetic Parkinsonism in an isolated mountain village which turned out to be the first Parkinson's mutation described in Eastern Africa. A paper is being written about it."

In May of 2019, Bhwana accepted an invitation to fly to Vancouver, at Louise's instigation, to receive her extensive research papers regarding epilepsy.

A consistent supply of antiepileptic drugs (AEDS) has long been problematic for the clinic. In 2019, the ROW Foundation, a partner of OWP Pharmaceuticals, began donating an ongoing supply of the AED Subvenite® (lamotrigine USP) to ensure the clinic will not run short.

In conjunction with NIMR, Dr. Bhwana hopes to build a new, well-equipped centre in Mahenge which, he says, "will be the fingerprint of the great work that Mama doctor did in her days . . . and it will involve the community strongly in all activities because epilepsy is still a highly stigmatized disease and there is a continuing need to educate the community."

In July of 2019, Dr. Bhwana was delighted to accept the gift of a new motorbike from the Provision Group. This enables him to make "house calls" to patients who are not able to come to the clinic, as well as respond more readily to emergencies in the surrounding villages— operating as a roving "bush doctor" in the same way Dr. Louise Aall worked in 1959.

SIXTY YEARS AFTER Mama Doctor encountered the *maskini* boy who believed his life would be ruined by "moon madness," her revitalized clinic for epileptic patients at Mahenge operates with renewed hope.

Louise blows the spores off a dandelion in her front yard at Tsawwassen, British Columbia, during a visit from Dr. Dan Bhwana and Alan Twigg in 2019.

CHRONOLOGY

April 2, 1931—Louise Mathilde Aall is born in Oslo, Norway, as the second child of Lily Weiser-Aall, PhD, an ethnologist who became the guiding force at the Norwegian Folk Museum, and Anathon Aall, PhD, an internationally renowned professor of philosophy and psychology.

1941–1945—The family flees to their country house called Ospeteig near Roa, Norway, for the duration of World War II, where Louise attends to and comforts her increasingly hallucinatory father, secretly cared for by a Norwegian physician, Dr. Askerud. Her father dies of Parkinson's disease in 1943. Louise almost dies from a burst appendix.

1946–1948—While her brother and sister are allowed to return to Oslo, Louise and her mother remain in Ospeteig. Louise teaches herself to read Swedish and Danish and to play the piano. She develops a lifelong admiration for Dostoevsky's novels *The Idiot* and *The Brothers Karamazov*. She vows to become a doctor.

1948–1950—Exclusively home-schooled prior to the war, Louise struggles to complete secondary school. She has minimal fraternization with other students during her late teens. Due to her inability to excel in mathematics, she is unable to gain entrance to the University of Oslo.

1951–1954—She studies medicine at the University of Tübingen, Germany, where she learns to enjoy the company of other students. This will be regarded as one of the happiest periods of her life.

1954—After a torchlight procession from Oslo University to city hall, she is among 20,000 well-wishers who sing a Norwegian hymn to honour Nobel Peace Prize Laureate Dr. Albert Schweitzer and his wife.

1954–1955—She studies medicine at Saarland University, now in Germany, but at the time, linked to France. The teaching was done in both French and German.

1955–1958—She enrols at the University of Zurich and completes all her medical exams. She becomes deeply involved with a sensitive, like-minded but troubled young man who dies in her arms.

1958—She returns briefly to Norway, as promised, to take over the rural medical practice of Dr. Askerud, who had attended to her dying father, enabling him to take an unprecedented month-long holiday.

1958–1959—She studies tropical medicine at the Swiss Tropical Institute in Basel, Switzerland, and receives her Diploma of Tropical Medicine. She accepts a minimal salary to conduct research work in Africa.

1959–1960—She commences medical fieldwork in the British Trust Territory of Tanganyika, initially at the Geigy Institute of Tropical Medicine at Ifakara, then at approximately twenty Catholic mission stations and outlying dispensaries throughout the Ulanga District, travelling in trucks, and biking or walking for days to get from one place to the next.

1960—She lays the groundwork for her future epilepsy clinic at Mahenge by treating 20 men and 15 women suffering from severe tonic-clonic seizures at the Catholic Mission at Kwiro, operated by Swiss Capuchins. The drugs phenobarbital and phenytoin, which were the only anticonvulsive medications available in Tanganyika at the time, turned out to be astonishingly effective. Not only were the frequency of seizures greatly reduced, in some cases attacks ceased completely.

1960–1961—She accepts an urgent request from the Norwegian Red Cross to co-manage an over-crowded 200-bed hospital at Matadi, in the Congo, with severely ill-patients during the bloody upheaval of civil war. Most of the Belgian population had fled. She earns the Henry Dunant Medal and Citation of the League of Red Cross Societies, Geneva, Switzerland.

1961—Awaiting a Dutch freighter and delayed for a week, she opts to fly to Lambaréné in Gabon where she becomes pediatric assistant to eighty-six-year-old Dr. Albert Schweitzer who had first established his jungle hospital in 1913. She lives in staff quarters without electricity or running water, shares many intimate conversations with Schweitzer, listens to him play Bach melodies at night on his organ, and witnesses how Schweitzer chose not to replicate the standards and practices of a European hospital. "My unforgettable time in Lambaréné turned out to be decisive in my eventually choosing psychiatry as a speciality." When she returns by freighter to Dar es Salaam, there is a message from Dr. Schweitzer telling her she is missed.

1962—Having returned to Europe, she finds her fundraising meeting with the Chief of Mental Health for WHO in Geneva ("an elderly gentleman" close to retiring age) is unsuccessful and demeaning. His dismissal of her credibility because she's female with "beautiful eyes" and a mere M.D. fuels a resolve to become a psychiatrist.

Her chief supporter is Professor Manfred Bleuler in Zurich. She writes personal letters to the Honourable Prime Minister of Tanganyika, Mr. Rashid Kawara, the Health Minister, Mr. Derec Bryceson, the regional government representative for the Ulanga District, Mr. C.M. Kapilima, as well as others, but these appeals for them to collaborate with WHO do not generate any traction. Seeking alternate recognition, having treated approximately 200 *kifafa* patients, she publishes the first of her many papers, "Epilepsy in Tanganyika," in a Canadian journal, *Review and Newsletter, Transcultural Research in Mental Health Problems* (Montreal, McGill University), to be followed by similar articles for German (1964) and Scandinavian (1965) journals.

1963—At the Swiss Institute for Epilepsy in Zurich, while undertaking her further neurological training under Professor H. Landolt, she meets an Austrian colleague who is an avid photographer. Apprehensive about returning to Africa alone, she agrees to let him accompany her for a return to Mahenge—without knowing his first name. After witnessing the expansion of antiepileptic treatments to approximately 200 patients in Mahenge, she leaves a Swiss Catholic nun from Kasita in charge, with three helpers. After prolonged restraint, she accepts intimacy with her escort, Wolfgang Jilek, in Dar es Salaam.

1963—After marrying Wolfgang Jilek, with wedding ceremonies in Oslo and Vienna, she and her husband sail to Canada on the Cunard Line with immigrant visas conferred by a sympathetic embassy official after they had applied only for student visas. They were independently motivated to study transcultural psychiatry and epidemiology under Professors E. Wittkower and H.B.M. Murphy at McGill University in Montreal.

1964—Tanganyika and the island of Zanzibar merge to form the Republic of Tanzania.

1964—Dr. Jilek-Aall and husband successfully re-write their medical exams for Canadian accreditation; both study psychiatry at McGill University. She publishes the first paper in medical history to identify the "head nodding" syndrome in children who later develop epileptic seizures — having learned that mothers in Tanzania recognize this phenomenon as *amesinzia kichwa* (Swahili: "he/she is nodding the head) — and understand that it is a precursor to generalized seizures for their child. Her treatise is largely ignored or discounted by WHO. Fifty years later the phenomenon will be verified and studied, with no recognition of her pioneering work.

1965—Dr. Albert Schweitzer dies.

1965—Louise receives her McGill diploma in psychiatry; she undertakes neuropsychiatric research (Carbamazepine-psychotropic treatment of epilepsy) at the Institut de Recherche Psychiatrique, Joliette, Quebec; she obtains a Specialist Certification and later becomes a Fellow of the Royal College of Physicians of Canada. The couple discover the beauty and diversity of British Columbia during their cross-Canada vacation journey in a Volkswagen. They decide to settle there.

1966—Both psychiatrists receive their licences to practise medicine in B.C. and become the only psychiatrists in the Fraser Valley until 1975. They open an office in Chilliwack and build their first home at nearby Harrison Lake. In conjunction with Chilliwack Hospital, they coordinate mental health clinics from Langley to Hope. They co-found the Section of Native Peoples

Mental Health of the Canadian Psychiatric Association. They are active in the World Psychiatric Association's Transcultural Section for neuro-psychiatric and ethno-psychiatric research.

1969—She commences studies in anthropology and sociology at the University of British Columbia, Vancouver, Canada, resulting in a Master of Arts degree in 1972.

1971—A World Health Organization initiative to improve mental health leads to a decision by the government of Tanzania to take over the independent epilepsy clinic in Mahenge as of 1972. One psychiatric nurse is hired to handle all patients with mental illness or epilepsy. Finally, a dilapidated room in a warehouse, outside of the main hospital, is allotted for patients with epilepsy.

1972—Having gained the trust of Fraser Valley First Nations, Louise and her husband co-publish "Transcultural Psychotherapy with Salish Indians," *Transcultural Psychiatric Research Review* 9: 59–62.

1975—She becomes clinical assistant professor, Department of Psychiatry, University of British Columbia. The couple moves to Delta, B.C. and builds their second home in Tsawwassen, nearer to Vancouver. From 1975 to 1995 she works variously at Vancouver General Hospital, Shaughnessy Hospital and B.C. Children's Hospital.

1978—She delivers one of the first of her public presentations on epilepsy in Africa at the Epilepsy International Symposium, Vancouver.

1979—After a preliminary visit to an orphanage in Bogota, Colombia, she returns to Bogota to formally adopt a four-year-old girl from the orphanage, who became Martica Ilona Jilek (born approximately 1975). A birth date of June 28 is selected.

1979—She releases her first book, *Call Mama Doctor* (Hancock House), later translated and published in Japan, China and Hungary. It is dedicated to her mother, Dr. Lily Weiser-Aall, "who inspired my interest in anthropology and in folk medicine."

1982–1986—Louise becomes a clinical associate professor in the UBC Department of Psychiatry; and she presents papers at the National Centre for

Epilepsy, Oslo-Sandvika, Norway, 1981 and 1983.

1984—She serves as a mental health volunteer in Papua New Guinea where Wolfgang Jilek has been appointed as a World Health Organization consultant.

1986–1987—She is a clinical professor, UBC Department of Psychiatry.

1988—She serves as UNHCR assistant and volunteer psychiatrist in refugee camps in Thailand, where Wolfgang Jilek has been posted as a UNHCR Refugee Mental Health Coordinator.

1989—With Dutch funding, Dr. Henry Rwiza conducts an epidemiological survey of convulsive disorders in the Ulanga District and confirms the prevalence rate from 8 to 20 per thousand in Mahenge area villages, some exceeding 40 per thousand. Dr. Rwiza, from the University of Dar es Salaam, has recently finished his specialist qualifications in the Netherlands where he was introduced to Dr. Jilek-Aall's publications about Mahenge by Dr. H. Meinardi, director of Epileptology at the Instituut voor Epilepsiebestrijding Meer & Bosch-De Cruquiushoeve, Heemstede, the Netherlands.

1990—She publishes *Working with Dr. Schweitzer: Sharing his Reverence for Life* (Hancock House), based on her journal and drawings from 1961.

1990—She revisits Tanzania after an absence of almost thirty years, working with Dr. Henry Rwiza of the Muhimbili Medical Centre, University of Dar es Salaam, to lay the groundwork for a more extensive Ulanga District field study into the etiology and clinical characteristics of *kifafa* and the reasons for the extraordinarily high prevalence rate. She makes presentations on epilepsy at Muhimbili University College of Medicine, Dar es Salaam, and at an International Conference on Genetics and Epilepsy, Minneapolis.

1991—She delivers presentations at the WPA International Symposium on Cultural Psychiatry, Budapest, Hungary, and at a preparatory conference for a UBC/Dar es Salaam project on seizure disorders. She receives the news in September that her research proposal with Dr. Rwiza has been accepted for funding by the International Development Research Centre (IDRC) of Canada. It entails funding for three years.

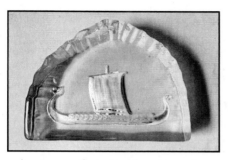

Louise was first cited for pioneering work in Africa when she received this carving at the 20th International Epilepsy Congress, Oslo, Norway, 1993.

1992—She returns to Mahenge as Principal Investigator and Canadian Team Leader for a joint Canadian-Tanzania Epilepsy Research Project, determining 52 percent of patients became free of seizures due to treatments; co-founds Tanzania Epilepsy Association.

1993—She writes: "I finally discovered that the infestation with the filaria worm *Onchocerca volvulus* seemed to be much higher in people suffering from epilepsy than in healthy people of the same region." In November Sister Josefata sends a letter to say tireless colleague Dr. Rwiza has suffered a stroke in Dar es Salaam and has been flown to London where he is treated and recuperates.

1994—Louise founds a Mahenge branch of the Tanzania Epilepsy Association and integrates a health education program at the clinic.

1995—After her articles in *International Epilepsy News* (1991, 1993) and *Epilepsia* (1992), she next publishes "Neurofiliasis: Can Onchocerciasis cause Epilepsy?" in *Recent Advances in Tropical Neurology* #100 (Amsterdam: Elsevier Science Publishers 1995). It is later the basis for a chapter called "Neurofiliasis" in *Neurology in Tropics* (New Delhi). She once more re-asserts: "It would be of utmost importance to carry out research to confirm the association between epilepsy and onchocerciasis, as *Onchocerca volvulus* is a common parasite also in other parts of Africa as in most developing countries. Eradication of *Onchocerca volvulus* has been the task of WHO in many parts of Africa, not because of the possible connection with epilepsy, however, but because of the better-known 'river blindness' caused by the filaria."

1997—At the 22nd International Epilepsy Congress in Dublin, Ireland, the International Bureau for Epilepsy and the International League Against Epilepsy confer on her, in absentia, their Ambassador for Epilepsy Award.

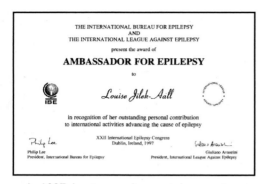

THE INTERNATIONAL BUREAU FOR EPILEPSY
AND
THE INTERNATIONAL LEAGUE AGAINST EPILEPSY

present the award of

AMBASSADOR FOR EPILEPSY

to

Louise Jilek-Aall

in recognition of her outstanding personal contribution
to international activities advancing the cause of epilepsy

XXII International Epilepsy Congress
Dublin, Ireland, 1997

Philip Lee
President, International Bureau for Epilepsy

Giuliano Avanzini
President, International League Against Epilepsy

In 1997, Louise was honoured at another International Epilepsy Congress when she received an Ambassador for Epilepsy award from the International Bureau for Epilepsy and The International League Against Epilepsy, in Dublin, Ireland.

2001—The couple co-write Chapter 14, "Culture-specific Mental Disorders," for *Contemporary Psychiatry Vol. 2: Psychiatry in Special Situations* (New York: Springer pp. 218–245), not specifically regarding epilepsy.

2003—Louise returns to Mahenge and oversees renovation of her clinic. She is stabbed twice in the chest by a gang of young muggers in Dar es Salaam while walking near a hotel with her daughter. Martica helps her to receive emergency medical treatment.

2005—She returns to Mahenge as co-investigator in the research project "Collaborative Study on Onchocerciasis and Epilepsy," with her daughter and International Coordinator Prof. Dr. E. Schmutzhard (Medical University of Innsbruck, Austria) and colleagues Dr. William Matuja (Tanzania) and Dr. Andrea S. Winkler (Germany). For the first time, children with "head nodding" syndrome (later officially dubbed Nodding Syndrome) are taken to the Aga Khan Hospital in Dar es Salaam for electro-encephalolographic and magnetic resonance studies, confirming the epileptic disorder she discovered at Mahenge almost 45 years before.

2006—She attends a conference on "Medicine in Tanzania" at the Medical University of Innsbruck.

2009—Martica Jilek and her mother meet with Father Achilles Ndege and Father Placid Kindata in Mahenge to create an ongoing rehabilitation program that will enable treated epileptics to gain dignity and independence as paid agricultural workers. Once derided as *maskini*—the useless ones, the ones who are a burden to others—selected workers are able to reintegrate into mainstream society.

2010 —She co-publishes her scientific paper, "Clinical Characteristics and Sociocultural Aspects of People with Head Nodding in Southern Tanzania" in *Tropical Doctor*, reasserting her pioneering work in the subject.

2011—According to the website of the World Health Organization, "Jilek et al (1962) first described several children with attacks of 'head nodding' in Mahenge," but reportage of a WHO, CDC Atlanta and UNICEF initiative to investigate Nodding Syndrome in Southern Sudan makes no reference to Jilek-Aall's pioneering work in the field or her identification of the syndrome in the early 1960s.

2012—Having first visited Mahenge with Dr. Jilek-Aall in 2009, Ken and Nancy Morrison create the Provision Charitable Foundation in Richmond, B.C., to fund health care and education services in Tanzania, including the epilepsy rehabilitation programs. Clients of Provision Accounting Group had already contributed half the purchase and delivery price for a vehicle for Mahenge, in conjunction with a Catholic charity in Europe called MIVA, delivered in 2011, when the Morrisons made their second visit to Mahenge.

2013—She co-publishes her final scientific paper, "Nodding Syndrome: Origins and Natural History of a longstanding Epileptic Disorder in Sub-Saharan Africa" in *African Health Services* #13. Thousands of cases are reported from Tanzania, northern Uganda, and South Sudan but 21st-century researchers often opt to present their own works as groundbreaking.

2016—After a visit to Mahenge in 2014, medical student Julianna Shinnick of Philadelphia, born with epilepsy, returns to Mahenge for a month and files a report on the progress of microfinance projects (tailoring, carpentry) and includes the following statistics: ten million people in Africa live with epilepsy and 90 percent of these people remain untreated (Boer, 2008). In the Mahenge region the prevalence rate of epilepsy is 19 to 36 per 1,000 versus 7.4 per 1,000 in the U.S. (Jilek-Aall, 1990). Excluding South Africa, the continent has only nine MRI machines in 2005 compared to 8,000 in the U.S. In the areas of Mahenge and nearby Ruaha, 65 percent of focus group participants in a study by Dr. Louise Jilek-Aall still believed people with epilepsy should not work or attend school (Winkler, 2010).

2017—Dr. Wolfgang Krahl strives with Dr. Gabriella Escheu and Dr. George Rieder to develop a conference to be held at Mahenge via the International Network of Cooperation in Mental Health. It does not materialize.

2018—Wolfgang Jilek's heart is failing him; he is hospitalized, and he has severe circulation problems. Doctors suggest amputating one of his legs. He resists and returns home in August, greatly assisted by a homemaker, but remains in much discomfort.

2019—Dr. Dan Bhwana makes his first trip outside of Tanzania in order to visit Louise at her home in Tsawwassen, British Columbia, at her expense. The primary purpose of this journey is to receive her research materials and medical records regarding epilepsy, and to consult with her about managing and improving the clinic.

RESEARCH & SCIENTIFIC PAPERS
(SELECTED)

THE GROUNDBREAKING work of Dr. Louise Jilek-Aall has not always been credited by those who have followed her path. For instance, in a 2017 report from the director of National Institutes of Health for the U.S. Department of Health & Human Services entitled "Rare Disease Mystery: Nodding Syndrome May Be Linked to Parasitic Worm," there are no references made to Dr. Louise Jilek-Aall's pioneering work regarding the syndrome in the early 1960s or her published works pertaining to the filaria worm *Onchocerca volvulus*. Here is a checklist of her most important research articles. It should be noted her surnames include Aall, Aall-Jilek and Jilek-Aall.

Aall, Louise. (1962). "Epilepsy in Tanganyika," *Review and Newsletter, Transcultural Research in Mental Health Problems*, 13: 54–57 (Montreal: McGill University).

Aall-Jilek, L. (1964). "Geisteskrankheiten und Epilepsie im tropischen Afrika," *Fortschritte der Neurologie und Psychiatrie*, 32: 213–259.

Jilek, W.G. & L.M. Aall-Jilek. (1964). "A Blind Interpretation of Rorschachs in the Wapogoro of Tanganyika," *Transcultural Psychiatric Research Review*, 1: 139–142.

Aall-Jilek, L.M. (1965). "Epilepsy in the Wapogoro Tribe in Tanganyika," *Acta Psychiatrica Scandinavica*, 41: 57–86.

Jilek, W.G. & L. Jilek-Aall. (1967). "Psychiatric Concepts and Conditions in the Wapogoro Tribe of Tanganyika," *Contributions to Comparative Psychiatry*, ed. N. Petrilowitsch, vol. 5 (1): 205–228. Karger, Basel / New York, 1967.

Rajotte, P., W.G. & L. Jilek-Aall, A. Perales, N. Giard, J-M Bourdeleau & L. Tétreault. (1967). "Propriétés anti-épileptiques et psychotropes de la Carbamazépine," *Union Médicale*, 96: 1200–1206.

Jilek, W.G. & L.M. Jilek-Aall. (1968). "The Problem of Epilepsy in Rural Africa: 'Kifafa' in a Tanzanian Tribe," presentation at Colloque de l'Epidémiologie de le Epilepsie en Afrique, Marseille, September 3, 1968.

———. (1970). "Transient Psychoses in Africans," *Psychiatria Clinica*, 3: 337–364.

———. (1970). "The Problem of Epilepsy in Rural Africa," *Transcultural Psychiatric Research Review*, 7: 43–48.

———. (1972). "Una Clinica neuropsiquiátríca en la Selva Africana, Sinopsis Comparativa de la Epilepsia en el Peru y Tanzania," *Revista Medica Peruana*, 35: 173–181.

Jilek-Aall, L.H. (1976). "Kifafa: A Tribal Disease in an East African Bantu Population," *Anthropology and Mental Health*, ed. J. Westermeyer, The Hague: Mouton.

Jilek-Aall, L.M., W.G. Jilek & J.R Miller. (1979). "Clinical and Genetic Aspects of Seizure Disorders Prevalent in an Isolated African Population," *Epilepsia*, 20: 645–650.

Jilek-Aall, L.M. & W.G. Jilek. (1989). "Epilepsy and its Psychosocial Implications in Africa," *Clinical Psychology in Africa*, eds. K. Peltzer & P.O. Obigbo, pp. 184–202, University of Nigeria, Enugu, Nigeria.

Jilek-Aall, L. & H.T. Rziwa. (1991). "The Mahenge Epilepsy Project in Tanzania: Prospects for a Brighter Future in Epilepsy Sufferers," *International Epilepsy News*, 105: 24–25.

Jilek-Aall, L. & H.T Rziwa. (1992). "Prognosis of Epilepsy in a Rural African Community: a 30-year Follow-up of 164 Patients in an Outpatient Clinic in Rural Tanzania," *Epilepsia*, 33: 645–650.

Jilek-Aall, L. (1995). "Neurofiliasis: Can Onchocerciasis cause Epilepsy?" *Recent Advances in Tropical Neurology* #100. Amsterdam: Elsevier Science Publishers.

Jilek-Aall, L., M. Jilek, J. Kaaya, L. Mkombachepa, & K. Hillary. (1997). "Psychosocial Study of Epilepsy in Africa," *Social Science & Medicine,* 45 (5): 783–795.

Jilek-Aall, L. (1998). "Neurofiliasis," *Neurology in Tropics.* New Delhi: B.I. Churchill Livingstone.

Jilek-Aall L. (1999). "Morbus sacer in Africa: Some Religious Aspects of Epilepsy in Traditional Cultures," *Epilepsia,* 40 (3): 382–386.

Jilek-Aall, L. (2003). "Forty Years of Experience with Epilepsy in Africa," pp 37–52, *The Brainstorms Village: Epilepsy in Our World,* eds. S.C. Schachter and L.F. Andermann. Philadelphia: Lippincott, Williams & Wilkins.

Winkler, A.S. & L. Jilek-Aall (2008). "The Head Nodding Syndrome: Clinical Classification and Possible Causes," *Epilepsia,* 49 (12): 1–8.

Winkler, A.S., Michael Mayer, Michael Ombay, Bartholomayo Mathias, Erich Schmutzhard & Louise Jilek-Aall. (2009). "Attitudes towards African Traditional Medicine and Christian Spiritual Healing Regarding Treatment of Epilepsy in a Rural Community in Tanzania," *African Journal of Traditional, Complementary and Alternative Medicines,* 7 (2): 162–170.

Winkler A.S. & L. Jilek-Aall, et al. (2010). "Clinical Characteristics and Sociocultural Aspects of People with Head Nodding in Southern Tanzania," *Tropical Doctor,* 40: 173–175.

Koenig R. & L. Jilek-Aall, et al. (2010). "The Role of Onchocerca volvulus in the Development of Epilepsy in a Rural Area of Tanzania," *Parasitology,* 137: 1559–1568.

Mayer, Michael, Silke Schnaitmann, Michael Ombay, Bartholomayo Mathias, Erich Schmutzhard & Louise Jilek-Aall. (2010). "Belief Systems of Epilepsy and Attitudes toward People Living with Epilepsy in a Rural Community of Northern Tanzania," *Epilepsy & Behavior,* 19 (4): 596–601.

APPENDIX
LETTERS WRITTEN TO DR. AALL (1992)

Susan *(19-year-old woman)*

I was in grade nine of a Catholic secondary school for girls. The teachers were nuns who had very strict rules. We were not allowed to see boys while we boarded at the school, but I had a boyfriend and I would sneak out at night to be with him.

One late evening while sitting on the wayside waiting for him, somewhat guilty and scared, I suddenly felt dizzy. My stomach was grumbling. I had pains everywhere, and my heart was pounding. Then I blacked out. When I first came to, I could not figure out where I was. There were people standing around, staring at me. Nobody spoke to me. In the dim light I could see shock and disgust in their faces. I could not say a word, my head hurt so. I got up and went home. Avoiding my parents, I just went right to bed and fell into a deep sleep.

The next day, I realized that I must have had an attack of *kifafa* and was overcome with despair and shame. From then on, my life became a nightmare. People told my parents what had happened. I was not allowed to return to school. Teachers and students would refuse to be in the same room with me. I was not permitted to talk to anyone about my illness. My boyfriend never came to see me again. I was so sad and lonely and had nobody to help me, but the sense of guilt I felt toward God and about what I had brought upon my family made me suffer without complaint.

My seizures continued. I was taken to a healer who made me swallow some concoctions that tasted bitter and caused me to vomit. I was told that the *kifafa* spirit was sitting in my stomach in the form of a toad, and if I could throw it up and get it out, I might be cured.

When these treatments did not help, my parents kept me at home. I had to hide in a hut when people visited my family and was only let outside at night when it was dark.

I dreaded the seizures, because I was afraid of getting hurt when falling and because of the pain and confusion they caused. I learned to expect most attacks when there was no moon in the sky; I would be extra cautious then with the fire and with fetching water. During the time of my seizures I would have bad dreams, mostly about people or animals chasing me while I tried to run away. As soon as I felt a touch, I would wake up in terror and have an attack. I found out that during the day my stomach would rumble and my mouth filled with saliva just before a seizure, so I was lying down quickly. But it happened also that I had no time to lie down.

One evening I fell with my arm in the open fire in front of the hut. I woke up with terrible pain and was rushed to the hospital with bad burns. That is how I got to the Mahenge Epilepsy Clinic and got to know Dr. Jilek-Aall. I am no longer afraid to talk about my illness. I only wish that others who suffer from *kifafa* will get medical treatment so they can find a way out of the terrible life they live.

Jera (24-year-old mother)

I had my first seizure shortly after the birth of my child. I had been sleeping and dreamed that I was washing myself. As I was pouring water over my shoulders, the water suddenly turned into blood. I woke up with a cry and had a seizure.

I knew it was *kifafa*. In my family there are several persons who have *kifafa*, and they say this dream appears before a seizure. My husband was from a village where they did not know my family. I had moved to his people with him. *Kifafa* was never mentioned there, and now I was so afraid he would find out.

I secretly went to the *mganga* (healer) in my parents' village, who gave me medicine from a root to rub on my forehead in order to protect me from that dream. But I had another attack, and this time I could not hide it.

My husband was furious. He gave my baby to his brother's wife, returned me to my parents, and demanded back the bridal price he had paid them to marry me. My parents had to comply, for it is our custom that a man can do this if he is not satisfied with his wife.

My family was not happy to have me back. Everybody felt ashamed of me, and I was devastated. My seizures came only once a month, but I had two or three at a time. I did not really feel sick. I could get up right away and continue whatever I had been doing before the seizure started. I helped my parents as much as I could to make up for the failed marriage, but I was very unhappy. I was always thinking of my baby and longed for my husband.

One day I could not stand it any longer. I set out to visit him and to see my child. I could not believe that he would refuse me, for we had been living well together. As soon as the people of his village saw me coming, they became very upset. They must have known what happened and were afraid of catching *kifafa* from me. Before I could reach my husband's home, they shouted at me, "Go away!" They began to threaten me, and finally some of the people picked up stones and threw them at me. I had to run for my life until I was well out of the village.

I cried all the way to my parents' place but did not tell anybody where I had been. Shortly afterwards, my husband came to see me. He felt bad about what had happened to me in his village. He told me he had heard of the Mahenge Epilepsy Clinic and had inquired about *kifafa* treatment there. He had been assured that my type of seizures could most probably be fully controlled by medication, and he was encouraged to take me to the clinic.

We went to the clinic. I was astonished to see the very small white tablets and just could not believe that they would be able to control *kifafa*. But my parents, who had also come along, hoping for a reunion of myself with my husband, insisted that I give the medicine a try. My mother made sure I took the medicine regularly every day.

To my great surprise, no attacks occurred the next time they were expected. I was filled with hope, and when months passed without further seizures, I mustered the courage to look for ways to earn some money. Within a year I had earned enough to pay back my own bridal price to my parents. When my husband heard this, he immediately took me back, and when he saw that I had no more seizures, he let me have my child again.

I never forget to take my tablets. I have been free of seizures for several years now, I am well accepted in my husband's family, and the villagers are no longer afraid of me.